Nationalism and the Nation in the Iberian Peninsula

Competing and Conflicting Identities

Edited by
Clare Mar-Molinero and Angel Smith

BERG

Oxford • Washington, D.C.

First published in 1996 by
Berg
Editorial offices:
150 Cowley Road, Oxford, OX4 1JJ, UK
22883 Quicksilver Drive, Dulles, VA 20166, USA

Berg is an imprint of Oxford International Publishers Ltd.

Library of Congress Cataloging-in-Publication Data

A catalogue record for this book is available from the Library of Congress.

British Library Cataloguing-in-Publication Data

A catalogue record for this book is available from the British Library.

ISBN 1 85973 180 5 (Cloth)
1 85973 175 9 (Paper)

Typeset by JS Typesetting, Wellingborough, Northants.
Printed in the United Kingdom by WBC Book Manufacturers, Bridgend,
Mid Glamorgan.

Contents

Contents

Editors' Preface

In March 1995 the University of Southampton was the venue for a conference with the title of *Nationalism and National Identity in the Iberian Peninsula*. The aim behind the conference and the subsequent book was to bring together a wide range of specialists on Spain and Portugal in a cross-disciplinary approach to the discussions of nationalism and national identity. All but two of the following chapters were originally presented at this conference as papers. Chapter 1 has since been written by the editors to provide a coherent framework for the various themes of these papers, and Chapter 11 by Josep Llobera was included although the author had been unable to attend the conference. We believe that the present volume does indeed reflect its cross-disciplinary genesis with contributions from a wide spectrum of areas including history, social anthropology, sociology, sociolinguistics, political sciences and cultural studies. These varied approaches are manifested in the diversity of methodology and analysis employed.

We are grateful to many people for helping and supporting the organisation of the conference and for the preparation of this book. The Instituto Cervantes, the Spanish Embassy and the Instituto Camões all gave generous grants which allowed us to invite speakers from a wide international field.

In the production of the book we would like to thank our colleague Alan Freeland for his advice and help in reading various draft chapters and pointing us in the direction of the relevant literature on Portugal. We would also wish to thank all those who have contributed to this volume; whilst their opinions may not always be our own, we take sole responsibility for the overall shape and argument of the book. We are also very appreciative to Kathryn Earle of Berg Publishers during the drawn-out coordination of this project.

Clare Mar-Molinero and Angel Smith
Southampton

Notes on Contributors

José Alvarez Junco holds the Principe de Asturias Chair of Spanish Culture and Civilisation at Tufts University. He is the author of *La comuna en España* (1971), *La ideología política del anarquismo español* (1976) and *El emperador del Paralelo* (1990), and has edited *Populismo, caudillaje, y discurso demagógico* (1987). His current research interests are especially in nation-building processes in nineteenth- and early twentieth-century Spain.

Sebastian Balfour is Reader in Contemporary Spanish Studies at the London School of Economics. He is author of *Dictatorship, Workers and the City. Labour in Greater Barcelona since 1939* (1989) and *Castro* (1994, 2nd edn) and a number of articles and chapters on twentieth-century Spanish history. He is preparing a book entitled *The End of the Spanish Empire. The 'Glorious' Disaster and the Crisis of the Liberal Monarch in Spain, 1898–1923*.

Alan Freeland is a Senior Lecturer and in charge of Portuguese and Brazilian Studies at the University of Southampton. His main research interests are in nineteenth-century literature. His publications include a study of Eça de Queirós's masterpiece *Os Maias* (*O Leitor e a Verdade Oculta),* (1989) and the first edition of this novelist's consular letters from Cuba, England and France, *Correspondência Consular* (1994). He is also the author of the BBC television course *Discovering Portuguese: An Introduction to the Language and People* (2nd edn 1995). His current research focuses on the construction of Portuguese national identity since the Romantic period, drawing on a range of fictional and historiographical representations.

Helen Graham is a Lecturer in the Department of History at Royal Holloway, University of London. She is author of *Socialism and War: The Spanish Socialist Party in Power and Crisis, 1936–1939* (1991) and has edited (with Paul Preston) *The Popular Front in Europe* (1987), (with Martin Alexander) *The French and Spanish Popular Fronts: Comparative Perspectives* (1989) and (with Jo Labanyi) *Spanish Cultural Studies: An Introduction* (1995). She has published various articles on the Spanish Left in the 1930s and is currently writing a book on the Second Spanish Republic during the Civil War.

Tracy Henderson is a research student in the School of Modern Languages at the University of Southampton. She is completing a Phd on language policies in Galicia and has made many research trips to Galicia for her research. She has given papers at various conferences on Galician language policies, and has articles on the subject in press.

Josep R. Llobera teaches anthropology and sociology at Goldsmiths College of the University of London, where he is a Reader. He has done research in Catalonia and Barbados. He has published extensively in the field of the history of the social sciences and nationalism. His latest book is *The God of Modernity: The Development of Nationalism in Western Europe* (1994).

Jeremy MacClancy is Senior Lecturer in Social Anthropology in the School of Social Sciences, Oxford Brookes University. His publications include *To Kill a Bird with Two Stones: A History of Vanuatu* and *Consuming Culture* (1986). He is the editor of *Sport, Ethnicity and Identity* (1996) and co-editor (with C. McDonaugh) of *Popularizing Anthropology* (1996). At present he is completing a manuscript on the evolution of Carlism since the Civil War.

Clare Mar-Molinero lectures on Spanish and sociolinguistics at the University of Southampton. She has published many articles on language planning and language policies in the Spanish-speaking world, as well as on language teaching methodology. She is author of the BBC stage two radio Spanish course *Paso Doble*. She has a textbook on Spanish sociolinguistics currently in press, and is preparing a book on language and nationalism in the Spanish-speaking world.

Michael Richards is a research fellow of the British Academy and teaches in the Department of History at the University of Sheffield. His doctoral research was about violence and economic relations under Francoism. He is currently writing a study of pathologies of development and a social history of the Franco years.

Francisco J. Romero Salvadó is currently Lecturer in Modern European History at London Guildhall University. He has published several articles on contemporary Spanish politics and is currently writing a history of twentieth-century Spain.

Notes on Contibutors

Angel Smith is Lecturer in Modern Spanish History at the University of Southampton. He works in the area of social and cultural history. He has written a number of articles on the Catalan and Spanish labour movement, and published *An Historical Dictionary of Spain* in 1996. At present he is working on a history of Catalan labour between 1899 and 1933, and is editing a book on labour, ethnicity and nationalism.

Benjamín Tejerina Montaña lectures in Sociology in the Faculty of Social Sciences of the University of the Basque Country. He has published various articles on language conflict, the relationship between language and collective identity and sociological theories of social conflict. He is currently researching in the areas of the political dimension of collective identity, particularly in the context of the Basque Country and Spain's 'State of Autonomies'. He has published *Nacionalismo y Lengua: los procesos de cambio lingüístico en el País Vasco* (1992), his revised doctoral thesis.

AbdoolKarim A. Vakil is a Lecturer in Portuguese History at King's College, University of London. His current research and publications are mainly in the areas of nineteenth- and twentieth-century cultural and intellectual history, with particular reference to historical representations and national identity. Two major collections of historical studies, *Oliveira Martins: História, Ciências Sociais e Mitologia Nacional* and *The Strangers Within: Orthodoxy, Dissent and the Ambiguities of Faith in the Portuguese Renaissance*, both co-edited with Professor Helder Macedo, will be published in 1996.

Alan Whitehead is Professor of Public Policy at Southampton Institute. He lectures and researches in sub-national government and has published widely on aspects of local politics and administration in the UK and Europe. He also has considerable practical experience of local government having served as Leader of Southampton City Council from 1984 to 1992. He is currently a member of the UK Labour Regional Policy Commission.

The Myths and Realities of Nation-Building in the Iberian Peninsula

Angel Smith and *Clare Mar-Molinero*

Introduction

The objectives of this chapter are twofold. First, we aim to provide an overview of the development of nationalist movements in Spain and Portugal in order to set the contributions which follow within a broader context. Second, we intend to cover some areas in rather greater depth: in particular the rise of peripheral nationalisms in Spain from the late nineteenth century, and the causes behind the very different nationalist identities and conflicts which developed in Spain and Portugal.

These two countries offer multiple insights into the development of modern nationalism. Since the Middle Ages they have formed the two major states in the Iberian Peninsula. Spain is by far the largest of these states, with over four times Portugal's population and over five times its area, though with respect to economic development, social structures and political movements many historical similarities can be discerned. However, in the modern era the terms of the nationalist debate have been enormously different. Between 1580 and 1640 they were united in a single state, and only after revolt in Portugal did they go their own separate ways. This has determined a certain asymmetry in the state nationalist discourses which developed in the nineteenth century: while reunification with Portugal would occasionally surface in Spanish political debate, fear of Spanish imperialism would be a defining characteristic of Portuguese national identity. More surprisingly at first sight, while from the end of the nineteenth century Spanish nationalism would find itself contested within Spain itself by a number of alternative nationalist discourses, the Portuguese claim to nationhood has, at least within the country itself, remained virtually unchallenged.

In order to understand these contradictions more fully one has to look back to the forging of these states in the Middle Ages and early modern era. Both Spain and Portugal underwent a process of early state-formation, their territories carved from the advance of the Christian armies southwards at the expense of the Peninsula's Moorish inhabitants. From 1249 Portuguese territorial boundaries were almost identical to her present-day frontiers, while the Kingdom of Spain was established through the alliance between the Crowns of Castile and Aragon in 1479, and completed with the incorporation of Navarre into Castile in 1512. In both cases a single territory was defined and a single language came to predominate. In Portugal, by the early sixteenth century, Portuguese had evolved from its language of origin, Galician, into a clearly separate tongue, and was spoken throughout almost the whole of the country (Graça Feijó 1989: 38–9; Chapter 14). In Spain matters were more complex but, as Clare Mar-Molinero (Chapter 4) points out, government and state elites increasingly used a single vernacular language, Castilian,[1] which by the sixteenth century had also become the major vehicle of literary culture.

Nevertheless, there were also important differences between the two states. As we have noted, the Kingdom of Spain was the result of a pact between the Crowns of Castile (itself forged out of the alliance between several different kingdoms) and Aragon (a loose confederation of the territories of Catalonia, Valencia and Aragon), and until the early eighteenth century there was no attempt at meaningful centralisation (Linz 1973: 38–49). Hence the three territories of the Crown of Aragon retained their own *Cortes* (parliament) and the Basque Country and Navarre their own systems of administration (the *fueros*). Moreover, the common people continued to speak a multiplicity of languages (see Chapter 4). In contrast, the construction of the Portuguese State was the result of the conquest of the south of the country by a nucleus of population originally based in the north-west of the Peninsula (Graça Feijó 1989: 38), and there would be no foral-type administrative divisions. The results would be of great importance in the age of nationalisms. José Álvarez Junco (Chapter 5) has suggested that an 'ethno patriotic' sense of Spanish identity probably existed in Spain by the eighteenth century. However, other authors have argued that in areas such as Catalonia, within the context of institutional autonomy and a separate language, alternative identities could persist and indeed grow (Simon i

---

1. We prefer to use the term Castilian rather than Spanish language as it is, of course, just one (though the most widely spoken) of the languages used in Spain. The term Spanish rather than Castilian is itself a construct of sixteenth-century Spanish 'proto nationalism' (the Dictionaries of the *Real Academia Española* only used the word Spanish rather than Castilian from 1925), and implies either that there should be no other languages spoken in Spain (the right-wing Spanish nationalist perspective), or that areas where other languages are spoken should not form part of Spain (the peripheral nationalist separatist viewpoint).

Tarrés 1993: 8–16; Ettinghausen 1993). These interpretations are not necessarily incompatible, but in the nineteenth century a preexisting sense of specificity could, if conditions were right, be used by the new ideologues of nationalism. In contrast, as we shall see, in the Portuguese case there would be no memory of distinctive administrative and linguistic boundaries on which to hang an alternative nationalist discourse.

These dichotomies formed an influential backdrop to the attempt by Portuguese and Spanish governments to forge fully-fledged nation-states during the nineteenth century. At the level of state and government policies there were similarities between the Portuguese and Spanish experiences. However, while in Portugal, by the early twentieth century, few doubted that the country formed a single nation, in Spain the road to the construction of a modern nation-state was to prove littered with obstacles. Indeed, Spain was the only European country to be considered without doubt a nation-state by European nationalist ideologues in the mid-nineteenth century (unlike the Austro-Hungarian and Ottoman Empires), which by the early twentieth century was facing a series of internal nationalist challenges.

The Failure of the Spanish Liberal Nation-State Project

The partial failure to forge a nation-state in the nineteenth and early twentieth centuries is thoroughly analysed by José Alvarez Junco, Sebastian Balfour and Francisco Romero Salvadó (Chapters 5, 6 and 7). As Alvarez Junco emphasises, in Spain, as throughout the rest of Europe, the nation-state-building process was carried through by liberal politicians who needed to construct new legitimacies following the overthrow of absolutism. Liberal regimes governed in Spain between 1833 and 1923. However, their nationalising policies were a shadow of those pursued by the major Western European powers. In the first place, the poverty of the Spanish State, poor communications, the inadequate education system and a restricted cultural market ensured that the construction of a national identity out of a multiplicity of local references was very incomplete. Furthermore, the dominant liberal tradition proved enormously conservative, and its power-base rested on local oligarchs rather than on sections of public opinion. Consequently, it preferred to try to maintain the traditional legitimation provided by the Catholic Church rather than resorting to the dangerous game of mobilising the masses behind nationalist goals.

The years 1898 to 1923 were to see the final failure of this conservative liberal nation-state project. The defeat of Spain and loss of Cuba in war with the United States was without doubt a crucial turning point. Sebastian Balfour argues that the months following the outbreak of hostilities had, in urban areas, seen a considerable upsurge in patriotic fervour. This indicates that despite the tardiness of the Spanish State some sense of national consciousness had grown up. With defeat, however, came great disillusion. Balfour points out that in its aftermath it would prove far more difficult to enthuse the population with dreams of imperial conquest. At the same time the Restoration regime was discredited and though it was able to limp on until 1923 it remained incapable of structuring a coherent national ideal. On the contrary, as Romero Salvadó explains, between 1898 and 1923 governments were still wedded to the old *caciquista* system of politics, and particularly from 1914 were faced with a growing opposition from both the democratic and revolutionary Left and authoritarian Right, and, as we shall see, from new peripheral nationalist parties. The regime was finally swept away by the military coup launched by General Miguel Primo de Rivera in September 1923.

There were, as Alvarez Junco states, more radical liberal nationalist ideologues, in general linked to the liberal professions. By the late 1860s, exasperated by the Bourbon monarchy's alliance with the most reactionary strand of liberalism, many of them turned to republicanism. The republicans structured an alternative nationalist cosmology in which the people were portrayed as the true repositories of Spain's supposedly democratic-nationalist traditions, while the Church and monarchy were seen as the chief blocks to the country's national regeneration. There were two major strands within the republican movement. In the first place, federal republicanism which, especially in Catalonia, displayed certain particularist features (see below, p.5, and Chapter 10). On the one hand there developed a more centralist, Spanish republican movement. This gave a boost to Spanish nationalism because it provided a democratic alternative to the backward-looking rhetoric of elites (Blas 1991). And taken together with the dissemination of a radical-democratic vision of the Spanish nation by many of the leading writers of the day, this ensured that a liberal nationalist alternative to official nationalism took root in sectors of the urban middle and lower classes. At the same time, however, as Alvarez Junco explains, the existence of competing national discourses also resulted in the fracturing of national identity. The Carlists and conservative liberals could not agree on the same king and radical liberals favoured a republic. Each in turn had their own symbolic apparatus of flags and anthems.

Federalism, Traditionalism and the Romantic Movement: A Challenge to the Spanish Nation?

The very concept of a Spanish nation was for the first time thrown into some doubt in the second half of the nineteenth century. Already in the mid-nineteenth century opposition had been voiced to the centralising tendencies of the liberal state. On the Left, many progressive liberals came to adopt federalism as their creed, and between 1868 and 1873, under the influence of Proudhonian doctrines the first major republican party called itself the Federal Republican Party. Its leading thinker, Francesc Pi i Margall, saw Spain as the nation, but believed that it should be reconstructed on the basis of its 'old provinces', which had retained their individuality and should therefore be given a high degree of autonomy.[2] These federalists were not, then, nationalists *avant la lettre*, but in recognising the personality of the regions they could help lay the basis for future particularist and nationalist thought (López Cordón 1975; Trías and Elorza 1975). This was very clear in the case of Catalonia where in the 1880s the ex-federalist, Valentí Almirall, developed a programme in favour of Catalan autonomy (Trías Vejerano 1975; Figueres 1990).

At the same time, the republicans also championed the possible future unification of the Iberian peoples in a single confederation. This was supported most enthusiastically by the federalists, and was justified in ethnic and historical terms with the claim that the Iberian Peninsula had constituted a single Iberian race before the Roman invasion (Cirujano Marín, Elorriaga Planes and Pérez Garzón 1985: 87–8). This ideal was, indeed, as Alan Freeland points out in Chapter 3, also to be found in the writings of Portuguese republicans, for whom a loose Iberian confederation could provide protection against possible Spanish aggression and allow Portugal to play a more central role in European history. Within the dominant moderate liberal tradition, however, these ideas found little echo. Though the loss of Portugal in the 1640s was oft-lamented, it was realised that with England acting as the guarantor of her sovereignty any attempt at intervention would be doomed to failure. Indeed, the rather passive European foreign policy which Spain was forced to pursue throughout the nineteenth century was increasingly justified in racial terms. As social Darwinism came into vogue from the mid-century, it was argued in Britain and Germany that the northern European Aryan races were superior. Concomitantly, Spanish

---

2. Pi stated, 'almost all of them were nations in their day. They still retain their specific physiognomy and some are distinguished from the rest by the particularity and unity of their language, customs and laws' (Pi i Margall 1877, 1936 edn: 274).

liberals became increasingly aware of Spanish relative backwardness, and pessimistic as to the role the country could play in European affairs.

Hence the leading Spanish statesman of the second half of the century, Antonio Cánovas del Castillo, explained his policy of withdrawal (*recogimiento*) with reference to the supposed 'decadence of the Latin races' (Jover Zamora 1981: 317).

On the Right, traditionalist and conservative thinkers also criticised liberal centralism, contrasting it with reference to the supposed liberties of 'the peoples' of Spain in the Middle Ages (Mañé y Flaquer 1886), and therefore supported the claim for the restitution of medieval privileges such as the *fueros*, and the decentralisation of the state administration.[3] The traditionalist, particularist current, which drew on the writings of Le Play and Taine, was especially pronounced in the Basque Country and Catalonia, but was also to be found in Galicia, Valencia and Aragon (Solé Tura 1974: 55–94: Cirujano Marín, et al. 1985: 127; Riquer 1987: 78–84). In the Basque Country, where the *fueros* were not abolished until 1876, they were strongly defended by the traditionalist–Catholic Carlists and later by middling landowners (the *jauntxos*), whose local power they had protected. Javier Corcuera argues that both these movements tended to foster a 'pre-nationalist' consciousness in sectors of the population because they created an 'us' and 'them' mentality, in which the 'them' could be identified with Castilian liberalism (Corcuera Atienza 1979: 51–8, 180–4).

Traditionalists also drew on European Romanticism, which exalted Classical Antiquity and the Middle Ages and emphasised the cultivation of one's own particular language and legends, with the result that in both Catalonia and Galicia from the 1850s cultural revival movements grew up – the *Renaixença* and *Rexordimento* – which mythologised and glorified these regions' past (Chapters 4 and 14). Similarly in the Basque Country so-called *fuerista* writers, took up myths which had been built up from the sixteenth to the nineteenth centuries and spun tales of the independent spirit of the Basque peoples, who had descended from Tubal, nephew of Noa, and who, by bravely fighting off the Romans, had retained their original language (Jauristi 1986). Their organicist vision of their own territory, which postulated the forging of a particular race with its own character through a combination of spirit,

---

3. The traditionalist historian, Víctor Gebhardt, argued in favour of 'the right which Catalonia, Navarre, the Basque provinces and the other regions of Spain which feel at ease with the remnants of their national existence have to live their own lives' (Cirujano Marín et al. 1985: 129). In quite similar terms the conservative representative of Catalan industrial interests, Juan Mañé y Flaquer, stated in 1855: 'Spain is a federation of peoples (*pueblos*), of nationalities, of distinct races, with different traditions, different customs and different languages' (Riquer 1987: 78–9).

customs and language, certainly helped lay the basis for future ethno-cultural nationalisms. Significantly, however, Portuguese Romantic writers never pursued themes which could, in the future, be taken up by anti-state nationalists. On the contrary, a major theme in Portuguese Romantic literature was Luís de Camões, the sixteenth-century poet who, in the nineteenth century, became the symbol of national identity (Chapter 3).

It can, therefore, be seen that in Spain by the second half of the nine-teenth century the centralist liberal vision was widely challenged. This was not unique to Spain. Nevertheless, it may be argued that the failure of the liberal state to command the allegiance of much of the nineteenth-century intelligentsia, and its weak integration of the sub-altern classes into the dominant conservative-liberal conceptualisation of the nation, allowed a particularly lush undergrowth of antagonistic ideological plants to grow. Furthermore, the diverse historical memories and traditions provided fertile soil for a 'regional' cultural production which sat uneasily with myths of Spanish nationhood. As we shall see, with the injection of European theories of race and nation into the Spanish body politic, not only were alternative nationalist ideologies build on these foundations, but social groups alienated from the dom-inant oligarchy could come to see their grievances in nationalist terms.

Inventing the Alternative Nations

Nationalist currents grew up throughout much of Spain during the sec-ond half of the century. Their intellectual pedigree was never uniform, and even within particular territories competing nationalist ideologies and even movements were to grow. Nevertheless, it was the case that the dominant current to a large extent adapted what has been referred to as German cultural nationalism, and, therefore, postulated what were seen as a series of ahistorical, immutable, markers, such as the race, spirit, culture and language, which determined the shape of the nation, viewed as an organic whole above and beyond the individual (Alter 1994: 9; Chapter 4). This was perhaps in part inevitable as non-statist nationalists had to seek other markers of identity (Máiz 1984: 146), but it also reflected the growing conservatism of much European intellect-ual thought from the mid-nineteenth century (Hobsbawm 1992: 102–4). The result was an exotic cocktail of racial nationalist theories and hist-orical exegesis which were meant to provide the passport to nationhood.

In Andalusia from the late 1860s a group of ethnologists and folk-lorists linked to Antonio Machado y Núñez, Professor of Natural His-tory at the University of Seville, developed the theory that the And-alusians were an amalgam of Arab and Christian blood, and therefore of an entirely separate national category from their Castilian neighbours (Moreno Navarro 1981: 237–8). From the mid-nineteenth century the father of Galician nationalism, Manuel Murguía, argued that the Galicians were in fact of Celtic-Swabian descent, and therefore a subgroup of the superior central European Aryan race. This set them apart from the inferior Spanish-Semitic race who had unjustly dominated them (Máiz 1984: 136–80). From the late nineteenth century, moreover, Galician nationalists maintained that this Celtic community also encompassed Portugal – as we have noted, both the Galician and Portuguese languages had the same origin and were still close – and that they should, therefore, be reintegrated within a single nation (Beramendi 1991: 160–3; Chapter 14). Similarly, in Catalonia nationalists developed the argument that Catalans were of European Celtic or Aryan stock, while the Castilians were Semitics of African descent (Marfany 1995: 205). In the 1890s in the Basque Country, Sabino Arana set out his beliefs that the Basques formed a pristine European race, which had remained unconquered in the Cantabrian mountains and Pyrenees throughout the ages. Nevertheless, nationalist demands based purely on race were more convincing in some cases than in others. Basque nationalists could, indeed, present a strong case for millennial isolationism combined with distinct physical features. This was far more difficult for Catalans and Galicians to argue, and this no doubt helps explain why these two movements laid greater stress on markers such as spirit, language, laws and history to justify nationhood (Chapter 4).

As in the Spanish nation-state case, each of these antagonistic nationalist theories needed to appeal to History for justification. However, unlike liberal Spanish nationalists, who saw the building of the Spanish nation as a cumulative process, these anti-state nationalists, drawing on the writings of the nineteenth-century Romantics, appealed to a past Golden Age when their people had lived freely and in harmony (Smith 1991: 66–8). These narrators of the alternative nations then charted the fall, brought about by growing influence and conquest by Castile (portrayed as the oppressor nation), and went on to describe the bravura struggles of the subjected people at the hands of their subjugator. This, however, was, of course, only the prologue to redemption at the hands of the new nationalist movement in the process of organisation.

Depending on the racial stereotype and preconceptions of the territory's history the mythological narration would, nevertheless, vary enormously. In the case of Andalusia nationalist ideologues painted an idyllic picture of the centuries of Moorish domination, in which the arts, culture and civilisation had flourished. This was brought to a brutal close by conquest (not reconquest as in the Spanish nationalist narrative) at the hands of the barbarous Castilians (Cortes Peña 1994: 228–

42). In Galicia early integration into the Crown of Castile meant that the Golden Age tended to be placed in the supposedly ethnically pure, Aryan, pre-Roman past. This was also the case in the Basque Country, where Sabino Arana portrayed the people as living in a rural arcadia until the ninth century when the *Señorío de Vizcaya* and the Crown of Castile united. They still, according to Arana, valiantly defended their independence, but were slowly sapped by intermarriage with Castilians. The fall would then come with the undermining of the *fueros* by Spain in 1839 (Granja Sanz 1994: 97–139). In Catalonia, on the other hand, for nationalist historians writing from the turn of the century the Golden Age was to be found in the Middle Ages, when between the twelfth and fourteenth centuries the Aragonese Confederation (in which Catalonia had been the dominant partner) had indeed been a major Mediterranean power, and Catalan a respected language of culture on a par with Castilian and the various dialects of Italian. Here the fall began with the Caspe Compromise and the consolidation of the Castilian Trastamara dynasty, and the Union of the Crowns between Fernando and Isabella in 1479 which linked Catalonia to Castile. The following two centuries were seen as witnessing a process of inefficient and ruinous Castilian centralisation with culminated in the War of Succession, portrayed as a war of national liberation, and which in turn provoked the 1714 *Decreto de Nueva Planta*, through which all Catalonia's political institutions and liberties were abolished (Solé Tura 1974: 156; Simon i Tarrés 1994: 210).

These nationalist historiographies were not equally convincing. The Catalan nationalist account formed the basis for the development of a powerful historiographical current, which culminated in Ferran Soldevila's three volume *Història de Catalunya* in 1934/35. On the other hand, Sabino Arana's disquisitions on Basque history were not taken seriously by historians even in the late nineteenth century. Nor, it may be suggested, are all mythical histories equally effective. Where, as in the case of Catalonia and the Basque Country, one could appeal to institutions which had existed in the relatively recent past and which were still retained within the historical memory of at least the proposed nation's educated classes, then the imagination of the new national community could be more effectively propagated.

The Portuguese Counter-Model: An Unchallenged Nation-State

The Portuguese experience certainly lends credence to this claim. As has been noted, there were many similar elements in Portugal's and Spain's nineteenth-century evolution. In Portugal the early nineteenth century also saw a liberal revolution against the old order, and from the mid-nineteenth century the country came under the sway of elite, oligarchic politics. As in Spain two parties rotated in government, their power resting on the rural *caciques* (Gallagher 1983: 14–17). It would also be mistaken to believe that the Portuguese authorities carried out a programme of nation-building any more effectively than their Spanish counterparts. Thus, for example, throughout Europe in the nineteenth century education played a key role in forging a new national consciousness, but in Portugal the education system remained rudimentary, and, in European terms, illiteracy rates were extremely high. Futhermore, the fact that anarchism, a passionately anti-state and internationalist creed, tended to be the dominant current within the labour movement until the 1930s also indicates a relatively weak national integration. As in Spain regional variations in social structure and socio-cultural identities, patterns of religious worship and political allegiance were also highly pronounced, with the additional feature that two of the regions bordering on Spain were more similar to their Spanish counterparts than to other areas in Portugal itself. The Alentejo in the south was a land of great landed estates (*latifundia*), which bore a pronounced resemblance to the southern Spanish *latifundista* belt in Andalusia, whereas the Minho region in the north-west of the country, a region of tiny peasant plots and a highly religious peasantry, was akin to Galicia (Pina Cabral 1989: 11). Similarities could also be discerned in the division of political and economic power; in both Spain and Portugal the political capital (Madrid and Lisbon respectively) was not the industrial powerhouse. This was Oporto in Portugal and Barcelona in Spain.

Moreover, a similar division opened up between liberal-conservative elites and liberal-democratic republicans. Even the terms of the divide were comparable; while the conservative elites' power rested primarily on the *latifundistas*, and secondarily on finance and big business, the republicans recruited from the urban middle and lower classes, who felt excluded from power, and from intellectuals disgusted at the stultifying conservatism of the ruling order.

Like all nineteenth-century state nationalists, the Portuguese liberal intellectuals presented a vision of their history as a process of national awakening, and in this march towards nationhood the great fifteenth-century Portuguese maritime Discoveries were assigned a central role. It is on this nationalist discourse, and especially its appropriation by the republicans, that the chapters in this volume by AbdoolKarim Vakil and Alan Freeland centre. As Vakil explains, from its foundation in 1880 the Republican Party was to mount a determined challenge to the ruling regime. The central ideological weapon in its armoury was the successful move to hegemonise nationalist discourse and present itself as the only force which could forge a national 'imagined community'. The assault began with the organisation of celebrations to commemorate the tercentenary in 1880 of the sixteenth-century poet and symbol of Portuguese national identity, Luís de Camões. The central theme of these celebrations was the Portuguese Discoveries, which were presented as Portugal's monumental contribution to scientific progress and the expansion of European civilisation. In this way the republicans looked to link the Discoveries to their own political agenda, arguing that only they could recapture this era of progress and modernisation. In contrast, like their Spanish republican counterparts, they presented the monarchist parties as backward-looking, neglectful of empire and unable to construct the nation-state. Vakil stresses the success of this 'cultural politics', and how the Discoveries from this date became central to any definition of national identity. In this respect similarities can be discerned with Spain, where the dominant oligarchic parties were also both unable and unwilling to attempt to enlist the new techniques of mass politics (the modern party, press, mass meetings) to mobilise behind nationalist discourse (Chapter 5). Nevertheless, as Vakil points out, this did not ensure the republicans' permanent hegemonisation of the cultural-political symbol. Following the overthrow of the monarchy, during the First Republic (1910–26) it became the contested terrain around which rival liberal-democratic and conservative formations attempted to mobilise. The Right looked to promote a rival interpretation of the Discoveries which stressed the country's Christian Catholic mission. As we shall see, the Spanish Second Republic (1931–6) was to see a quite similar set of debates.

While in these respects, then, many similarities between Portugal and Spain can be pointed to, it is essential to note that in the Portuguese case conservative and liberal renditions of nationalism were not challenged by anti-Portuguese nationalist discourses. Certainly Portuguese nationalism was both obsessive and uncertain. This was, as Alan Freeland shows, reflected in the nationalist Romantic and historiographical writers of the nineteenth century, who painted a picture of decline from the mid-sixteenth century, and who were preoccupied by perceived threats to Portugal's national identity. However, this was the result of a sense of backwardness, and the fear of attack from without rather than undermining from within. The major enemy was, of course, Spain. Nationalist historiographers portrayed the Portuguese people as having fought bravely to throw off Spanish rule and oppression, but possible Spanish intervention remained in the back of politicians' and intellectuals' minds. This was, as Alan Freeland points out, not fanciful in the context of the second half of the nineteenth century, when Portugal's small size and population made her claim to nationhood questionable (indeed in 1801, during the 'war of the oranges', in alliance with France Spain had seized the Alentejo district of Olivença). Nevertheless, fear of Spanish designs on Portugal persisted well into the twentieth century. Gallagher (1983: 150), for example, argues that in the late 1960s discontented officers were constrained from toppling the rapidly weakening Salazarist regime for fear of possible Spanish intervention. The other major preoccupation for Portuguese nationalists was, Freeland tells us, the uncertain British alliance. This was forged as early as the thirteenth century, and by the seventeenth century had become of key importance in deterring possible Spanish threats to independence. It had resulted in the establishment of a close trading relationship and heavy British investment in the Portuguese wine trade. Yet at the same time it placed Portugal in a position of weakness, her very national survival dependent on the politics of a foreign power, and it afforded the Portuguese no special treatment when it came to British foreign policy. This became clear in 1880 when an attempt by Portugal to link her colonies in Mozambique and Angola was met by the so-called British ultimatum: a threat to declare war if the plan were not abandoned. On the other hand, it may be argued that this siege mentality, fostered by both the nationalist Left and Right, has in itself played a significant role in stimulating the nationalist cohesion of Portuguese society.

The Rise of Peripheral Nationalisms in Spain

The history of the peripheral nationalisms in Spain in the early twentieth century tends to bear out this link, discussed in the previous sections, between the rise of nationalism and historic/linguistic markers of identity. Between 1890 and 1936 only the Catalan, Basque and to a far lesser extent Galician nationalist (*Galeguista*) movements were able to structure effective political parties with an ample social base. These were also the three areas in Spain in which indigenous languages other than Castilian were spoken (see Chapter 4). Viewed from this perspective there seems little doubt that the fact that the monolingual Castilian-speaking community – concentrated in Castile and the south – made up about 75 per cent of Spain's population at the end of the nineteenth century (Riquer 1994: 110) served at least to limit the intensity of the anti-Spanish nationalist challenge.

Yet language and historical identity is in itself insufficient as an explanatory model. This is indicated by the fact that much of the Catalan industrial and commercial elite had abandoned Catalan in the eighteenth century, but in the early twentieth century they became the bank-rollers of the major Catalanist party, the *Lliga Regionalista*. At the same time,

Catalan was widely spoken in the Balearic Islands and Valencia, but strong nationalist movements did not grow up in these territories prior to 1936. Furthermore, Galician was far more widely spoken than Basque and even Catalan, yet nationalist parties were weaker than in either of these two territories.

This was a reflection of the fact that nationalism was also about power, and became the vehicle of groups who felt they had been marginalised from the structures of central government and believed themselves to be the victims of its policies. Nationalism could, in particular, attract the rural and urban middle classes, who favoured ideologies which though attacking the abuses of central government did not call into question the essentials of the social order. Nevertheless, this left the door open to considerable variations in social support, as a comparison of Catalanism and Basque nationalism makes clear.

Catalanism developed in urban Catalonia from the 1880s, picking up support amongst lower-middle and middle-class social strata, industrialists – who following the 'Disaster' of 1898 were exasperated at the regime's seeming inability to defend their interests – and anti-liberal rural property owners (Riquer 1987: 78–84; Marfany 1995; Chapters 6 and 10). This diverse base of support was reflected in the fact that while the dominant strand within early twentieth-century Catalanism, represented by the *Lliga*, had strong traditionalist, anti-democratic, roots (Solé Tura 1974: 209–31), rather than look back to the *ancien regime*, the party saw itself as the motor for the industrialisation of Catalan and, by extension, Spanish society (Erlich 1992/3: 43–50).

In contrast Basque nationalism always retained a heavy Catholic-conservative slant. Sabino Arana was an extreme anti-liberal traditionalist, who saw Catholicism and the rural peasantry as the soul of the Basque people. In the early years the *Partido Nacionalista Vasco* (PNV), founded by Sabino Arana in 1895, therefore became a refuge for declining petty bourgeois and artisanal groups, whose way of life and livelihood were under threat from the rapid industrialisation of the Vizcaya region from the 1870s. This helps explain the virulent racism which the PNV directed at the immigrant 'Spanish' labour force (Elorza 1978: 132–8). Nevertheless, from the turn of the century a more modern middle-class grouping known as the *Euskalerriacos* gained influence within the party. Unlike the emerging steel, mining and financial elites, which became closely linked to the central Spanish oligarchy (Harrison 1977: 371–93), the new grouping represented those sectors integrated into the territory's new industrial economy, such as shopkeepers and shopworkers, office workers and the professions, who were, nevertheless, excluded from centres of administration by the elites' operation of *caciquismo* (Corcuera Atienza 1978; Mees 1989: 71–99).

The populist, vaguely anti-capitalist egalitarian rhetoric of the followers of Sabino Arana also allowed the PNV to develop a significant base amongst the indigenous Basque working class.

On the base of this middle-class discontent both Catalanism, and to a lesser extent Basque nationalism, were to grow rapidly. Already in the first decade of the twentieth century Catalan nationalism represented a serious challenge to the central state, and in the Second Republic during the 1930s the PNV emerged as the most powerful single party in the Basque Country. In comparison Galician nationalism or *Galeguismo* for long remained a movement of competing liberal and conservative political elites in search of a base. Only during the Second Republic did a unified party, the *Partido Galeguista*, formed in December 1931, make a significant impact, although it remained at a considerable distance from the statist Right and Left parties (Beramendi 1991: 164–70). In part the relative failure of *Galeguismo* can be put down to the fact that the territory had been integrated into the Crown of Castile early, and there was no historical memory of institutions of self-government on which nationalists could hang their discourse, as in the case of Catalonia with the medieval parliament and in the Basque Country with the *fueros*. More important was probably the underdeveloped rural nature of much of the Galician social structure, which meant that communications remained poor and localism strong (Máiz 1994: 173–208). In this case then the problems faced by Spanish nationalism in spreading its discourse also restrained its competitor. Furthermore, the dependency of the peasantry on landed elites meant that Galicia was prime territory for rural *caciques* linked to the central state.

In other territories anti-Spanish nationalists had even less success. Valencia provides an especially interesting case study. Catalan was not only spoken in Catalonia itself but also in Valencia, the Balearic Islands and the French *département* of Roussillon (which had formed part of Catalonia until 1659, and came to be referred to by Catalan nationalists as *Catalunya Nord*). The demand for a close association between the 'Catalan countries' remained an important element within Catalanist discourse. The response in Valencia was, however, disappointing. The first pan-Catalanist *Valencianista* groups[4] were set up in 1907, and after 1914 Right and liberal-Left *Valencianista* parties were formed, with a base amongst urban industrialists and the middle and lower-middle classes. Yet they were to remain minoritarian. On the one hand, one can point to the fact that the linguistic base of Catalan was significantly eroded in some parts of Valencia in comparison to Catalonia. Just as

4. Valencian historians refer to pan-Catalanist Valencian nationalism as *Valencianisme Politic*.

important was the political context. The *Valencianistes* faced a Spanish nationalist republican movement known as *Blasquismo* (so-called after the republican Valencian novelist, Blasco Ibañez), and the dominant agrarian elites also showed great hostility. This was a consequence of antagonistic economic interests, for while Catalan industrialists and the *Lliga* championed economic protectionism the orange and wine exporters of Valencia favoured free trade. The key aspect for our study is that from the turn of the century this polemic was to a large extent fought out in nationalist terms. The political representatives of agrarian elites and the *Blasquistas* argued that Valencia needed to forge links with Murcia and the Spanish agrarian interior, and presented the Catalanists and by extension Catalonia as their natural enemies. Hence, a discourse was forged which alerted to Catalonia's 'imperialist' designs on Valencia, and stressed the existence of a separate Valencian spirit and identity, shown in their own bilingual culture, in the specificity of the Valencian language (presented, despite limited grammatical variations, as separate from Catalan) and in the cordial relations obtaining with the rest of Spain. It was the fact that variants of this discourse were promoted by both the urban Left and agrarian Right which reduced the political space open to *Valencianisme*, and ensured that an antagonistic Valencian/Spanish identity would coalesce in wide sections of the public (Cucó 1974; Martínez Serrano and Soler Marco 1977: 24–30; Fabra i Sanch 1977: 31–6; Pérez Moragón 1983: 57–82).

In a weaker position still were the *Andalucistas*, who under the Left-liberal leadership of Blasco Infante between 1910 and 1936 were unable to build a significant social base. On the one hand, they could expect no sympathy from the Andalusian landholding elite, which was one of the pillars of the Restoration regime and later, during the Second Republic, rallied behind the parties of right-wing Spanish nationalism. On the other, the land-hungry peasantry backed the anarchists and Socialists (Cortes Peña 1994: 222–3). Moreover, Andalusians had been depicted by Spanish nationalists as central to the Spanish national character, and it seems likely that these stereotypes were assimilated as the dominant self-image of elites and the urban middle classes.

Though, like the Spanish nationalists, the alternative nationalist movements tried to paint a picture of national unity, even in the Catalan and Basque case, the reality was rather different. In both areas nationalists had to contend with Spanish nationalist republican movements, and from 1914 in particular, they were faced with the consolidation of an independent class-based labour movement under Socialist and anarchist hegemony (Chapter 10). This not only affected the peripheral nationalisms. As José Alvarez Junco suggests, the weakness of Spanish state-building helps explain the strength of anarchism. Yet as Angel Smith notes, peripheral nationalists had the additional problem that though Socialists and anarchists described themselves as internationalists they tended to see the consolidation of the established nation-states as laying the foundations for further material and social progress on the road to communism. This together with the strong traditionalist elements often present within the anti-state nationalist ideologies in the early twentieth century led to a vision of them within much of the leftist and working-class press as backward and reactionary.

This was most starkly brought out in the Basque Country where the immigrant Socialist movement remained – as would be expected given the racist rhetoric of the PNV – vehemently anti-Basque nationalist (Fusi Aizpurúa 1979). In Catalonia the situation was more complex, but a similar set of problems could to a degree be perceived. This is the subject of Angel Smith's chapter in this volume, where he argues that the fact that from the turn of the century the *Lliga* hegemonised Catalanism produced a generally negative reaction in working-class circles with only the most reformist elements coming under nationalist tutelage. Only during the Second Republic when the republican *Esquerra Republicana de Catalunya* (ERC) became the dominant Catalanist party could the movement attract wider working-class sympathy (Ucelay da Cal 1982).

All nationalisms fashion idealised national cultures (Díaz-Andreu 1996), and the anti-Spanish nationalisms had, of course, also to invent (or at least recycle) their own, alternative (both competing and antagonistic) cultures and traditions. This process went, as might be expected, furthest in Catalonia and the Basque Country. In Catalonia, from the turn of the century, Catalanists propagated a nationalist rendition of rural folk songs, presented as *the* authentic songs of the new nation, and adopted the *sardana* (in fact the folk-dance of the Empordà region of the Costa Brava) as *the* national dance. At the same time, the mountain of Montserrat and its Benedictine convent were converted into the spiritual heartland of Catalonia. In 1899 a Catalanist adaption of the folk-song, *La guerra dels segadors* (commemorating the revolt of the peasantry against Castilian domination in 1640), was adopted as the national song. Then, from 1901, Catalanists began celebrating 11 September as the national day, in homage to the desperate defence of the city of Barcelona against the advancing Castilian army in 1714. This was accompanied by the setting up of an ever denser network of clubs, hiking and choral societies (Marfany 1995: 293–353). At the same time an attempt was made to Catalanise the major cultural and intellectual forums of debate in Barcelona, and to codify and standardise the

Catalan language. In the Basque Country, meanwhile, in the 1890s Sabino Arana invented the major symbols of the Basque nation, including the country's name (*Euskadi*) and flag (the *ikuriña*). Henceforth from the first years of the new century the PNV would function as a 'party nation', setting up a series of political-recreational associations known as *batzokis*. The work of the other nationalist movements was naturally less intense. In Galicia, nevertheless, the tradition of the *Xogos Florais* (oral poetry contests) of the late nineteenth century was continued, and combined with an interest in literary output in Galician, work on developing linguistic norms and the production of various literary-nationalist magazines, which were to become the organs of the emerging political groups. The *Valencianistes*, for their part, as might be expected, functioned as rather a pale shadow of their Catalan counterparts.

The symbols, activities and commemorations have, in large measure, remained through to the present day as the hallmarks of the alternative nations. However, this should not lead one to assume that the nationalist movements were politically and culturally static. Their nationalist *volksgeist* could be grafted onto both traditionalist, liberal and leftist political discourses (Beramendi 1991: 137–8), and all the major movements were to have more conservative and democratic wings. As we have seen, in Catalan and especially Basque nationalism in the early twentieth century more traditionalist currents predominated. Galician and Andalusian nationalists, on the other hand, tended to be more liberal, probably because their associations and parties were staffed by urban intellectual elites, rather disconnected from urban and rural property owners and Catholic opinion. However, as the century progressed, peripheral nationalism moved to the Left. This was most clearly the case in Catalonia, where by the Second Republic the hegemonic nationalist party was the republican ERC, but even in the Basque Country during these years the PNV began to move in a more Christian-democratic direction (Fusi Aizpurúa 1979; Granja Sanz 1986).

Behind this shift a general factor could be seen at work. A new vociferous Spanish Right had grown up from the first decade of the twentieth century (see below, pp.19–21), which was viscerally opposed to any form of home rule and, in these circumstances, it became clear that only the Spanish Left would accede to a decentralisation of the state. This encouraged peripheral nationalists to see themselves as the 'democratic' opposition to authoritarian Spanish nationalism, and to develop contacts with Spanish republican and Socialist groups. Furthermore, in Catalonia, the only area in which elites played a powerful role in the autochthonous nationalist movement, growing social conflict from 1914 led them to seek military support from

Madrid, thereby discrediting in Catalanist eyes the conservative *Lliga*, a party which they strongly influenced.

Surprisingly at first sight, given that according to certain nationalist doctrine each nation should have its own state, of these parties only the PNV took an unambiguously separatist stance, yet even in this case the more possibilist, *Euskalerriaco*, wing favoured autonomy within Spain, and the party was in practice to accept an autonomy statute from the Republic during the Civil War. In general these parties, seemingly building on ideas first developed by the federalists, worked for the formation of a decentralised Iberian confederation of 'nations' (e.g. Catalonia or the 'Catalan Countries', Castile, Andalusia, Galicia and Portugal), which could also be enlarged to take in, depending on the schema, the 'Latin races' or even the whole of Western Europe (Solé Tura 1974: 195–206; Pérez Moragón 1983: 70; Beramendi 1991: 160–3; Cortés Peña 1994: 72–3). In large measure, it seems, this was the result of pragmatism: only through civil war or foreign intervention could full-blown independence be achieved, and such independence might, indeed, adversely affect the nationalist parties' middle-class base. Another factor involved was also possibly the fact that a degree of Spanish identity was to be found throughout most of Spain, leading to reluctance to call for total succession. Indeed, the leading figures of the weaker nationalist parties especially, such as the *Andalucistas*, tended to use a confusing vocabulary in which it was unclear whether Spain or one's own territory were the nation. Whatever the causes, this stance in favour of home rule did mean that during the Second Republic it seemed possible that a solution would be found to Spain's 'national problem' through the granting of autonomy statutes. An autonomous Catalan government (the *Generalitat*) began to operate from late 1932, Galicia voted in favour of its own autonomy statute a little before the start of the Civil War, and the Basques were granted a statute by the Republican authorities during the war itself. The assumption of power by the Franco regime would, however, lead to this process being aborted.

The State Nationalist Left and Right in Spain and Portugal, 1910–1974

From the late nineteenth century, in both Spain and Portugal, the world of elite oligarchic politics entered into crisis as the urban masses took to the political stage. At the same time, underdevelopment and colonial humiliation (in Portugal in 1890, in Spain in 1898) produced a pessimistic assessment of the nation's place within the new imperialist world order. As we have seen, in both countries it was the republicans who promised to attack what they saw as the institutional roots of backwardness, and who fashioned modernising nationalist discourses. The Spanish Second Republic and Portuguese First Republic, however, showed the limits of this rhetoric.

In her analysis of nation-building during the Spanish Republic and in the Republican zone during the Civil War (1936–9), Helen Graham (Chapter 8) argues that the objective conditions that faced the Republic were daunting. In social and cultural terms Spain was highly fragmented, and the parties of the Left were enormously divided. The republicans' project also had serious limitations: first, they had a narrow base of support amongst the progressive urban middle classes; second, the rather conservative republican leadership's nationalist discourse tended to centre on parliament itself, rather than reaching out to the populace.

The limits of the republican project were, nevertheless, most crudely exposed during the Portuguese First Republic, when republican governments extended the franchise no further than the middle classes, became divided into three groupings which fiercely competed for power, and like the monarchists before them became enmeshed in a system of patronage and nepotism. Hence, there could be no possibility of forming a broad inter-class alliance for reform, and by the early 1920s even the middle classes and intelligentsia were becoming weary of political bickering and strife (Wheeler 1978).

The difficulties of the Republican nation-state projects in Spain and Portugal gave new opportunities to the Right to reconquer state power. As in other European countries the early years of the twentieth century saw a revival of right-wing politics, and the structuring of new anti-liberal, authoritarian, state-nationalist right-wing movements and theories of the nation-state. This was, of course, a response to the growth of mass politics and democratisation, the appearance and development of leftist political parties, the rise of labour, and, particularly in Spain, the growth of peripheral nationalisms and the fear of egalitarian reforms. It was the final loss of the levers of state power in Spain and Portugal which galvanised the Right into action. Thus it is no coincidence that both the Spanish and Portuguese Republics were overthrown by military coups, and that dictatorships, closely linked to social elites, were subsequently installed in their place.

In Spain, as both Balfour and Romero Salvadó point out (Chapters 6 and 7), the Spanish nationalist authoritarian Right began to grow from the turn of the century. Rightist proposals found the greatest echo amongst military officers and, later, conservative civilian politicians, who feared that liberalism was leading to chaos and anarchy, and, as Michael Richards explains (Chapter 9), they received ideological cover from anti-democratic currents within 'regenerationist' thought. It was this counter-mobilisation which was to lead to the establishment of first the Primo de Rivera dictatorship (1923–30), and then the Franco regime (1939–75). The Right fashioned its own national discourse, which drew on nineteenth-century Catholic traditionalism, and then integrated twentieth-century fascist thought. It eulogised the *Reconquista* and the conquest of the Americas, during which Spain (seen almost exclusively in terms of Castile) fulfilled her destiny by spreading the Christian, Catholic faith. In contrast, the nineteenth and early twentieth centuries were viewed as a period of decline in which the country was infected by the foreign viruses of liberalism, socialism and communism. Only a reconstruction of the country's essential Catholić self, then, could provide the basis for Spain to reconquer her past glories. The Right's project was therefore highly exclusivist. The Catalans and Basques were seen as Spaniards who had to be brought back to the fold by any means, and the Left was portrayed as an anti-nationalist cancer which had to be extirpated.

As Michael Richards shows, this project reached its apogee in the early years of the Franco regime, when autarky combined with insti-tutionalised violence were utilised as weapons in the fight to cleanse Spain of decadent, foreign influences, and lay the basis for a triumphal rebirth of Spain as a powerful, unified, Catholic state. The result in the early years was not only the fierce repression of the Left, but also of all manifestations of what were seen as anti-Spanish cultures and languages, with the result that the use of Catalan, Basque and Galician was severely restricted (see Chapter 4).

Right-wing Portuguese nationalism was not far removed from this ideological universe. The early twentieth century saw the growth of rightist parties, the most influential of which were the Lusitanian Integralists, who tried to wrest from the republicans their hegemony over nationalist discourse. Hence, they presented a reading of the Dis-coveries which emphasised Portugal's Catholic mission over scientific endeavour. The instability of the Republic combined with a growth of labour unrest from 1914 was used by the Right to argue that order was needed to ensure Portugal's future. It was finally overthrown in a mil-itary coup in 1926 which, because of Republican mismanagement, at first had quite wide-ranging middle- and upper-middle-class support.

There were to be a number of significant divergencies between the Portuguese dictatorship and the Franco regime. As there had been no need to fight a civil war to ensure a conservative return to power in Portugal, repression was far less severe, and the military never felt the need to retain the reins of power to the same extent. Hence, it was to be a civilian politician in the shape of António de Oliveira Salazar who

Myths and Realities of Nation-Building

would consolidate a *de facto* personal dictatorship, the so-called *Estado Novo*, from 1930 (Gallagher 1983: 38–61). However (especially after the end of the Franco regime's 'semi-fascist' phase of 1939–45), many similarities could be discerned between the traditionalist, Catholic nationalist rhetoric of both regimes. In Portugal this was reflected in the *'Fatima'* cult, with Salazar pictured, by its clerical promoters, as the Messiah which Our Lady in her miraculous visitation of 1917 had promised would rescue Portugal from catastrophe (Gallagher 1983: 94).

Nationalism and Nation-Building in the New Spain and Portugal

Repression of the peripheral nationalist movements did not however lead to an eclipse of nationalist aspirations in these territories. As Michael Richards points out in this volume, the Franco regime was never able to convince the social milieu linked to the Republican project, with the consequent frequent recourse to violence and repression. Social elites throughout Spain spoke Castilian, and amongst parts of the non-politicised middle class, especially in the Basque Country and Galicia, there was also a tendency to use Castilian within the home environment in order to socialise children in the language of the public sphere.

Yet at the same time, as Llobera, Tejerina Montaña and MacClancey make clear (Chapters 11, 12 and 13), in both Catalonia and the Basque Country there was a stubborn cultural resistance within the old nationalist communities. This was accompanied by a redefinition of the nationalist discourse. The consequences of fascist and especially Nazi rule were to discredit, throughout Western Europe, the language of race – totally generalised in Spanish and Portuguese political circles in the early twentieth century – with the result that new markers of identity had to be emphasised. In the Basque Country and Catalonia this coincided with further rapid industrial development from the 1950s, the influx of a new wave of 'Spanish' immigrants and the consequent further dilution of the native population. The combined result was that in the 1960s a new generation of nationalists placed a greater weight on language and culture as markers of identity. The switch in emphasis was most obvious in the Basque Country, where race had been the totally defining characteristic of early twentieth-century discourse. These markers proved more flexible because one could become part of the nationalist community through education rather than birth.

In the highly repressive atmosphere of early Francoism it was, in general, difficult for nationalist sympathisers to go much further than transmit their vernacular, and cultural and political beliefs, through family and friendship networks, but from the 1950s nationalists began the work of creating a cultural space through various types of associations. In the Basque Country, as Benjamín Tejerina Montaña shows (Chapter 13), the redefinition of nationalism and the growing threat posed to the survival of the Basque language (Euskera) galvanised younger nationalists into action, with great effort expended on the creation of a network of Basque language schools known as *ikastolas*.

In Catalonia, on the other hand, effort was put into restructuring Catalanist hicking clubs, choral dance societies and the like, which had been decimated by the onset of Franco's rule. This was then followed in both areas by a successful move to reestablish a book industry in the vernacular. From the transition to democracy, as the nationalist movement broadened, this growth in nationalist activity was accompanied by the reestablishment of commemorations designed to affirm the respective nation and, later, the resurrection of a Basque and Catalan nationalist landscape of toponyms and monuments. This question is central to Josep Llobera's chapter (Chapter 11), which analyses the role played by the 11 September and 23 April (the Day of the Book) in contemporary Catalan culture. As Llobera emphasises, historical and cultural memory is central to the reproduction of a national project, and commemorations have a key role to play in this reproduction.

This re-consolidation of a nationalist counter-culture was accompanied by the rise of left-wing nationalist projects. This, as has been indicated, was not totally new. We have already noted the tendency for nationalist movements to move Left in the early part of the century. However, the 1960s saw, amongst segments of Spain's radicalised anti-Francoist student youth, the linking of Marxism to demands for the freedom of the oppressed nation. Rather like the anti-colonial guerrilla forces of Central and Latin America and Africa, the new generation of radical nationalists maintained that their social elites had sold out to the colonial power (Castile or Spain), and that it was the downtrodden people who would simultaneously carry through a national and socialist revolution (Sullivan 1988: 41; Máiz 1994: 195–6). Such rhetoric could be seen in a number of movements founded from the late 1950s: ETA in the Basque Country; the *Unión del Pobo Galego* (UPG) in Galicia; the *Partit Socialista d'Alliberament Nacional dels Països Catalans* (PSAN) in Catalonia; and the *Partido Socialista Andaluz* (PSA) in Andalusia. It was, however, only ETA that would seriously resort to armed struggle against the Franco regime, stimulated by the violent rhetoric and intransigence inherited from the nationalism of Sabino Arana, fear of the disappearance of the Basque language and the extreme radicalisation of the political climate (Clark 1984).

The rise of these leftist nationalisms led to divisions within the nationalist communities, which, as we shall see, would be particularly severe in the Basque Country. However, in the 1960s and early 1970s the emphasis was on unity. As the Francoist regime weakened under pressure from a broad-ranging front of workers, students and the progressive middle classes and intelligentsia, so the peripheral nationalist movements were able to establish a wide social base. Because of the repressive centralism of the Franco regime and the anti-Spanish nationalisms' identification with the anti-Francoist struggle, the demand for autonomy and respect for one's own language and 'culture' came to be seen as consubstantial with the democratisation of the Spanish State. The flip side of the coin was the crisis of Spanish nationalism, which was viewed as innately imperialistic and authoritarian outside conservative circles, with the result that in the heady years of 1973–8 demands for autonomy were voiced throughout Spain. This was also reflected in the programmes of the Spanish leftist parties such as the Spanish Socialist Workers' Party (PSOE), which used an anti-state nationalist vocabulary and called for the establishment of a federation of Iberian nationalities within the Spanish State, rather than regions within the Spanish nation (Gillespie 1989: 303).

Under these circumstances a transition to democracy necessitated a decentralisation of state power and a recognition of the peripheral nationalisms. This was finally carried through by a group of ex-Francoists, led by Adolfo Suarez. Originally, it appears, they had planned to give some form of autonomy to Catalonia, the Basque Country and possibly Galicia, but faced with an overwhelming clamour for home rule they decided that only a decentralisation of the entire state structure would afford Spain any degree of stability. This was reciprocated by the other major political parties, who collaborated in drawing up the new Constitution of December 1978. This, as Clare Mar-Molinero and Alan Whitehead show (Chapters 4 and 15), was very much a compromise document, through which Spain was divided up between seventeen autonomous regions, though with the central state retaining a high degree of financial control, and which recognised certain linguistic rights of minorities, while maintaining Castilian as the hegemonic language. As Alan Whitehead explains, future developments are very much dependent on the evolution of the European Union, though trends are already in progress which indicate an evolution of the present 'State of the Autonomies' (*Estado de las Autonomias*), towards a system within which the major cities and regions will attain a high degree of independent decision-making capacity.

As is to be expected there was no pressure for an equivalent decentralisation of the Portuguese State following the revolution. On the mainland the sense of Portuguese identity remained strong, and with the exception of the Atlantic island chains of Madeira and the Azores (see below, p.25) the Constitution of 1976 proposed only a limited administrative decentralisation to newly created regions (Braga da Cruz 1992: 154–62).

Since the mid-1970s anti-Spanish nationalisms have again become consolidated in Catalonia and the Basque Country. In both these areas wide sections of the middle class have – as in the 1930s – voted nationalist, and Catalanism in particular has attained at least some sympathy in working-class quarters. Hence in both these communities nationalist parties have controlled the autonomous parliaments. In Catalonia the centre-liberal *Convergència i Unió* has won all the elections to the autonomous government since 1980. Furthermore, while the Catalan branch of the Spanish Socialist Party, the *Partit Socialista de Catalunya* (PSC-PSOE), has been successful in general elections and controls the Barcelona local government, its majority wing also shows pronounced Catalanist sympathies.

In the Basque Country, within the regions of Alava and Guipúzcoa the PNV has also reemerged as the dominant political force, but here the nationalist community has been more bitterly divided. Not only did the PNV split, with the foundation of a rival centre left nationalist party, *Eusko Alkartasuna* (Basque Unity), in 1984, but also ETA and its political front, *Herri Batasuna* (HB), have remained highly active. These divisions within the nationalist community have also to be seen in cultural terms, as becomes clear in Jeremy MacClancy's chapter. In the Basque Country, while the PNV has come to accept the autonomy statute, ETA has maintained its terrorist strategy under the political cover of HB. As MacClancy points out, in the process HB has developed a highly radicalised urban subculture, whose spearhead is the community's disaffected youth. In contrast the PNV's 'party nation' subculture is more conservative and middle class, firmly oriented indoors in the party's premises, the *bazokis*, in which Basque cultural activities are promoted (Landaburu Gorka 1995: 30–3). As MacClancey and Tejerina Montaña indicate, the bitterness of this divide, along with the continued dominance of the Castilian language, casts a shadow over the future of Basque nationalism.

Indeed, over much of Spain after the turbulent mid-1970s the nationalist tide has receded somewhat. Outside Catalonia and the Basque Country the middle classes have continued to vote for statist parties. Furthermore, with the decline of left-wing politics since the late 1970s, the Marxist nationalist discourses (again with the partial exception of the Basque Country and to a lesser extent Catalonia), which during the Transition could be heard throughout Spain, have become increasingly marginal. The result has been that nationalists have once again sought in vain for a solid social base. In Galicia, during the Transition, nationalism remained very much the prerogative of the Left. The historical weakness of *Galeguismo* within the urban middle classes and social elites was reflected in electoral victories for UCD and, more recently, the Partido Popular. Nevertheless the late 1980s and early 1990s have seen something of a revival. Tracy Henderson argues in her chapter that the consolidation of Galician autonomy has been accompanied by other substantial shifts in nationalist thinking. As has been seen, in the early twentieth century Galician nationalists looked to the establishment of a confederation with Portugal. However, by the 1980s the dominant current, the *Independentistas*, stressed the uniqueness of the Galician language, while the minority current, the *Reintegracionistas*, tried to forge closer links with Portugal. The battle has been fought out in terms of the norms of Galician orthography, but behind the dispute are two very different visions of Galicia's 'imagined community'. It seems clear in this case that the change in focus is very much the consequence of the attainment of autonomy, and the utopianism of any proposed link-up with Portugal.

In other areas, nationalist currents have in general tended to collapse with the consolidation of democracy and granting of the autonomy statutes. This has been the case in Andalusia where the PSA, which had gained five seats in the March 1979 elections, fell away in 1982, and the PSOE firmly established itself as the hegemonic party in the region. One may speculate that this was a consequence of the fact that a vote for the PSA in the late 1970s was a vote against inefficient central-isation, but the weak consciousness of ethnic separateness made the party's long-term future bleak. In Valencia, pan-Catalanist *Valencial-isme* also revived in the 1970s, but was organisationally linked to the far Left and has, as a result, remained very much a minority current.

The exception to this trend has been the case of the Canary Islands where in the 1980s nationalist parties gained ground (Hernández and Mercadé 1986: 433–5; Pomares 1989). In this case there are parallels with the Portuguese Atlantic islands of Madeira and the Azores, where clear regionalist tendencies have emerged, with the result that in the democratic Constitution of 1976 they were both granted the special status of autonomous regions, with their own legislative powers (Braga da Cruz 1992: 154–5). These movements represent the frustrations of distant island communities, exasperated by what they see as the ignor-ance and lack of interest of the metropole in solving their problems.

The democratic context has also necessitated a redefining of Spanish and Portuguese nationalist discourses, which could no longer be based on the backward Catholic imperialist rhetoric of the Francoist and Salazarist dictatorships. In Spain this has been reflected in the evolution of the PSOE, which came to power in 1982. From the mid-1970s the

PSOE moved to the centre of Spanish politics, and dropped its old class-based Third Worldist rhetoric for a social-democratic programme of economic and social modernisation. One result of this was that by the mid-to-late 1970s the party once again referred to the Spanish nation rather than state. The Socialists extolled Spain's European vocation and reforming impetus, and showed a respect for the country's cultural and linguistic pluralism. In symbolic terms this has been reflected in the importance given to the bicentenary of the death of the reforming king, Carlos III, in 1988, and, of course, the celebration in 1992 of the five hundredth anniversary of the so-called 'discovery' of America by Christopher Columbus (García Cárcel 1994: 176). During these celebrations, the 'discovery' of the Americas was seen in terms of technological and scientific advance, and the expansion of Western civilisation. At the same time, Spain was presented as a bridge between Europe and Latin America. This reworking of Spanish nationalism has, indeed, been rather successful. This has clearly been aided by Spain's relatively smooth transition to democracy, integration into the EU and rapid economic growth, with the result that it is probably easier to be proud of being Spanish today than at any time since the late eighteenth century.

Relatedly, the organisation into a 'State of the Autonomies' has, to a significant degree, served to defuse national/regional tensions. The combined effect of these factors has been the consolidation of dual identities in Catalonia, the Basque Country and Galicia, making it possible for one to feel part of both one's community and Spain (Giner and Moreno 1990: 190). At the same time, there has without doubt in recent years been a steady growth in attachment to a European identity combined, of course, with the culturally homogenising influx of a non-national specific culture through, for example, US films, television, food and dress.

Under the new democratic regime the Portuguese nationalist discourse has also adapted to new times. The 1970s saw the old fears emerge that the Portuguese identity was under threat: first, because of the economic dynamism of the Spanish economy since the 1950s, which had left Portugal trailing in her wake; and second, as a result of possible absorption within the European Community. Yet, following the success of the anti-colonial movements in Mozambique and Angola, who were granted independence in the mid-1970s, it became clear that Portugal's future lay in Western Europe. Hence, like Spain, Portugal joined the EC in 1985, its governments adopting the rhetoric of democratic modernisation. This has also meant again taking up themes from the early twentieth-century republicans, such as the Discoveries, portrayed once again in the Portuguese pavilion of the Spanish Expo of 1992 in terms of scientific advance and technological knowledge;

while of course, as in the case of Spain, old imperialistic rhetoric needed to be replaced by an emphasis on cooperation, Portugal therefore casting herself in the role of a key player in North–South dialogue.

Hence, in both Spain and Portugal, nationalism has, as in the past, both adapted and redefined itself. The majority currents of both statist and anti-statist nationalisms have, seemingly, fused with liberal-democratic values, and work within a parliamentary framework. Furthermore, the integration of both Spain and Portugal within the EU is leading to the lessening of the historic rivalries and enmities between the two countries. Both the confederal Spanish system and the more centralist Portuguese variant reflect the divergent historical paths they have followed, but each, in their own way, seems capable of channelling nationalist tensions. The most difficult challenge is the one facing Spain. The problem of ETA terrorism seems intractable and, at the other extreme, authoritarian undercurrents can still be detected in some renditions of Spanish nationalism. At the same time, processes of regionalisation within the EU are likely to put further power in the hands of the 'historic communities'. There are no easy 'solutions' to the question of Spain's future configuration, but one may suggest that both state and non-state nationalists need to show flexibility. Spanish nationalists, perhaps, need to accept that within the bounds of the Spanish Constitution further steps down the path to a federal state are likely, while peripheral nationalists must realise that any open challenge to the future existence of the nation-state can only lead to polarisation and possible violence.

References

Alter, Peter (1994), *Nationalism*, 2nd edn, London

Beramendi, Justo G. (1991), 'El Partido Galeguista y poco más. Organización e ideología del nacionalismo gallego en la España de la Segunda Republica', in Beramendi, Justo and Máiz, Ramon (eds), *Los nacionalismos en la España de la Segunda República*, Madrid, pp.127–70

Blas, Andrés de (1991), *Tradición republicana y nacionalismo español, 1876–1930*, Madrid

Braga da Cruz, Manuel (1992), 'National Identity in Transition', in Herr, Richard (ed.), *The New Portugal: Democracy in Europe*, Berkeley, pp.151–62

Cirujano Marín, Paloma, Elorriaga Planes, Teresa, and Pérez Garzón, Juan Sisinio (1985), *Historiografía y nacionalismo español, 1834–1868*, Madrid

Clark, Robert P. (1984), *The Basque Insurgents: ETA, 1952–1980*, Reno

Corcuera Atienza, Javier (1978), 'La burguesía no monopolista en el origen del nacionalismo vasco', in Tuñón de Lara, Manuel (ed.), *La crisis del estado español, 1898–1936*, Madrid, pp.109–52

—— (1979), *Orígines, ideología y organización del nacionalismo vasco, 1876–1904*, Madrid

Cortes Peña, Antonio Luis (1994), 'El último nacionalismo. Andalucía y su historia', *Manuscrits*, no.12, pp.213–43

Cucó, Alfons (1974), *El valencianismo político, 1874–1939*, Barcelona

Díaz-Andreu, Margarita (1996), 'Constructing Identities through Culture. The Past in the Forging of Europe', in Jones, S., Gamble, C. and Graves, P. (eds), *European Communities: Archaeology and the Construction of Cultural Identity*, London, pp.48–61

Elorza, Antonio (1978), *Ideologías del nacionalismo vasco, 1876–1937*, San Sebastian

Erlich, Charles E. (1992/3), 'Catalonia (1898–1914): Regional Identity as a Means of Regenerating the Greater State', *The ASEN Bulletin*, no.4, pp.43–50

Ettinghausen, Henry (1993), *La Guerra del Segadors a través de la premsa de la época*, 3 vols, Barcelona

Fabra i Sanch, Miguel-Angel (1977), 'Cara i creu d'una burgesia: bloc català-valencià o valencianisme des de Madrid', *L'Avenç*, no.5, pp.31–6

Figueres, Josep María (1990), *Valentí Almirall: forjador del catalanisme polític*, Barcelona

Fusi Aizpurúa, Juan Pablo (1979), *El problema vasco en la Segunda República*, Madrid

Gallagher, Tom (1983), *Portugal: A Twentieth Century Interpretation*, Manchester

García Cárcel, Ricardo (1994), 'La manipulación de la memoria histórica en el nacionalismo español', *Manuscrits*, no.12, pp.175–81

Gillespie, Richard (1989), *The Spanish Socialist Party: A History of Factionalism*, Oxford

Giner, Salvador and Moreno, Luis (1990), 'Centro y periferia: la dimensión étnica de la sociedad española', in Giner, Salvador (ed.), *España: sociedad y política*, Madrid, pp.169–97

Graça Feijó, Rui (1989), 'State, Nation and Regional Diversity in Portugal: An Overview', in Herr, R. and Polt, J.H.R. (eds), *Iberian Identity: Essays on the Nature of Identity in Portugal and Spain*, Berkeley, pp.37–47

Granja Sanz, José Luis de la (1986), *Nacionalismo y Segunda República en el País Vasco*, Madrid

—— (1994), 'La invención de la historia. Nación, mitos e historia en el pensamiento del fundador del nacionalismo vasco', in Beramendi,

Justo G., Máiz, Ramón and Núñez, Xosé M. (eds), *Nationalism in Europe. Past and Present*, vol.2, Santiago de Compostela, pp.97–139

Harrison, Joseph (1977), 'Big Business and the Rise of Basque Nationalism', *European Studies Review*, vol.7, no.4, pp.371–91

Hernández, Francesc and Mercadé, Francesc (eds) (1986), *Estructuras sociales y cuestión nacional en España*, Barcelona

Hobsbawm, Eric (1992), *Nations and Nationalism since 1780*, 2nd edn, Cambridge

Jauristi, Jon (1986), *La tradición romántica. Leyendas vascas del siglo XIX*, Pamplona

Jover Zamora, José María (1981), 'La época de la Restauración: panorama político-social, 1875–1902', in *Historia de España dirigida por Manuel Tuñón de Lara*, vol.8, *Revolución burguesa, oligarquía y constitucionalismo, 1834–1923*, Barcelona, pp.271–319

Landaburu, Gorka (1995), 'PNV: cien años de nacionalismo', *Cambio 16*, 24 July, pp.30–3

Linz, Juan José (1973), 'Early State-Building and Late Peripheral Nationalisms Against the State: The Case of Spain', in Eisenstadt, S. N. and Rokkan, Stein (eds), *Building States and Nations. Analysis by Regions*, vol.2, London, pp.32–116

López Cordón, María Victoria (1975), *El pensamiento político-internacional del federalismo español*, Barcelona

Máiz, Ramón (1984), 'Raza y mito celta en los orígines del nacionalismo gallego', in *Revista Española de Investigaciones Sociológicas*, no.25, pp.136–80

—— (1994), 'The Open Ended Construction of a Nation: The Galician Case in Spain', in Beramendi, Justo G., Máiz, Ramón and Núñez, Xosé M. (eds), *Nationalism in Europe. Past and Present*, vol.2, Santiago de Compostela, pp.173–208

Mané y Flaquer, Juan (1886), *El regionalismo*, Barcelona

Marfany, Joan Lluís (1995), *La cultura del catalanisme*, Barcelona

Martínez Serrano, Josep A. and Soler Marco, Vicent (1977), 'L'anticatalanisme al País Valencià', *L'Avenç*, no.5, pp.24–30

Mees, Ludgar (1989), 'Nacionalismo vasco y clases sociales. Algunos datos sobre la base social del nacionalismo vasco entre 1903 y 1923', *Estudios de Historia Social*, nos 50–1, pp.71–99

Moreno Navarro, Isidoro (1981), 'Primer descubrimiento consciente de la identidad andaluza, 1868–1890', in Bernal, Antonio-Miguel (ed.), *Historia de Andalucía*, vol.VIII, *la Andalucia contemporánea, 1868–1981*, Madrid/Barcelona, pp.233–51

Pérez Moragón, Francesc (1983), 'El valencianisme i el fet dels Països Catalans (1900–1936)', *L'Espill*, no.19, pp.57–82

Pi i Margall, Francesc (1877, 1936 edn), *Las nacionalidades*, Madrid

Pina Cabral, João de (1989), 'Sociocultural Differentiation and Regional Identity in Portugal', in Herr, R. and Polt, J.H.R. (eds), *Iberian Identity: Essays on the Nature of Identity in Portugal and Spain*, Berkeley, pp.3–18

Pomares, F. (1989), *El año de las elecciones*, Santa Cruz de Tenerife

Riquer, Borja de (1987), 'Els corrents conservadors catalans i la seva evolució cap al catalanisme polític', *L'Avenç*, no.100, pp.78–84

—— (1994), 'La debil nacionalización española del siglo XIX', *Historia Social*, no.20, pp.97–114

Simon i Tarrés, Antoni (1993), 'Patriotisme i nacionalisme a la Catalunya moderna. Mites, tradicions i consciències collectives', *L'Avenç*, no.167, pp.8–16

—— (1994), 'Els mites històrics i el nacionalisme català. La història moderna de Catalunya en el pensament històric i polític català contemporani, 1840–1939', *Manuscrits*, no.12, pp.195–211

Smith, Anthony D. (1991), *National identity*, Harmondsworth

Solé Tura, Jordi (1974), *Catalanismo y revolución burguesa*, 2nd edn, Madrid

Sullivan, John (1988), *ETA and Basque Nationalism: The Fight for Euskadi, 1890–1986*, London

Trías, Juan J., and Elorza, Antonio (1975), *Federalismo y reforma social en España, 1840–1870*, Madrid

Trías Vejerano, Juan J. (1975), *Almirall y los orígines del catalanismo*, Madrid

Ucelay da Cal, Enric (1982), *La Catalunya populista. Imatge, cultura i política en l'etapa republicana, 1931–1939*, Barcelona

Wheeler, Douglas L. (1978), *Republican Portugal. A Political History, 1910–1926*, Wisconsin

Part I

Centrist State-Building: The Imposition of a 'National' Hegemony

2

Nationalising Cultural Politics: Representations of the Portuguese 'Discoveries' and the Rhetoric of Identitarianism, 1880–1926

AbdoolKarim A. Vakil

In the contemporary academic discussion and literature of nationalism and national identity, as even a cursory survey of indices and bibliographies will rapidly suggest, Portugal and the Portuguese historical experience have not by and large received much attention. The references that it has merited, with few exceptions, only seem all the more to justify this neglect. The recognition of the physical and historical stability of Portuguese territorial boundaries; the ethnic, religious and linguistic homogeneity of its people; its long history as a continuous political unit and the richness of its high cultural production have, as it were, 'naturalised' its classification as a 'genuine nation-state'. Yet, and for these very reasons, it could be argued that Portugal presents a provocative case for thinking through some of the central questions in the current debate on nationalism.

From the comparative-historical perspective its interest could be said to reside not only in an additional area for the study of European nationalism and nation-building, but more specifically in a de-centring effect of reversing the terms of reference by studying nationalism in an 'old nation'. Assuming both the longer historical canvas afforded by its eight centuries and its ethnic homogeneity enables us to sharpen the analysis of continuities and discontinuities at the specifically cultural and political level, and thus to address some of the questions at the heart of the current academic debate. In particular, it enables us to displace the rather simplistic concern with concrete territorial state borders, in favour of a more complex analysis of the production and articulation of other incongruous and shifting administrative, secular and ecclesiastical, cultural and economic referents, and the processes by which they emerge, are experienced, imagined and represented. But also to

problematise the debate over elite versus mass consciousness by his-
toricising politicisation over a longer continuous period; to test the
relation between modernisation and nationalism by relating weak industrialisation and literacy to the *lack* of a nation-building imperative (Reis
1993); to ponder the reification and reinvention of tradition and of pre-
modern culture and symbolism in the appropriations and representations of culture and the past by modern nationalism.

Within the scope of a volume on the Iberian Peninsula, moreover,
the comparative approach is even more illuminating. It is not simply
through the expression of 'Iberian' nationalist doctrines, or even of the
necessarily Peninsular geo-political concerns reflected in the doctrines
of individual nationalisms, that their historical interaction forces itself
upon us; but also at the more general level, in the very parallels and
differences of their historical experiences, particularly over the last two
centuries.[1]

With regard to the theory of nationalism, more specifically, the significance of the Portuguese case, I would suggest, stems even more
directly from its marginalised status in the literature. Its relevance in this
respect may thus more readily be brought out by explaining and prob-
lematising that neglect.

Briefly stated, in the ideology of nationalism the establishment of the
nation-state represents its teleological end-point; in academic study by
and large, nationalism constitutes an object of analysis in situations of
conflict characterised by the ideological expression, or effective mobilisation, of a 'real' or perceived absence of congruence between nation
and state. In both, therefore, national*ism* falls short of the nation-state
and the nation-state, conversely, falls beyond the scope of discussion.
In these terms, then, Portugal's marginalisation would thus seem to stem
directly (if by default) from her ascribed status as a paradigmatic nation-
state. Addressing the Portuguese case, therefore, may well require a
more radical inversion of the terms of debate.

Following this suggestion, I would like in particular to explore here
some aspects raised by the discussion of the nation as an 'imagined
community' (Anderson 1983). One direction in which this can be done
is by arguing for the extension of the study of 'nationalism' to include
the continuing processes of production and reproduction of the 'national' and the 'imaginary' of imagined national communities – what
Michael Billig has more recently come to label 'banal nationalism'
(1995).

Another direction stems from reading the discursive strategies of
national identity – the logic and strategies of contesting and totalising

---

1. For which the best comparative introduction remains Payne 1973.

claims to national representation – back into the analysis of politics. This implies both locating the nationalist rhetoric at the heart of factional claims to political representation and legitimation (Verdery 1993: 41) and widening the analysis of party politics into the more encompassing discursive field of what Lebovics calls the 'wars over cultural identity' (1992).

It is in the context of this political and cultural struggle for the hegemonic definition of national identity that the study of representations of the 'Discoveries' proposed in this chapter finds its justification. Its heuristic power resides in the combination of the centrality of the 'Discoveries' in Portuguese history and culture and in discourses of collective self-representation, with the polysemy and inter-discursive foundation of its symbolism. The centrality and near universality of the representations provides us with both a point of entry from which to unfold the contending historical and cultural images of the nation within which these representations are framed, and a common point of reference by which to differentiate them. The richness of the symbolism of those representations, their inter-discursive framing and, particularly, their cultural and aesthetic formulation, on the other hand, effectively impair their reductive translation into narrowly political terms. Focusing on representations of the 'Discoveries', therefore, may suggest a more subtle reading of the cultural politics of the period.

Our first concern, then, must be to open out the study of nationalism and to locate the discursive construction of national identity within the cultural politics of a fully constituted nation-state such as Portugal.

Nation, Identity and Ideology

In a statement which directly relates the discussion of nationalism and national identity to the theme of the 'Discoveries', Vasco Graça Moura, at that time just recently appointed to the presidency of the Government-nominated *National Committee for the Commemoration of the Portuguese Discoveries* (CNCDP), declared that 'Portugal. . .unlike other countries which may organise commemorations, has no need to affirm its national identity. It has a national identity defined eight centuries ago; [its] commemorations are not so much about the affirmation of national identity but rather about shaping its physiognomy' (1989: 33).

This rather disingenuous downplaying of the ideological function of the commemorations may to some extent be explained in terms of both the only too recent experience of the political mobilisation of historical commemorations under Salazar, which Graça Moura explicitly alludes to, and the more immediate need to reinvent the CNCDP's image after the rather crude nationalist line imprinted upon it by his predecessor, Commander Serra Brandão. Yet, by contrasting the current commemorations against previous ideological appropriations, these points of reference, unwittingly, only impress all the more the need to place both Graça Moura's words and his interpretation of the Quincentenary within the Portuguese tradition, history and ideologies of national commemoration.

In this regard, the first and crudest ideological level of Graça Moura's words concerns the denial of the socio-political function of the current commemorations. The distance which indeed does separate them from the commemorative rhetoric of the New State initiatives should not be allowed to obscure other very real levels of continuity. Continuities, of form and function and of themes and images, which transcend specific political orientations and which, in this respect, stretch back to the late nineteenth-century invention of the Portuguese 'Discovering' tradition. Nor should the significant differences in context, in the form and force of mobilisation, and in the ideologies which they served, veil the politically significant congruence between the representations of the 'Discoveries' projected in each of the commemorative periods and the national self-image of the State promoting them; in this case the CNCDP's Quincentenary version of the 'Discoveries' as 'inter-cultural dialogue' and the main lines of Prime Minister Cavaco Silva's national and international projection of Portugal's image.[2]

What Graça Moura's claim denies, then, at this first level, is the relation between the institutional recycling of the signification of the 'Discoveries' – through what Andrew Wernick calls the 'promotional intertext' (1991: 92–5) – and the processes of social, political, academic, commercial and educational production and reproduction of collective memory and national representations within which, and by which, national identity is forged.

A second and more insidious ideological level of Graça Moura's words, however, stems from its effect as a performative statement, producing the very function it disclaims. The denial of the need to affirm

2. The ideal of Lusophone community and cooperation, one of Cavaco Silva's government's major foreign policy drives, has often been tied in his speeches to the commemoration of the 'Discoveries' conceived as a North–South cultural dialogue (Cavaco Silva 1989 and 1991). This interpretation of the 'Discoveries' draws particularly on the work of the historian L.F. Barreto (1988 and Barreto and Garcia n.d.). Cavaco Silva's *Portugal: A Pioneer of the North–South Dialogue* (1989) was distributed at the Council of Europe, and directly echoed in his speech there. This vision of the 'Discoveries', which feeds the new post-colonial orthodoxy of the Portuguese as cultural mediators, thus replaces that of racial mediators favoured by the New State (Alexandre 1979: 7–8).

national identity with the claim that it is of eight centuries standing, in other words, constitutes a performative reenforcement of that very postulated identity and an imputation of its historical and unquestionable existence.

With regard to the claim itself – that Portuguese national identity dates from eight centuries ago – two complementary points may be noted. The first concerns the disassociation of national identity and 'Discoveries' by casting the former back in time – reinforced by the supporting claim that 'long before the Discoveries we already had a national identity'. Implicit in this statement, however, is a refutation of contending positions which define Portuguese national identity specifically in terms of the 'Discoveries'; in other words, an ideological intervention in a politically charged debate over national tradition.

The second aspect concerns the stress on the eight centuries as vindication of the nation by the reification of history as temporality: a celebration of age-old nation and national identity by the very denial of their historicity. The 'we' of 'we' who 'already had a national identity', correspondingly, completes what Balibar calls the 'retrospective illusion' (Balibar and Wallerstein 1991: 86): the translation of the succession of generations in a retrospectively defined territory as the transmission of 'an invariant substance' denoted by the name of the community. Together, then, they collapse and conflate the synchronic and diachronic dimensions of Portuguese history and Portuguese*ness* into the 'Portuguese' national community.

Finally, Graça Moura (1989) recognised the function of the commemorations in defining 'the physiognomy of national identity'; yet, since he defines Portuguese national identity as eight centuries old and explicitly refutes the need for its commemorative affirmation, the matter of 'defining its physiognomy' would appear to be, essentially, rather inconsequential.

In short, at the heart of Graça Moura's statement, in the claim that unlike others Portugal has no need to affirm its national identity, there lie both an essentialist definition of the nation (as concrete, unproblematic and self-evident) and of national identity (as ahistorical), and their immediate contradiction through both the ideological reaffirmation of that identity and the attempt at shaping it (in its relation to the 'Discoveries').

Clearly, therefore, it is an antithetical definition of the nation as an 'imagined community', as a discursive construct, that, in the very act of repressing it, the essentialist definition of the nation actually ends up revealing. Contrary to its rhetoric, therefore, the nation is not a 'natural' or concrete entity, it exists rather only in and by the process of its continued and contested affirmation in collective representations, translated and inscribed in myriad more or less concrete symbols and symbolic practices. It exists, then, specifically *as* what Graça Moura dismisses as its physiognomy; subject, therefore, to challenge not only from rival definitions of 'the national' of national community, but to alternative, commensurate and incommensurate bids for community identification – from race, religion and gender to clan, class and party.

The suggestiveness of this notion, in conclusion, stems from the fact that re-reading political history in the light of this definition of the nation points to the specific importance of the struggle for hegemony over the representation of national identity as the key to legitimation. The force of this argument, however, as with the premise and validity of the notion of a *national* imagined community itself, are strictly predicated on the logic of modernity.

Modernity, Imagined Community and Identitarian Rhetoric

For the sake of clarification it may be convenient, within the limited context of the question being addressed, to differentiate between two definitional genealogies of modernity in the current literature. In one, modernity is essentially centred on the impact of the twin political and industrial revolutions of the end of the eighteenth century, and squarely tied to their interrelated consequences over the 'long nineteenth century'. In the other, the analysis of modernity is extended back into the conditions of possibility for these transformations to occur; into, that is, the proto-manifestations of modernity in the processes of secularisation, state formation, the military revolution, print culture, the emergence of the modern-world system and of capitalism. One aspect that may be noted in respect of the latter version, perhaps most manifestly in Portuguese historiography, is the consequent historical privileging of the 'long sixteenth century' and the 'Renaissance period', and hence, by synecdoche, of an interrelation between the 'Discoveries' and modernity.

A correlative to this temporal widening of the frame of analysis is the broader compass imposed by a cultural perspective on each of the two – political and economic – strands of modernity. Thus, the analysis of the political, for one, is recast from its more immediate focus on political revolution, the institutionalisation of liberal constitutional regimes and the transfer of sovereignty from the King to the nation, to the archaeological investigation of their conditions of possibility (Chartier 1991; Baker 1990). The analysis of the socio-economic, for its part, is equally reformulated more widely to include, in addition to the analysis of uneven processes of industrialisation, urbanisation, migration and quantitative change, a focus on the more general cognitive and onto-logical disruptions induced by the accelerated rhythm of change.

Transition to modernity, then, taken as shorthand for the complex interrelation of convergence and mutual redefinition of the processes referred to in each of ᴠ ese two strands, can thus be seen to describe both the concrete embodiment of the nation and its fictionɑlisation: the slow processes of articulation and integration of econon ⸝ and social spaces in the constitution of the national ⸍nomy and territory; and the slower processes of detachment and reattachⵏ ⸍ent of individual and communal identities to progressively wiⵑer and less concrete spheres culminating in the symbols of the nation – the privileged foci of ident-itarian rhetoric.

The 'transition' then, culturally and economically, imported both the redefinition of the political and of the politicised; the reframing of sub-jectivities and of socio-political identities. This redefinition was, at one level, partly effected through the re-articulation of elite political sociabilities but, at another, increasingly dependent on the effective negotiation of political enfranchisement. The management of the trans-ition, then, from the cognitive-ontological to the narrowly political, was predicated on the redimensioning of the integrative mechanisms of imagined community: the mobilisation of the language of symbolic politics; the abstraction from concrete social, economic and cultural differences and the exclusive nationalisation of solidarity.

In Portugal the parameters of this process may be taken as the period stretching from the enlightened-absolutist reforms of the Marquis of Pombal, in the third quarter of the eighteenth century, to the social, economic and political transformations of the post-1974 transition to democracy. In a historical process with many illuminating parallels to that of nineteenth-century Spain (see Chapter 5), key moments of this process may be signposted by reference to the revolution of 1820, at one end, and the emergence of republicanism in the last quarter of the century, at the other.

The abolition of Absolutism and the institutionalisation of the liberal regime must be interpreted in the context of the Napoleonic invasions (1807–10) and the consequent flight of the Portuguese Court to Brazil and the establishment of a British protectorate in Portugal; of the trans-formation of politics both by the agency of the military and secret societies, and by the revolution of the word (in journalism and parliamentary oratory). It must be seen, finally, by casting the 'pro-nunciamento' of 1820, and its aborted constitutional radicalism, against the international context of the Holy Alliance and the Brazilian dec-laration of independence (1822), and the protracted periods of civil war and then political factionalism and instability at home which lasted till mid-century.[3]

It is within this process of the contested affirmation of a new political order, framed by the imperatives of civic patriotism and education, that, from the perspective which concerns us here, the culture of romanticism, literary and artistic production, historiography, the historical novel, the cult of monuments, and the discovery of popular traditions attain their significance. It is partly through them, and primarily through serialised novelistic production and the new relation between texts and readers, that the imagining of society and the contemporary gained shape (França n.d.; Lourenço 1978; Silva 1987).

Later, it was, in the wake of this mid-century period of social peace and material development (known as the 'Regeneration' of 1851–68), and in the context of the period of intense intellectual renewal and foreboding economic crisis of the last quarter of the nineteenth century, that the politicisation of the petty bourgeoisie, on the one hand, and the fears over the incipient political organisation of workers, on the other, gave Republicanism a growing audience (Cabral 1988; Serrão 1979). But it was in the logic of modernity – the evolution of large-scale social integration and indirect relationships (Calhoun 1991), the primacy of symbolic politics, and the identitarian transformation of the civic patriotism of early liberalism – that republicanism found its language and strategy. In the name of the nation and the people, Republicanism posed its challenge to the representative legitimacy of both the liberal parties of constitutional monarchy and the rival socialist, Marxist and anarchist movements, which appealed to either more segmented or more universal identities (Freire 1992; Matias 1989).

Excluded from the political mechanism by the restrictive practices of the rotating parties and their electoral networks of patronage-clientele (Almeida 1991; Vidigal 1988), the republican challenge to the State in the name of the nation became constituted as a discourse of morality. The nation correspondingly became defined as a moral community and nationalism as redemption (Catroga 1991).

Correspondingly, as a bid for integration formulated in cultural terms, the literary, the historical and the aesthetic came to play a fundamental role. Addressing a massively illiterate population, however, the festive and the symbolic, the mythic and the oral became equally important in complementing the unprecedented mobilisation of the

3. For discussion of some of these aspects see Alexandre 1993; Bernardino 1986; Bethencourt 1991; Justino 1988; Pereira, J.E. 1991; Pereira, M.H. et al. 1982; Reis 1993; and Verdelho 1981.

press and the printed word. This cultural bias and populist media in turn impacted upon the content of the politics.

It is in its double nature as both a *political* bid to nationalise the masses and as a *nationalist* bid to politicise them, that the repressed contradiction at the heart of the identitarian rhetoric becomes exposed. The mould of a specific, factional, politically cast identity is presented as if an image in a mirror, inviting recognition as national identity. It is this double *misrecognition* (Laclau and Zac 1994) of individuals constituted as political subjects in the mirror of a collective and national self-identity that constitutes the logic of legitimation by identitarian rhetoric.

For various reasons – ranging from the discursive legacy of republicanism itself, its framing as moral regeneration and its messianic dimension (Medina 1990; Serrão 1990; Wheeler 1978), to the oligarchic structure of the political regime and the relatively undifferentiated nature of the cultural and political elites of the period – this logic of identitarian legitimation came to play an unparalleled determining role in the period of the First Portuguese Republic.

In brief, the politics of identitarianism, as the struggle for hegemonic definition of a national imagined community, is predicated on the evolution of systems of indirect communication; it is not merely a product of modernity, but a response to it. However, it is not reducible to George Mosse's 'nationalisation of the masses' (1975). If it arose, in the case of Portugal, precisely through such a populist bid on the part of the Republicans in opposition – as a challenge to the limitations of a political system from which they were excluded – in the period of the first Republic itself it continued, in its most important versions, to be only indirectly, if at all, related to mass mobilisation. In this latter period the battle over cultural definitions of national identity became instead the instrument of intense rivalry among shifting cultural groupings vying for the moral leadership of the nation.

The nature, style and content of this cultural politics of the Republic was, however, largely established in the oppositional republican framing of a commemorativist and symbolic politics in the last two decades of the nineteenth century.

The 'Discoveries' and the Commemorativist Politics of Identity

The Camões Tercentenary of 1880 constituted the founding moment of this new political discourse. As the tercentenary itself is the subject of Chapter 3, my remarks on this event here will be strictly limited to its contribution to the reconfiguration of political discourse.

Theorising the centennial in positivist terms, the republican conception of commemoration entailed two more or less explicit political effects. The first stemmed from the very principle of commemoration, namely the celebration of merit; antithetical by definition to the monarchist principle of heredity, merit thus struck to the very foundation of the legitimacy of the monarchy. The second was the appropriation and secularisation of ritual for the self-worship of the community. As Teófilo Braga put it, the nation commemorates great men as representative figures and 'each people [*povo*] elect the genius which is the synthesis of their national character' (1884: 388). Ultimately, therefore, in commemorating Camões the people were commemorating themselves in effigy.

If the self-commemoration seemed transparent, however, that transparency was itself an ideological construct. The ideal self-image presented, in which the nation was invited to recognise itself, implied two ideological operations. Firstly, the interpellation of individuals as individuals to accept as real a bond of community – 'national character' – which exists only in the imaginary, but which was presupposed by the very act of collective 'self-recognition'. Secondly, the acceptance of this 'image of the nation' as a self-image, as if reflected in a mirror. A notion made explicit by the organisers' claim that 'we held up to the great national soul the mirror in which it saw itself' (Costa et al. 1880: 135). By effacing its own role in the construction of that representation, a factional image is thus presented as reflected self-image.

Another fundamental aspect of the commemorative ideology resides in the fact that the nation whose identity the Republicans reveal is not the nation as it exists but the nation as project: the nation defined in a republican reading of history as future-oriented identity.

What the republicans elected in the celebration of Camões, then, was the epic story of the 'Discoveries' in the *Lusiadas*.[4] What they claimed to reveal as the national character of the Portuguese was therefore its 'colonial' mission. What they conjured up for contrast was the image of a once glorious country, now decadent, ruled by a monarchy neglectful of its people, of its history and of its empire.

In short, what republicanism achieved, through an effective mobilisation of festivals, print and press, was the projection of the reductive and totalising circularity of identitarian politics: the nation = the people = Camões; Camões = national tradition; national tradition = paradigmatic historical moment = 'Discoveries'; 'Discoveries' = colonialism; decadence = neglect of national tradition and of Empire = Monarchy;

---

4. For a brief but illuminating survey of ideological readings of Camões and the *Lusiadas*, see Rebelo 1990.

regeneration = national tradition + colonialism = Republicanism; Republicanism, therefore = the people = the nation = regeneration.

This circularity was further reinforced under the impact of the British Ultimatum of 1890 when, as the republicans once again appropriated and shaped the public manifestation of discontent through the press and street politics, the Monarchy and the two liberal monarchist parties were successfully depicted and near universally acknowledged as neglectful of the empire and of the glorious national tradition (Teixeira 1990).

From the narrow perspective of the point being argued here the achievement of republicanism in its contribution to the organisation of the 1880 commemorations and after, or more precisely in the appropriation of their meaning, was not the transformation of republicanism itself into a viable or even a potential political force (consequent as indeed this proved to be), but the enduring definition of both the terms of discourse of modern politics in Portugal, and of the cultural discourse of Portuguese national identity; and more significantly, the conflation of the two. The measure of the success of this redefinition of political discourse along nationalist lines produced through the festive and commemorative may be seen in some expressions of its institutionalisation.

Firstly was the generalised adoption of commemorative politics forced upon all contenders as the very form of political expression in public space and as a means of politicisation of new and traditional constituencies. Thus, whereas the republicans decided to capitalise on the success of 1880 by commemorating the centenary of the Marquis of Pombal's death as an anti-clerical celebration in 1882, the Catholics, among whose essays in political organisation was the formation of the short-lived Catholic Parliamentary Centre in 1894, and the commitment to the creation of a broad-based social movement in 1895 (Cruz 1980), responded this latter year with the celebration of the seventh centennial of the birth of St Anthony. The socialists, whose rhetoric over the 1882 commemorations had been largely indistinguishable from the republican (Bebiano 1983), also proved their understanding of the new politics promoting the May 1 celebrations; the ideological split between the 'possiblist' and Marxist factions and the criticism of the anarchists, with the first seeking to capitalise on its symbolism primarily as a festive ritual against the more narrowly political proposals of the latter two, is also revealing in this regard (Catroga 1989). Correlatively, whilst Camões and Pombal had been celebrated against the State, in 1894 the King associated himself with the commemorations of the birth of Prince Henry 'the Navigator' in Oporto, as a gesture of appeasement for the bloody suppression of an aborted republican revolt in that city three years earlier.

Second were the interpenetration and eventual standardisation (of the techniques, rhetoric and images) of two commemorative practices: the national celebration of historical dates and national self-presentation at international expositions, both instrumentalised by the State for the promotion of national identity and its representations, internally and externally.

Following closely from this last comes the adoption of practices standardised in the Great Exhibitions in England, the United States and France consisting of associating national narratives with visual popular entertainment, such as the re-enactment of 'historical' tableaux and fairground and circus shows, and more importantly, in the organisation of ethnographic exhibitions. These were of particular importance in bringing the empire and particularly its products to the direct experience of the population while reinforcing the rhetoric of a civilising mission through the stage-setting of the displays.[5]

Fourth was the incestuous relation between a certain largely ephemeral 'literary' production, historical commemorations and the symbolic investment of urban public space in the construction of the national imaginary. This was particularly important in the creation of visual and poetic images, metaphors and symbols for political appropriation, but also fed back into the aestheticisation of the historical topoi evoked by the commemorations, and the transformation of material culture in public space through related statuary and toponyms.

In and through all of these, the overwhelmingly most evident aspect of the self-image projected of Portuguese identity was the primacy of the historical and of the place of the 'Discoveries' within it.

Surveying the literary and historiographical production, political and colonial pamphleteering, and the texts and images deployed in commemorations and exhibitions in the closing decades of the Monarchy, the thematic and visual stock of representations of the 'Discoveries' inherited at the onset of the Republican period may be schematically summarised with respect to four points of reference: their interpretation within a predominantly positivist philosophy of history, and their relation to colonialism, to national character and to national history and tradition.

Framed in a synthesis of romantic philosophy of history and positivist ideology, Portugal's golden age – the period of convergence of national and universal history when its cultural character was supposedly revealed – was equated with the Expansion and the spirit of the 'Discoveries'; an epoch of national affirmation but also of scientific

5. On the ideological role of Expositions see Schneider 1982; MacKenzie 1984; Rydell 1984; and Greenhalgh 1988.

pioneering and 'modernity'. In respect of this claim, two aspects of the decisive contribution of the 'Discoveries', and therefore of Portugal, were to be particularly influential: the assertion that the shift from the Mediterranean to the Atlantic, produced by the expansion, inaugurated the modern age; and the claim to having saved Europe from Muslim domination, and therefore civilisation from barbarism, just as classical Greece – whose mantle Portugal thus inherited – had saved it from the Persians.

As a direct consequence of both the republican political campaign over colonial questions, and the ensuing scramble for Africa, a continuity was proclaimed (and an ideological transposition generated), between the 'Discoveries' and the historical empire, on the one hand, and the contemporary colonial effort, asserted on historical rights, on the other.

The 'Discoveries' were also often drawn upon in support of a different cultural identity thesis in relation to its 'others' (and by implication, of different foreign policy alignments). Fundamentally, the 'other' were the Spanish. So, overwhelmingly, it is the sporadic and cruel nature of the Castilian enterprise, dependent, it was emphasised, upon the imported expertise of Columbus and Magellan and the fierceness of the 'conquistadors' in the Americas, that we find contrasted to the organic nature of the Portuguese expansion, with its pleiad of 'discoverers'. Against this demarcation of the different and irreconcilable 'ethnic' characters of the two peninsular peoples, however, an alternative trend celebrated their 'Iberian genius' accentuating, instead, the parallels in the expansion of the two nations and particularly its spiritual and civilising mission, against the prosaic rapacity and commercialism of Anglo-Saxon expansion, – the 'other' of Hispanic civilisation.

Finally, an oppositional tradition, less prominent and less popular certainly, but insidiously critical – damning even – should not be forgotten. Symbolically represented by the 'old man of Restelo' of Camões' *Lusíadas*,[6] on the one hand, and the '*arbitrista*' tradition of the seventeenth century, on the other, it received its paradigmatic modern formulation in the writings of Alexandre Herculano, (the single most important figure of nineteenth-century Portuguese historiography), and later in the historical, political and aesthetic writings of key figures of the generation of 1870.[7]

6. For a discussion of the episode of the Old Man of Restelo and some of its ideological readings see Moser 1980.

7. One such figure, Alberto Sampaio, and his critical historical vision of the 'Discoveries' is discussed in Medina 1980: 205–19.

Decrying the abandonment of the land and of the rural tradition in a search for easy riches, the various strands of this critical tradition were to be recovered and reinterpreted in the ideological debates of the 1910s and 1920s. More refined versions sought a more ambiguous and shifting spatial and temporal differentiation between 'Discovery' and conquest. But here, too, the potential lay for the interpretation of this line as a demarcation of the legitimate historical tradition of the nation, or more generally for championing this criticism either in the name of a more progressive developmental model or of a reactionary return to a rural community.

The First Republic and Identitarian Cultural Politics

Underlying the significance of the theme of the 'Discoveries' is the specific importance of cultural politics in the political life of the First Republic (Ramos 1994). In this regard, the pertinent aspects which characterise the nature of the political may be succinctly stated. Firstly, the emotional, symbolic propaganda of pre-1910 republicanism in opposition, while integrative when polarised by its target, proved, upon its practical realisation, fatally disappointing in proportion to the messianic emptiness of its rhetoric. Secondly, at the practical level too, once in power, the Republic's institutional continuities through its bureaucratic personnel, its restrictive and vitiated electoral practices, and the virtual monopoly of power by the dominant 'PRP' (Portuguese Republican Party, later Democratic Party), fed the frustration and resentment of disillusioned republican factions, as its policies did in relation to all other political competitors (Valente 1982, 1992; Lopes 1994).

Thirdly, and this is the key point, the prevailing intellectual climate, the strength of the paradigm of politics as a moral discourse, and of the imperative of national regeneration, determined the centrality of the cultural mediation of politics. From State and opposition, republican and monarchist, intellectuals, ideologues and politicians, the constant refrain was the lack of a binding ideal, the degenerative lack of cohesion and the imperative need to guide both state and civil society by the ideal of the nation.

From the perspective of the State this was translated into the creation of a new secular calendar, national flag, ceremonies, festivals, and ritual commemorations (Medina 1990). But the more fundamental issue was defined as the mass production of citizens through schools, the idea of 'Educação Repúblicana', of a civic, secular morality, and particularly, of an education in the history of the nation and its ideals (Campos Matos 1990; Fernandes n.d.).

Aside from the State, not necessarily in opposition to it but critical and expressive of both the manifest inability of the State to achieve these aims and perhaps even of its reluctance to do so, intellectuals and cultural movements bid for the definition of the civic ideal; in this they founded their claims to legitimacy on the specular logic of historical national identity.

However we may choose to map the spectrum of politico-cultural activity in this period – and the point is precisely the reductiveness of narrowly political readings – all the intellectual figures of the First Republic thought, discussed and polemicised over the questions of tradition, the modern, the meaning of nation and colonialism, but most importantly, of history, as both past and as discourse, and of time, its shape and direction. My point, then, is that as themes which necessarily polarise, reflect and refract all of these questions, the contemporary discussions over national identity, and more contentiously but also more sharply, over the 'Discoveries', most effectively offer an opening to the analysis of the wider ideological conflicts.

In the construction of discourses of national identity, history invariably plays a fundamental role. The past, or rather, its representations and misrepresentations are of foundational importance in radicating collective identities. In the case of Portugal the age of expansion will determiningly shape the interpretation of the historical course of the nation, the meaning of its history and its lessons. But if the 'Discoveries' constitute such a paradigmatic historical reference, if, that is, they must almost obligatorily figure as a referent of cultural identity in any political appropriation of the past, their specific representations must equally differentiate those same diverse political appropriations. Representations of the 'Discoveries', in other words, must both differentially reflect and define the political discourses in which they figure.

It is as such that an analysis of representations of the 'Discoveries', implicit or explicit, marginal or central can prove a good filter for the re-reading of the cultural politics of the First Republic.

The richness of the theme stems also from the ambiguous relation between its contemporary linguistic meaning and its historical reference. In other words, between the active, interventionist, historically innovative sense of 'discovery', the historical specificity of the 'Discoveries' in the Portuguese past, and the ideological construction of the relation between the two.

It is this richness, polysemy and ambivalence of the theme and representations of the 'Discoveries' that allows for their mobilisation in the name of the most radically opposite principles. But my contention is stronger. The point is not only the fact that these representations lent themselves to such use, but that, as a central historical and cultural reference, and one that was universally, though differentially shared across the spectrum of elite and popular culture, they were often the chosen ground for the waging of cultural battles over national identity and the mantle of tradition and, therefore, over legitimation.

It is thus that through the lens of a close reading we find the 'Discoveries' at the heart of the polemics and conflicts between the advocates of political modernity and traditionalism and between cultural and aesthetic modernists and traditionalists which dominate public debate in the years 1912/14 to 1924. This is the period when, with the Republic politically institutionalised, and monarchist political expression again tolerated, the cultural battle for the soul of the nation begins.

Within one of the most influential cultural movements of the period, the 'Portuguese Renaissance', established to some extent to complete the revolution at the cultural level through pedagogic means, a split soon became evident between the cultural traditionalists led by the poet Teixeira de Pascoaes, and his more European-minded collaborators, António Sérgio and Raul Proença. The titles of their 1915 books, *Civic Education* and *The Art of Being Portuguese*, offer one indication of the differences between Sérgio and Pascoaes, and of the fundamental incompatibility that was to drive him and Proença out of the movement. The poet Fernando Pessoa also dissociated himself from the '*Renascença*' to embark on a path of literary experimentation that was to take him through both various expressions of modernism and futurism, and of intense and heterodox political writing on the subject of the nation.

In 1914, the Action Française-style 'Portuguese Integralism' emerged within the monarchist ranks. Joining the political battle at the level of culture and ideas this movement, though initially polarised by the *Renascença*'s growing influence, was just as much in need of defining itself against the more conservative constitutional monarchists of the 'official' '*Causa Monárquica*'. Between these movements and their various political and literary forums, in complex paths of intellectual, aesthetic and political definitions of individual and group identity, shaped by (and shaping) the political developments of these years of growing authoritarianism,[8] the agenda of traditionalism to some extent cornered even cultural and political modernists into waging the political battle in their language, forced to wrestle over the nation's symbols.

António Sérgio, perhaps most sustainedly among the political modernists, drew upon the 'Discoveries' for symbols and metaphors of progress; on its history for lessons in praise of scientific planning and openness to progress, and on its consequences for the condemnation of the negative traits of Portuguese social structure and ideology.

8. For a suggestive discussion of the relations between the aesthetic and the political in this period see Cabral 1989 and Mosse 1990.

Raúl Proença, in the same camp, attempting to turn the tables on the reactionaries of Portuguese Integralism, looked to the 'Discoveries' for historical support in his re-definition of the Portuguese Tradition as cosmopolitan.

Within the monarchist camp, conversely, it was by reclaiming the greatness of the 'Discoveries' that the constitutional monarchists, in the person of the King's lieutenant, Aires de Ornellas, sought to prove themselves truer traditionalists than their more radical Integralist critics, who rejected the Expansion and its colonial legacy. From the latter, and particularly through their leading figure, António Sardinha, we learn an important lesson regarding the plasticity and the limits to political manipulation of cultural symbols. Defining Tradition in terms of a ruralist political ideal modelled on medieval corporative monarchy, Portuguese Integralism emphatically denounced the 'Discoveries' as an 'error', and as one of the root causes of the capitalist cosmopolitan modernity they so radically opposed. Unable to disentangle the 'Discoveries' from national history, and the colonial legacy from the national imaginary, the Expansion, reinterpreted in the post-First World War years as Catholic and Hispanist Crusade, came now to symbolise the Integralist's very attack on the Godless Republic and its betrayal of this true national tradition (Vakil 1995).

It is the same contradictory and open nature of the symbolism of the 'Discoveries', as dead past and example of modernity, that served Pessoa and Almada Negreiros in the expression of their Marinettian rejections of history in *Portugal Futurista* (1917); and Teixeira de Pascoaes and Fernando Pessoa in the investment of its representations with the expression of their messianic, poetic and esoteric searches for the national tradition and identity.

In the period of transposition and interpenetration of political, cultural and aesthetic discourses, shifting intellectual allegiances and even faster political change of the end of the monarchy and First Republic, the representations of the 'Discoveries' framed in and as the battle for the definition of 'True Portugal' (to paraphrase Lebovics) thus provide a particularly sensitive thread in the unravelling of modernist and traditionalist perspectives, and an even subtler index of shifting positions.

References

Alexandre, V. (1979), *Origens do Colonialismo Português Moderno*, Lisbon
—— (1993), *Os Sentidos do Império. Questão nacional e questão colonial na Crise do Antigo Regime Português*, Oporto
Almeida, P.T. de. (1991), *Eleições e Caciquismo no Portugal Oito-*

centista (1868–1890), Lisbon

Anderson, B. (1983), *Imagined Communities: Reflections on the Origin and Spread of Nationalism*, London

Baker, K.M. (1990), *Inventing the French Revolution*, Cambridge

Balibar, E. and Wallerstein, I. (1991), *Race, Nation, Class: Ambiguous Identities*, London

Barreto, L.F. (1988), *Portugal: Pioneiro do diálogo Norte–Sul/Pionnier du dialogue Nord–Sud/A Pioneer of the North–South Dialogue*, Lisbon

—— (1989), *Portugal: Mensageiro do Mundo Renascentista*, Lisbon

Barreto, L.F. and Garcia, J.M. (n.d.), *Portugal na Abertura do Mundo*, Lisbon

Bebiano, R. (1983), 'O 1º Centenário Pombalino. Contributo para a sua compreensão histórica', *Revista de História das Ideias*, VI:2, pp. 381–428

Bernardino, T. (1986), *Sociedade e Atitudes Mentais em Portugal (1777–1810)*, Lisbon

Bethencourt, F. (1991), 'A sociogénese do sentimento nacional', in Bethencourt, F. and Ramada Curto, D. (eds), *A Memória da Nação*, Lisbon

Billig, M. (1995), *Banal Nationalism*, London

Braga, T. (1884), 'O Centenário de Camões', *Ocidente*, LXXIII:416 (1972), pp.386–405

Cabral, M.V. (1988), *Portugal na Alvorada do Século XX. Forças sociais, poder político e crescimento económico de 1890 a 1914*, Lisbon

—— (1989), 'The Aesthetics of Nationalism: Modernism and Authoritarianism in Early Twentieth-Century Portugal', *Luso-Brazilian Review*, XXVI:1, pp.15–43

Calhoun, C. (1991), 'Indirect Relationships and Imagined Communities', in Bourdieu, P. and Coleman, J.S. (eds), *Social Theory for a Changing Society*, Boulder

Campos Matos, S. (1990), *História, Mitologia, Imaginário Nacional: a História no curso dos liceus (1895–1939)*, Lisbon

Catroga, F. (1989), 'Os Primórdios do 1º de Maio em Portugal. Festa, luto, luta', *Revista de História das Ideias*, 11, pp.445–99

—— (1991), *O Republicanismo em Portugal: da formação ao 5 de Outubro de 1910*, 2 vols, Coimbra

Cavaco Silva, A. (1989), *Construir a Modernidade. Discursos proferidos durante a vigência do XI Governo Constitucional*, Lisbon

—— (1991), *Ganhar o Futuro. Discursos proferidos durante a vigência do XI Governo Constitucional*, Lisbon

Chartier, R. (1991), *The Cultural Origins of the French Revolution*,

Durham
Costa, J.C.R. da et al. (1880), 'Ao Povo Português', in Cabral, A., *Notas Oitocentistas*, I, Lisbon
Cruz, M.B. da (1980), *As Origens da Democracia Cristã e o Salazarismo*, Lisbon
Fernandes, R. (n.d.), *João de Barros Educador Republicano*, Lisbon
França, J.A. (n.d.), *O Romantismo em Portugal. Estudo de factos socioculturais*, 6 vols, Lisbon
Freire, J. (1992), *Anarquistas e Operários. Ideologia, ofício e práticas sociais: o anarquismo e o operariado em Portugal, 1900–1940*, Oporto
Graça Moura, V. (1989), 'Entrevista', *Semanário/Revista*, 21 Oct.
Greenhalgh, P. (1988), *Ephemeral Vistas. The Expositions Universelles, Great Exhibitions and World's Fairs, 1851–1939*, Manchester
Justino, D. (1988), *A Formação do Espaço Económico Nacional: Portugal, 1810–1913*, 2 vols, Lisbon
Laclau, E. and Zac, L. (1994), 'Minding the Gap: the Subject of Politics', in Laclau, E. (ed.), *The Making of Political Identities*, London
Lebovics, H. (1992), *True France: The Wars over Cultural Identity, 1900–1945*, Ithaca
Lopes, F. (1994), *Poder Político e Caciquismo na 1ª República Portuguesa*, Lisbon
Lourenço, E. (1978), *O Labirinto da Saudade: Psicanálise mítica do destino português*, Lisbon
MacKenzie, J. (1984), *Propaganda and Empire*, Manchester
Matias, J. (1989), *Católicos e Socialistas em Portugal (1875–1975)*, Lisbon
Medina, J. (1980), *Eça de Queiroz e a Geração de 70*, Lisbon
—— (1990), *'Oh! a República!...': Estudos Sobre o Republicanismo e a Primeira República Portuguesa*, Lisbon
Moser, G. (1980), 'What did the Old Man of Restelo mean?', *Luso-Brazilian Review*, 17:2, pp.139–51
Mosse, G. (1975), *The Nationalisation of the Masses: Political Symbolism and Mass Movements in Germany from the Napoleonic Wars through the Third Reich*, Ithaca
—— (1990), 'The Political Culture of Italian Futurism', *Journal of Modern History*, 25, pp.253–68
Payne, S.G. (1973), *A History of Spain and Portugal*, vol.2, Madison
Pereira, J.E. (1991), 'Identidade Nacional. Do reformismo absolutista ao liberalismo', in Bethencourt, F. and Ramada Curto, D. (eds), *A Memória da Nação*, Lisbon
Pereira, M.H., Ferreira, M. and Serra, J. (eds) (1982), *O Liberalismo na Península Ibérica na primeira metade do século XIX*, 2 vols, Lisbon

Ramos, R. (1994), *A Segunda Fundação*, vol.6 of José Mattoso (ed.), *História de Portugal*, Lisbon

Rebelo, L.S. (1990), 'Camões – Man and Monument', in Taylor, L.C. (ed.), *Luis de Camões: Epic and Lyric*, Manchester

Reis, J. (1993), *O Atraso Económico Português, 1850–1930*, Lisbon

Rydell, R. (1984), *All the World's a Fair*, Chicago

Schneider, W. (1982), *An Empire for the Masses. The French Popular Image of Africa, 1870–1900*, Westport

Serrão, J. (1979), 'Introdução ao estudo do pensamento político português na época contemporânea (1820–1920)', in Serrão, J. (ed.), *Liberalismo, Socialismo, Republicanismo: antologia do pensamento político português*, Lisbon

—— (1990), *Da 'Regeneração' à República*, Lisbon

Silva, A.S. (1987), *Formar a Nação: Vias culturais do progresso segundo intelectuais portugueses do século XIX*, Porto

Teixeira, N.S. (1990), *O Ultimatum Inglês: Política externa e política interna no Portugal de 1890*, Lisbon

Vakil, A. (1995), 'Representations of the "Discoveries" and the Imaginary of the Nation in Portuguese Integralism', *Portuguese Studies*, 11, pp.133–67

Valente, V.P. (1982), *O Poder e o Povo: A Revolução de 1910*, Lisbon

—— (1992), 'Revoluções: A 'República Velha' (ensaio de interpretação política)', *Análise Social*, XXVII (115):1, pp.7–63

Verdelho, T. (1981), *As Palavras e as Ideias na Revolução Liberal de 1820*, Coimbra

Verdery, K. (1993), 'Whither "Nation" and "Nationalism"?', *Daedalus*, 122:3, pp.35–46

Vidigal, L. (1988), *Cidadania, Caciquismo e Poder: Portugal, 1890–1916, Estudos*, Lisbon

Wernik, A. (1991), *Promotional Culture: Advertising, Ideology and Symbolic Expression*, London

Wheeler, D. (1978), *Republican Portugal: A Political History, 1910–1926*, Madison

3

The People and the Poet: Portuguese National Identity and the Camões Tercentenary (1880)

Alan Freeland

Introduction

A key symbol in the official projection of Portuguese national identity is the sixteenth-century poet Luís de Camões. The anniversary of the date claimed to be that of his death, 10 June 1580, is celebrated as Portugal's national day, 'dia de Portugal, de Camões e das Comunidades Portuguesas'. The association here of the emigrant communities with Camões is a relatively recent change, made three years after the April revolution of 1974 and designed, in a newly democratic post-colonial Portugal, to draw into the nation the communities of emigrant workers and to refashion a national identity based on the more acceptable image of the Portuguese as emigrant, rather than coloniser.[1] Official interest in Camões is also evident in the publication in 1983, by the state-owned Imprensa Nacional, of a small volume, *Camões e a Identidade Nacional*, which brings together the speeches made by distinguished figures in Portuguese culture at the annual celebrations of the 10 June, between 1977 and 1982. And as we approach the end of the millennium and pass through successive quincentenaries that celebrate Portugal's fifteenth-century voyages, Camões is still a key symbol of Portuguese

---

1. The 1977 Camões Day ceremony, held in the symbolic setting of Guarda on the Spanish frontier and the first such ceremony to link the national day to emigration, is deconstructed by Eduardo Lourenço as follows: 'The final meaning of the Guarda ceremony is transparent: to focus the view of our past, the matrix we need in order to illuminate a diminished, anxious present, not around the image of the *Portuguese coloniser* that for five hundred years served us as a reference and an epic and moral viaticum, but around that of the *Portuguese emigrant*, its modern, acceptable version' (1978: 128).

The programme for the 1993 commemorations of the *Dia de Portugal* among the Portuguese community in London describes Camões as a poet, soldier and *emigrant – poeta, soldado e emigrante*.

nationhood. Recent evidence of his continuing potency is the transformation in 1992 of the Institute of Portuguese Language and Culture, the Portuguese equivalent of the British Council, into the Camões Institute, and its subsequent removal from the control of the Ministry of Education to that of Foreign Affairs. So the promotion of Portuguese language and culture abroad, now recognised as an aspect of foreign policy, takes place in the name of Camões.

Camões as a symbol of Portuguese national identity is largely a creation of the nineteenth century, particularly of the Romantics in the early decades and, later, of the intellectuals of the so-called 'generation of 1870'. For example, the historian and philosopher of history Oliveira Martins published a biography of Camões in 1872, and the poet has an important symbolic role in his *História da Civilização Ibérica* and *História de Portugal* (both 1879). Eça de Queirós, Portugal's major nineteenth-century novelist, sets the ending of *O Crime do Padre Amaro*, revised in 1879, beside the statue of Camões in Lisbon (Queirós 1880/n.d.: 499–500) – a statue first proposed in the 1850s and finally inaugurated in 1867 (Macedo 1985: 148–58). In particular, the tercentenary in 1880 of Camões's death provided an opportunity, skilfully exploited for propaganda purposes by the republican movement, to organise national festivities and to elaborate and strengthen the symbolism invested in the figure of the poet.

This chapter examines how the 1880 version of Camões relates to questions of national identity posed by the age-old fear of Spain, the ambivalent special relationship with Britain, and the beginning of a new phase of European imperialism in Africa. I shall refer particularly to two short texts. One is 'O Centenário de Camões', first published in 1880 in the periodical *O Positivismo*, by Teófilo Braga, an enormously prolific literary historian, the leading positivist in Portugal, and a republican theorist and activist who had two brief periods as president in the first Republic, from 1910 onwards. My other main source is *Luís de Camões e a Nacionalidade Portuguesa* (1880), by Teixeira Bastos, a lesser-known figure today, one of the group associated in the late 1870s and early 1880s with the positivist periodical mentioned above.

The Story of the Nation

In order to understand how Camões functions as a myth, and indeed in any approach to the subject of Portuguese national identity in the nineteenth century, we need to recall two pervasive patterns of metaphor that interconnect and reinforce each other: first, the tendency of the nineteenth century to think of society as an organism, in terms of analogies drawn from biology; secondly, the tendency in Portugal to see the world through a prism of messianic expectation. Both these patterns inform the story of the nation, within which Camões acts as a central character and, at another level, as a narrator of part of that story.

In outlining this narrative, I have in mind particularly the 1871 lecture by the Proudonian socialist Antero de Quental – 'Causas da Decadência dos Povos Peninsulares nos Últimos Três Séculos' ('Causes of the Decadence of the Peninsular Peoples in the Last Three Centuries') – which contains a succinct but thematically complex rendering of the story of the nation, in a structure inherited from earlier Romantic writers. The main features of this story of rise and decline are also to be found in the work of Oliveira Martins, who indeed alludes to Quental's lecture in a chapter title in his *História da Civilização Ibérica.*[2]

Nineteenth-century Portuguese writers tend to see their nation's history, in accordance with the organic model, as a temporal process of growth from a seed or birth located usually in a medieval world, though some writers project the antecedents further back in time (Quental 1871/1982: 258). This original Portugal, in its infancy as it were, is associated with creativity and spontaneity. It grows to maturity and its full flowering in the late middle ages and early Renaissance, and finds its outward expression in medieval lyric poetry, in gothic architecture, and specifically in such monuments as the monastery of Batalha. The voyages of discovery are seen as the continuation of this process of growth, though in some variants of the pattern they are the point at which the nation deviates from its natural evolution. The process of growth culminates in the Manueline period of the early sixteenth century. Then, within a few decades, the moment of perfection passes, and Portugal enters its decline. The causes of decay are partly internal and organic – the exhaustion of a small nation that overgrows itself in its maritime empire – and also partly external: growth is stifled by the imposition of a centralising monarchy and a repressive church, especially in its Jesuit arm. Whilst the onset of decadence is thought to lie in the mid-sixteenth century, the crisis in which it manifests itself is the defeat of the young King Sebastian at El-Ksar el-Kebir in 1578, the ensuing invasion of Portugal by Philip II in 1580, and the so-called Philippine occupation that lasted until 1640. Although the restoration of independence in 1640 is celebrated, it is seen by many as an *incomplete* restoration, that failed to halt the long process of decline.

2. The summary of this story of the nation in the following two paragraphs is taken from my recent publication, Freeland 1995.

Within this structure of growth and decay, the messianic pattern, with its connotations of death, resurrection and the second coming of Christ, is centred on the traumatic events of 1580. The Spanish invasion and occupation are compared to the biblical 'captivity' in which the nation waits for the return of the messiah, King Sebastian. But if the restoration of 1640 could not in fact restore Portugal to its former glory, then the nation that died in 1580 is still awaiting the 'great man' or the idea that will bring about its resurrection. Thus the republican discourse relating to the 1880 tercentenary, as we shall see, tends frequently to use terms such as awakening, revival and revitalisation (Vilela 1985: 415–16).

The Romantic Camões

Before considering the significance of Camões in the 1870s, and his relationship to this story of the nation, we need to look briefly at the Camões created by the Romantics (Macedo 1985; Monteiro 1985). For the liberal Romantics of the early decades of the century, he is the author of the national epic, *Os Lusíadas*, a work that tells the story of Portugal in the upward phase of its growth, from its origins to its culmination in the great voyage to India of Vasco da Gama. His lyric poetry, too, is given its place in the mythical structure: it is associated with an older popular native tradition, the *romanceiro*, overlaid in the sixteenth century by imported classical styles. Indeed, in Camões's work as a whole, the Romantics – as one would expect – stress aspects that break classical conventions. So his work is the expression of the national spirit, the product of the poetic genius whose sensitivity is in tune with the poetry of the people (Monteiro 1985: 125).

The biography of Camões is just as important as his work for the elaboration of the myth. In his characteristics and in the events of his life, he conforms to many of the features of the Romantic hero. He is an exceptional individual, surrounded by mediocrity, the target of petty intrigue at Court which leads to imprisonment and banishment, the soldier-adventurer who survives shipwreck in the Mekong Delta, swimming ashore with the manuscript of his poem, and whose travels – Ceuta, Goa, Macau, Mozambique – evoke an exotic oriental world, the first Portuguese empire. He is a victim of society, pursued by creditors, penniless, dependent in his final sickness in Lisbon on charity, buried in an unmarked pauper's grave. According to the ending of Almeida Garrett's poem, *Camões*, published in 1825, 'the Portuguese do not even know the humble place where Camões's ashes lie' (*'Nem o humilde lugar onde repoisam/As cinzas de Camões, conhece o Luso'* (Garrett 1825/n.d.: 168)).[3]

It is above all the timing of Camões's death which feeds the Romantic myth. He lives at the turning-point in the story of the nation, and his death in 1580 coincides with the loss of independence. Garrett's poem ends with the poet's death, and attributes to him the dying words: "'Fatherland, at least we die together".... And with the fatherland he expired' (*"'Pátria, ao menos/Juntos morremos..."* E expirou co'a pátria' (Garrett 1825/n.d.: 167)). The Romantic emphasis on his death is reflected also in a Requiem Mass composed in Paris by João Domingos Bontempo in 1818, and in a painting by Sequeira, *A Morte de Camões*, exhibited in the Paris Salon of 1824. Finally, in this Romantic version of the story, Camões and his work become the inspiration of national resistance during the sixty-year 'captivity' under Spain.

A Viable Nation?

The Romantic Camões is the product of writers and artists, often in exile themselves, living at a time when Portugal's survival as an independent state was again evidently threatened – by the Napoleonic invasions, the flight of the royal family to Rio de Janeiro, the British domination of Portugal under Beresford, the 'loss' of the second empire, Brazil, and the civil wars of the 1820s and 1830s. By comparison, Portugal in the 1870s would appear to be relatively secure. And yet the young Portuguese intellectuals who at the beginning of the decade set out to challenge the cultural and political establishment are obsessed with national decadence.

In the cycle of growth and decay described earlier, they see contemporary Portugal at the nadir of decline. The most pessimistic voice is that of Oliveira Martins, who starts from the assumption that Portugal is an 'organic' part of the 'body' of the Iberian Peninsula and, by implication, unviable once separated from the larger organism. Portugal, he claims, lacks clear definition based on natural territorial boundaries, or, in relation to Galicia, based on ethnicity and language. The country was created by the personal ambition of barons and princes, from bits and pieces – *retalhos* – of neighbouring kingdoms, especially Galicia and

---

3. Concern about the undignified resting-place of Camões is reflected in recurrent proposals, from the second decade of the nineteenth century onwards, to search for the poet's remains and transfer them to a national pantheon. Searches were made in the Lisbon convent of Santana in 1836, 1855 and 1880 (Braga 1891: 267–73; Macedo 1985: 145–6, 149; Medina 1986: 19, note 2). It seems safe to assume that any bones in the 'tomb of Camões', in the Jerónimos Convent at Belém, Lisbon, are not those of the poet.

León. In the final chapter of Book I of *História de Portugal*, he concludes his introductory characterisation of the nation with a description of its 'passive individuality': 'If anything in fact defines us, it is the lack of affirmation of our genius. What we may call our own individual qualities consist in the facility with which we receive and assimilate the qualities of others' (Martins 1879b/1987: 45).

The view that Portugal and its people lack identity is echoed in other writers of the period: imitation and importation of foreign culture are alleged to be vitiating the 'true' national culture. Ramalho Ortigão, in a satirical piece entitled 'To Mr. John Bull' (1876), written on the occasion of a visit of the Prince of Wales to Lisbon, notes the British influence on government, fashion, food and sport (Ortigão 1876/1925: 96–7). For Eça de Queirós, the threat to Portuguese culture lies in 'francesismo' – the slavish imitation of French models, a theme examined both in his essay entitled 'O "Francesismo"' and in his masterpiece, *Os Maias*, a novel much concerned with problems of personal and national identity.

These pessimistic interpretations of Portugal's viability are not shared by the positivists and republicans, at least as regards the possibility of future regeneration. Strongly influenced by Herbert Spencer's concept of social evolution, they tend to interpret the ills of the present as the transition to the future age of Science and Industry: 'We are going through an epoch of transition, a true period of crisis', as Teixeira Bastos puts it (1880: 4). The transition is a period in which the old order is disintegrating and a new society evolving. Here, as in many respects, positivism contains echoes of messianic beliefs (Medina 1986: 11–16), and the sense of a crisis of transition recalls the upheavals that will usher in the last age in chiliastic prophesy.

For the propagandists of 1880, the tercentenary would mark the beginning of the new age (Matos 1992: 60). Teófilo Braga writes that 'the Camões centenary, at this historic moment and in this crisis of spirits, has the significance of a national revival' (1880: 4). The commemoration of the tercentenary, according to Teixeira Bastos, 'shows that Portugal is awakening to historic life, and that the Portuguese people are beginning to be conscious of their nationality once more. . . The centenary festivity must be the shining threshold of a new era of national revival' (1880: 14).

A basic concept in these predictions is the notion of national feeling or national consciousness – *sentimento nacional, sentimento da nacionalidade, consciência nacional*. Teófilo Braga, publishing in 1891 a collection of earlier essays on Camões, gives them the title *Camões e o Sentimento Nacional*. In 1880, whether or not this consciousness is still alive in the people will be tested by their response to the commemoration. At the same time, the fact that the royal family and the government have given rather lukewarm support to the tercentenary proves – at least to the satisfaction of the republicans – that the institutions of the liberal constitutional monarchy do not represent or even recognise this national spirit. The emphasis on national feeling as an indicator of the cohesiveness of the community, and as an emotion that can be stimulated through the celebrations themselves, points to a conscious political manipulation of nationalism.[4] By publicising the programme of events planned in different parts of the country on 10 June, and by inviting municipalities and public bodies to be represented in the Lisbon procession (Braga 1891: 274–81), the organisers are encouraging a wide public to feel part of the 'imagined community' of the nation. This community includes the ancestors, present in the historic associations of the Camões myth.

The cultivation of national feeling in the tercentenary involves a theme of betrayal, and identifies an enemy within – who, we may infer, does not share the 'sentimento nacional'. In the Romantic period, themes of loyalty and betrayal are important in the work of Almeida Garrett, both in *Viagens na Minha Terra* and in *Frei Luís de Sousa*, the latter set at the end of the sixteenth century, in the context of the Spanish occupation. However, if this Romantic drama presents complex conflicts of loyalty, personal as well as political, the republican writers of 1880 are less subtle. According to Teófilo Braga, in the years leading up to 1580 Portugal was *betrayed* to the Spanish. The traitors are associated with the monarchy, the aristocracy and the church, especially the Jesuits. Camões, on the other hand, is identified with the national cause. When he returned to Lisbon in 1570, in the words of Teófilo Braga, 'the Jesuits dominated the conscience of the young monarch, King Sebastian, and were plotting with Spain the infamous incorporation of Portugal' (Braga 1884: 42). Eight years later, after the battle of El-Ksar el-Kebir, 'Camões realised that Cardinal Henrique, the blind tool of the Jesuits, was conspiring against Portugal's autonomy, and all the supporters of national independence gathered round the poet' (Braga 1884: 43).

> When the armies of Philip II entered Portugal in 1580, and *the aristocracy shamelessly sold themselves to the invader* [my italics], recognising his dubious claims, there was a national party of independence which resisted; one of that party was D. Francisco de Almeida, who was busy enlisting people for a national uprising, and it was to him that Camões wrote the famous words: 'at least I'm dying with the fatherland.' (Braga 1880: 3)

4. On the role attributed to collective emotion in positivist theory, see Matos 1992: 61–2.

The Spanish Threat

An important aspect of Portugal's perceived weakness in the 1870s was simply its small size. In an age in which large nations were forming, with the recent unification of Italy and Germany, Portugal failed to fulfil the 'threshold principle' (see Hobsbawm 1990: 30–2). Furthermore, the Franco-Prussian War seemed to usher in a new age of instability, in which the rule of international law was replaced by a social-Darwinist principle of struggle for existence. Thus João de Andrade Corvo, Portuguese foreign minister for much of the 1870s, warns of the threats to 'small nations' in a book published in 1870, during the war, and aptly entitled *Perigos* ('Dangers'). In Eça de Queirós's story 'A Catástrofe', set in a future Portugal under foreign occupation, the narrator recalls the outbreak of the general European war that led to this invasion: 'it seemed as though the terrible day had come when the small nations might disappear from Europe!' (Queirós 1925/1951: 226). In *Os Maias*, set mainly in 1875–6, Eça's characters claim from time to time that what the country needs is a Spanish invasion that would perhaps provoke a national revival (Queirós 1888/n.d.).[5]

Portugal was perceived to be vulnerable to the proposal for Iberian union (Catroga 1985) – an issue that had been reopened in 1852 by the publication of a work by D. Sinibaldo de Mas, *A Ibéria. Memória escrita em língua espanhola por um filo-português, e traduzida em língua portuguesa por um filo-ibérico*. To judge by the rate of publication of pamphlets on the Iberian question, it was at its height in the late 1860s and early 1870s (Medina 1973: 299–300). By the end of the decade it was no longer felt to be a real threat, at least from a federal republican perspective. Teófilo Braga refers to the principle of large nations and its enforcement in the peninsula as an unlikely hypothesis:

> If the principle of forming large nations artificially and by force were to prevail, the principle on which Napoleon III launched contemporary Europe into a state of war, Portugal would have to be united with Spain by violent means; the two peninsular monarchies have dreamt such adventures, which still feed the insane dream of Iberian union. Camões's poem, and his name,

5. On the 'Iberian question' in Eça's fiction, see Medina 1973.
In 1878 Eça outlined a plan for a novel, *A Batalha do Caia*, about a Spanish invasion of Portugal and the ensuing collapse of the nation (Queirós 1983: I, 166). 'A Catástrofe' would appear to develop the same theme on a smaller scale. However, in 'A Catástrofe', he goes to striking lengths to avoid confirming that the invader is Spain. The narrative refers to the *enemy* sentinel, army, uniform, flag, fleet, etc., in contexts where the reader expects an indication of nationality. Eça's suppression of this information does not, of course, prevent the reader, especially the Portuguese reader, from inferring that the invader is indeed Spanish (e.g. Medina 1973: 305).

would for ever be the eloquent protest against the assassination of a small nation, as they were in 1640. But western Europe is tending towards the stability of peace through democracy; the political form of western nations will be the republic, based on federation, in which ethnic and traditional differences are recognised. (Braga 1884: 21–2)

Teófilo Braga goes on to predict that, as Pi i Margall shows, the cantonalist aspirations in Spain will become disciplined into federal republics. Portugal will enter the confederation of Peninsular states 'with its own national autonomy, with Galicia as an integral part of its ethnic organism, and given its geographical position and moral superiority, it will then exercise a real hegemony' (Braga 1884: 22). That is, a confederation of peninsular states would provide a 'place' for Portugal that protects its separate identity, no longer threatened by a unified and more powerful Spain. Teófilo Braga and Teixeira Bastos see such an Iberian federation as part of a still larger grouping of Latin states that would include France and Italy. And, although the further intermediate stages are not made explicit, the process of forming larger and larger groups eventually places Portugal in the ultimate positivist family: humanity.[6]

Both in relation to Spain and in relation to 'humanity', Camões provides a badge of identity. 'When in any country in Europe they talk about Portugal, they confuse us unconsciously with Spain; but when you say "I'm from the land of Camões" immediately our national individuality is recognised' (Braga 1880: 2–3).

The Perfidious Alliance and Africa

The traditional defence against absorption by Spain was alliance with Britain. But this in itself restricted Portugal's autonomy. Indeed the sense of decadence in the final quarter of the nineteenth century was felt partly by contrast with a Britain that was the most powerful industrial and naval power of the age. One possible solution for Portugal that increasingly attracted interest lay in developing the African colonies. Portugal's foreign minister, Andrade Corvo, in the book mentioned above, *Perigos*, connects the three elements, Spain, Britain and Africa, in an argument that was to form the basis of his colonial policy for the decade. Taking seriously the possibility of enforced unification with

6. Underpinning this bold attempt to reconcile Portugal's particular identity with a place in a larger structure are perhaps Herbert Spencer's theory of social evolution as the transformation of the simple into the complex and his notion of 'coherent heterogeneity'. Social evolution, in Spencer's account, involves both increasing differentiation and the combination of heterogeneous elements into larger aggregates. By implication, evolution would seem to favour small nations combined in a federal structure. See Catroga 1985: 456–7; Homem 1989: 137–40, 153.

Spain, he set out to build on Portugal's position in Africa. His strategy aimed to strengthen Portugal's tenuous hold on the coasts of Mozambique and Angola, and to define colonial frontiers, working in collaboration and negotiation with Britain, which he regarded as the dominant power emerging in southern Africa.

Andrade Corvo was initially successful. He persuaded Britain to accept French arbitration in a dispute over Lourenço Marques (now Maputo): the resulting MacMahon arbitration of 1875 confirmed Portugal's claims and defined the southern frontier of Mozambique. However, a draft treaty of Lourenço Marques, negotiated in 1879 by Andrade Corvo and the British ambassador in Lisbon, became the target of fierce opposition attacks in the Portuguese parliament and press over the next two years. With the rejection of this treaty, and the defeat of Andrade Corvo's strategy of collaboration with Britain, Portugal in the 1880s followed a utopian course that laid claim to the vast interior between Angola and Mozambique, an area represented in pink on the so-called *mapa cor-de-rosa* of the period (Telo 1991: 30–40). This policy inevitably collided with the interests of Britain and Cecil Rhodes, provoking the 1890 'ultimatum' that forced Portugal into a humiliating climb-down. The consequences in Portugal were a wave of popular anti-British feeling, political and financial crisis, an abortive republican revolt in Oporto, and the composition of a chauvinistic song that begins 'Heroes of the sea, noble people', which is now the Portuguese national anthem, *A Portuguesa*.

In this gradual deterioration in Anglo-Portuguese relations, the Camões tercentenary celebrations in 1880, and the preparations for them, coincide with a stage when Andrade Corvo's more cautious, realistic colonial strategy for Africa was under opposition attack, and losing ground to the more confrontational policy that would lead to the crisis of the early 1890s. The 1880 celebrations take place against 'marked anti-British tension', generated by opposition to the treaty of Lourenço Marques (Catroga 1991: I, 46). Teófilo Braga seems to be alluding to this treaty, and to another dealing with Goa (1878), when he talks of the national territory being 'dismembered by fraudulent treaties' (1884: 53). In the festivities in Lisbon on 10 June 1880, the African significance was recognised in the civic procession to the statue of Camões. Among eight allegorical tableaux was one representing the colonies (Macedo 1985: 172).[7] The Camões myth elaborated by the republicans, with all the associations taken over from the Romantic version, contains implicit justifications for a revival of Portuguese colonialism in Africa.

---

7. I am grateful to AbdoolKarim Vakil for drawing my attention to this detail.

The Divine Mission

The broadest justification is the notion of a divine mission. The story of Portugal, as told in *Os Lusíadas* and retold in the nineteenth century, involves the nation being born out of conflict with two 'others': Spain, decisively defeated at Aljubarrota in 1385, and Islam, pursued southwards as the Christian kingdom is established in the twelfth and thirteenth centuries. The divine origin of the nation is represented in a foundation myth invented in the sixteenth century, according to which Christ appeared to Afonso Henriques on the eve of the battle of Ourique (1139), promising victory against the Moors in the coming battle and an independent kingdom for Afonso Henriques and his heirs. Although by the mid-nineteenth century the miracle of Ourique is dismissed by Alexandre Herculano as a 'pious fraud', the sense of Portugal's national mission is an important ingredient in the ideology that concerns us here.[8]

The sense of divine mission and the notion that a colonising role is part of being Portuguese, that the national territory somehow extends into Africa, is strengthened by the southerly direction of the formation of the nation. That is, its origins lie in the north, in the connections with Galicia, and in even more ancient roots in Germanic peoples.[9] The nation is formed by a drive from north to south, in pursuit of the 'infidel'. This pursuit of Islam within Portugal continues into North Africa, with the capture of Ceuta in 1415, and culminates in the voyages to the East, which according to Teófilo Braga and Teixeira Bastos 'saved modern civilisation from imminent ruin' by forcing the Ottoman Turks to divert their attention eastwards, away from Europe (Bastos 1880: 20–2; Braga 1880: 5–6). Expansion into Africa becomes a logical culmination of national destiny. The Infante Dom Henrique – Prince Henry the Navigator – in the words of Teixeira Bastos 'was the first to see in Africa a vast field for the Portuguese to *continue* [my emphasis] their great deeds and their acts of war in honour of the fatherland and religion' (1880: 16).

The divinity of this mission has a literal importance in the late nineteenth century, if we bear in mind the role of the missionary and the Christianising veil that European colonisers drew over their occupation of the African continent in the final decades of the century.

---

8. On the battle of Ourique as a foundation myth, see Buescu 1993.

9. The belief that Portugal's origins lie in the north of the country is apparent in the claim of the Minho town, Guimarães, birthplace of Afonso Henriques, to be the 'cradle of the nation' – *o berço da nação*.

Historic Precedence

Closely related to divine mission, in the case of Portugal, is the notion of historic rights as a justification for claiming colonies – the same historic argument that was rejected by the other European powers at the Conference of Berlin (1884–5). *Os Lusíadas* and the story of Camões's own travels are an implicit reminder that the Portuguese were the first Europeans to 'discover' vast areas of the world for trade and conquest. Teófilo Braga writes of Camões: 'he went forth into the vast domain of the Portuguese conquests, facing the dangers of sieges, naval battles, storms, shipwrecks, fever-stricken voyages, and the wretchedness of alien hospices' (1884: 27). Teixeira Bastos writes in similarly heroic terms: 'Vasco da Gama finally arrives in India in 1498; the sea route to the East was discovered, and about to begin was the famous Portuguese dominion of the sixteenth century, the vast empire of Afonso de Albuquerque. The tenacity, valour and heroism of our people had reached their highest peak; Portugal was in the vanguard of civilisation' (1880: 18–19).

Progress

Finally the organisers of the tercentenary deploy a series of comparisons between the age of Camões and the present, which depend on the positivist concept of progress. The age of the voyages is seen as the beginning of the modern age of science, and is echoed in the transition to the future age of Science and Industry, a transition which the positivists of 1880 believe they are living through. To celebrate Camões is to recall Portugal's past role in the great march of humanity, and to claim such a place once again.

Teixeira Bastos quotes approvingly a passage from Quinet's *Le génie des Religions* which suggests the significance of Camões for the industrial age. Camões deserves to be better known because, Quinet says, 'I don't know of any poet who better corresponds and who is associated with a greater number of ideas and feelings widespread in this century'. *Os Lusíadas* is an epic without battles which presents 'the eternal conflict of man and nature, that is, the struggle that the writers of our time so often speak of. . . . The poem that opens the modern era with the sixteenth century is the same one that, sealing the alliance of East and West, celebrates the heroic age of industry, a poem no longer of the pilgrim but of the traveller, above all of the trader, a true *Odyssey* among the factories, the nascent markets of the Great Indies, and the cradle of modern commerce' (Bastos 1880: 49–50). So Camões is the poet of modern industry, *Os Lusíadas* is the poem of commerce. This sounds innocuous enough, until we recall the nature of the relationship, in the late nineteenth century, between Europe and the markets of the 'Great Indies'.

The positivists and republicans of 1880, then, whilst incorporating in their Camões aspects of the Romantic myth, fit the poet into their model of history as evolution towards the new age of Science and Industry, and towards a republican confederation of peninsular states, in turn part of a Latin and even a Western European federation. Camões and his epic symbolise the collective effort of the Portuguese people that made possible their unique contribution to the development of modern Europe. Through the celebration of the Camões tercentenary, 'national consciousness' is to be revived, a revival that will eventually lead to the Republic. The Camões myth involves drawing analogies between past and present, retracing the three hundred years in which the nation has deviated from its true destiny. Concordances are suggested – between 1580 and 1880, between the lost empire of the East (and the lost Brazil) and a future 'new age', between those who betrayed the nation then and the monarchy and church now that impede the inevitable evolution towards this new era. We may infer that there is a strong link between the nostalgia for a lost empire, cultivated in the commemoration of the tercentenary, and the growth of public interest in Africa which helps to lay the foundations of the third Portuguese empire that ended on 25 April 1974 – though its terrible aftermath still haunts the people whose maps, in the shape of Angola and Mozambique, were drawn by Europe in the late nineteenth century.

References

Bastos, Teixeira (1880), *Luís de Camões e a Nacionalidade Portuguesa*, Biblioteca Republicana Democrática, vol.15, Lisbon
Braga, Teófilo (1880), 'O Centenário de Camões em 1880', *O Positivismo*, vol.2, pp.1–9
—— (1884), 'O Centenário de Camões', *Os Centenários como Síntese Afectiva nas Sociedades Modernas*, Oporto
—— (1891), *Camões e o Sentimento Nacional*, Oporto
Buescu, A.I. (1993), 'Vínculos da memória: Ourique e a fundação do reino', in Centeno, Y.K. (ed.), *Portugal: Mitos Revisitados*, Lisbon, pp.9–50
Camões e a Identidade Nacional (1983), Lisbon
Catroga, F. (1985), 'Nacionalismo e ecumenismo. A questão ibérica na 2ª metade do século XIX', *Cultura – História e Filosofia*, vol.IV, pp.419–63

—— (1991), *O Republicanismo em Portugal: da Formação ao 5 de Outubro de 1910*, 2 vols, Coimbra

Corvo, J. Andrade (1870), *Perigos*, Lisbon

Freeland, A. (1995), 'The *Sick Man of the West*: A Late Nineteenth-century Diagnosis of Portugal', in Earle, T.F. and Griffin, Nigel (eds), *Portuguese, Brazilian, and African Studies*, Warminster, pp.205–16

Garrett, Almeida (1825/n.d.), *Camões*, Oporto

Hobsbawm, E.J. (1990), *Nations and Nationalism since 1870*, Cambridge

Homem, A. Carvalho (1989), *A Ideia Republicana em Portugal. O Contributo de Teófilo Braga*, Coimbra

Lourenço, Eduardo (1978), *O Labirinto da Saudade. Psicanálise Mítica do Destino Português*, Lisbon

Macedo, J. Borges de (1985), 'Camões em Portugal no Século XIX', *Revista da Universidade de Coimbra*, vol.33, pp.139–80

Martins, Oliveira (1872/1986), *Camões, Os Lusíadas e a Renascença em Portugal*, 4th edn, Guimarães Editores, Lisbon

—— (1879a/1994), *História da Civilização Ibérica*, 12th edn, Guimarães Editores, Lisbon

—— (1879b/1987), *História de Portugal*, 19th edn, Guimarães Editores, Lisbon

Matos, S. Campos (1992), 'História, Positivismo e Função dos Grandes Homens no Último Quartel do Século XIX', *Penélope*, no.8, pp.51–71

Medina, J. (1973), 'Eça e a Espanha: Reflexos da Questão Ibérica na Obra de Eça de Queiroz (1867–1888)', *Arquivos do Centro Cultural Português*, vol.VII, pp.299–339

—— (1986), 'Zé Povinho e Camões. Dois Pólos da Prototipia Nacional', *Colóquio Letras*, no.92, pp.11–21

Monteiro, O. Paiva (1985), 'Camões no Romantismo', *Revista da Universidade de Coimbra*, vol.33, pp.119–37

Ortigão, Ramalho (1876/1925), 'A Mr John Bull', in *As Farpas*, 3rd edn, Lisbon, vol.2, pp.95–132

Queirós, Eça de (1880/n.d.), *O Crime do Padre Amaro*, 4th edn, Livros do Brasil, Lisbon. (*The Sin of Father Amaro*, trans. Nan Flanagan (1962/1994), Manchester)

—— (1888/n.d.), *Os Maias*, 2nd edn, Livros do Brasil, Lisbon. (*The Maias*, trans. Patricia McGowan Pinheiro and Ann Stevens (1965/1993), Manchester)

—— (1925/1951), *O Conde d'Abranhos* e *A Catástrofe*, Lello, Oporto

—— (1983), *Correspondência*, 2 vols, ed. Guilherme de Castilho, Lisbon

Quental, Antero de (1871/1982), 'Causas da Decadência dos Povos

Peninsulares nos Últimos Três Séculos', in Antero de Quental, *Prosas Sócio-Políticas*, ed. J. Serrão, Lisbon, pp.255–96

Telo, A.J. (1991), *Lourenço Marques na Política Externa Portuguesa, 1875–1900*, Lisbon

Vilela, M. (1985), 'Recepção de Camões nos Jornais de 1880', *Revista da Universidade de Coimbra*, vol.33, pp.403–18

4

The Role of Language in Spanish Nation-Building

Clare Mar-Molinero

Introduction

In this chapter I will investigate the role that language plays in defining nationalism and then see how far it is a salient marker in the nation-building process and nationalist movements of modern Spain. The importance of the role of language, like that of any other markers of nationalism, will depend to some extent on how we define nationalism: as the ideology of a self-defined group which aspires to some political formulation of the national community, or simply as a cultural phenomenon, the outcome of an awareness of shared characteristics. These varying views of nationalism are frequently described as 'political nationalism' and 'cultural nationalism' (Fishman 1972; Alter 1991) or 'subjective' and 'objective' nationalism (Alter 1991), and reflect very different roles for language. Political-subjective nationalism is described by Alter (1991: 15):

> a process of domestic political transformation generated the nation as a community of politically aware citizens equal before the law irrespective of their social and economic status, ethnic origins and religious beliefs. . ... [T]he unifying whole is formed by a uniform language, a uniform judicial and administrative system, a central government and shared political ideals. The sovereignty of the people is the foundation of state power.

The cultural-objective concept of nationalism, on the other hand, is based on external markers, such as one territory, shared history and heritage, race and common language, which a person has, whether they like it or not. This deterministic and exclusive concept is in contrast to the previous liberal-democratic one, and as Alter points out has frequently been seen as irrational and undemocratic. In terms of this political-cultural split it is quite often suggested that language is only an important element in the latter. I will argue that this is far from the case, not least in the Spanish context.

Two contrasting and persuasive commentators who highlight the role of language in nationalism are, on the one hand, Benedict Anderson (1983)[1] and, on the other, Elie Kedourie (1960), who develops the ideas of the eighteenth-century German writer Herder and his followers. Essentially the difference between the two positions is whether language is viewed as a subjective marker, which can be controlled and developed to serve nationalist purposes, or as an objective characteristic, 'given' by virtue of one's birth. In the case of the former, language is clearly used as a conscious part of the political processes in nation-building.

Anderson in his *Imagined Communities: Reflection on the Origins and Spread of Nationalism* argues very convincingly that a significant cause of the emergence of separate nations and their communities was the result of the increased use of the vernacular in public life and the spread of the print-word, even though literacy was restricted to a relatively small elite until the late nineteenth century. Anderson (1983: 47–8) identifies three important roles for the print-word in shaping modern nationalism and national identities. In the first place, the print-word entailed standardisation of a linguistic variety, ensuring that a 'norm' emerged which now could serve as means of communication across the nation, or identifiable community in a way Latin had previously done. Secondly, the previous dialectal diversity was now overcome and national languages were not only 'fixed' and serving as a unifier of diverse dialects, but this standard norm would also 'fix' language across time so as to create an historical basis for the nation in a way which previously could not have happened. Literacy and standardisation have allowed an accessibility to the past and future which previously did not exist. This new sense of time, both chronologically emerging from a shared past and simultaneous with a shared present community, is essential to the sense of nationhood (Anderson 1983; Williams 1984).

A third important aspect of the standardisation of the vernacular, according to Anderson, is that it helped create linguistic hierarchies, establishing new power relationships, as the chosen dialect, or those close to it, dominated the more deviant varieties. In turn this has put a high premium on the prestige of the print-word which is reflected in today's minority linguistic communities' desire to establish literacy in their languages.

---

1. For a detailed application of Anderson's ideas to the specific situation of Galician, see Chapter 14.

Another important role of print-language associated with nationalism is the way it helped underpin the political ideas of Europe after the French Revolution. Insofar as Rousseau and other intellectuals of the French Revolution are usually considered as being the original impetus for the ideas of politica. nationalism – those of democracy, the general will of the people and their collective right to be heard – language in its new standardised print form was instrumental in spreadin these ideas. As Anderson notes, the print-word pro ced 'blue-prints' (Anderson 1983: 79) and helped create the models of th new societies, where fraternity, equality and liberty were to triumph.

Gellner (1983) also sees the importance of language in the modernisation process that has helped create nations. He argues that literacy in the modern world is the essential entry required for full citizenship, and that this must be provided via the national education system. He describes all men as 'clerks' in their relationship to society and stresses how this role and its reliance on literacy has made people less mobile, only able to operate within the areas where the particular national language is spoken (Gellner in Hutchinson and Smith, 1994: 56). Indeed, the rise and standardisation of the vernacular languages also helped create clearly defined boundaries, as loss of intelligibility defined where the nation and its national language should stretch. Monolingualism amongst the elites, those in power, became more widespread, highlighting the sense of 'them' and 'us' so central to nationalism. It is this role of language, as exclusive and discriminating, which is typical of the discussions about linguistic nationalism associated with the writings of the father of cultural nationalism, Johann Gottfried von Herder.

Herder, writing in the latter half of the eighteenth century, was amongst the first to stress the importance of language as *the* marker of national identity. He both insists that 'language is the medium through which man becomes conscious of his inner self' (cited in Barnard 1969: 57) and extends the importance of language to say that it 'is the criterion by means of which a group's identity as a homogenous unit can be established' (cited in Barnard 1969: 58). For Herder and those who followed him, such as Fichte, language is the soul of a nation, without which a nation cannot exist. Furthermore, they believed that a nation could only have one language, as people can only truly express themselves through their native tongue. Herder stressed that since one community, i.e. nation, should possess one language, then this naturally bound its territory; there should be no expansion beyond these boundaries. He did not, however, believe, unlike Fichte, that any one language, not even his beloved German, was superior to others. He also found it perfectly natural that there should be many languages, but they should not be mixed. This emphasis on keeping language 'pure' from borrowing or mixing of other languages because of the complete congruence between people and their languages has profound implications. As Kedourie (1993: 61) says, 'two conclusions may be drawn: first, that people who speak an original language are nations, and second, that nations must speak an original language'.

Whilst Herder himself was largely interested in the cultural implications of the link between language and society, the logic of what he is saying may lead to clear political consequences. To quote Kedourie (1993: 62) once more:

> The test, then, by which a nation is known to exist is that of language. A group speaking the same language is known as a nation, and a nation ought to constitute a state. It is not merely that a group of people speaking a certain language may claim the right to preserve its language, rather, such a group, which is a nation, will cease to be one if it is not constituted into a state. . . . Again, if a nation is a group of people speaking the same language, then if political frontiers separate the members of such a group, these frontiers are arbitrary, unnatural, unique.

In this brief survey of theories of language in the development of nations and national identity, we are aware of the constant tension between the notion of 'nation' and that of 'state'. My working definitions for these will synthesise the current writings on nationalism to propose that a nation is a community of people with common attributes, such as language, race, religion, history, etc., and a self-awareness of this shared community. A state, on the other hand, is a politically constructed entity which imposes boundaries and has the ultimate power to defend and control these boundaries (to paraphrase Max Weber's well-known definition, cited in, e.g. Alter 1991: 11). The logical conclusion of both the strictly political nationalism of the French thinkers such as Rousseau and the cultural nationalism of Herder and his followers both point to a congruence between the nation and the state. As we know, in most parts of the world, including in nineteenth-century Europe where these ideas were formed, this is not an automatic congruence, and in fact leads to many conflicts and to a lack of satisfaction with the original theories.

Spain is an extremely obvious example of how the notion of the nation-state has often been imposed but has not, and does not, naturally emerge. And yet, if the inevitable implication of all forms of nationalism, including that which is culturally rather than politically formulated, is for a community to aspire to some form of political organisation, as Kedourie argues in the quotation above, and as many other commentators believe, then it would seem that the conflicts between nation-state hegemony and peripheral nationalism are impossible to resolve. The linguistic manifestations of these political aspirations are carried out through overt and covert language policies, and through Language Planning, the resources for which, even ironically, in the case of minority communities, must invariably come from the central state.

In the remainder of this chapter I shall sketch the context of Spain's conflicting nationalisms insofar as these reflect linguistic issues. I shall also show how and where the complex relationship between language and politics shapes these nationalisms through language planning, and how this may in fact doom minority groups ultimately to be cast in the image of and controlled by the central majority powers. From this discussion it will emerge that whilst we can observe language as both a subjective and objective feature in Spain's nationalism, ultimately language always has a political as well as a cultural role to play.

The Emergence of a 'National' Language in Spain

The end of the fifteenth century, it can be argued, marks the birth of modern Spain. This period heralds the beginning of the imposing of Castilian hegemony, a hegemony born out of solidarity in the face of the common Moorish enemy, throughout the newly formed state, and the repression of what were now perceived as minorities along the peripheries. Spanish nationalism and Castilian linguistic supremacy go hand in hand, but, nonetheless, they do not succeed in entirely eliminating non-Castilian communities.

Initially the so-called 'unification' of Spain created by the Catholic Monarchs' marriage and the annexation in 1512 of Navarre was a very loose concept, hardly akin to our present notion of 'nation'. This is reflected in the range of languages still in use across the Peninsula, although Castilian was indeed beginning to dominate. Its political superiority, as the language of the Court and government and the expanding Empire, was mirrored too during this period by the flourishing literary output in Castilian of Spain's Golden Age.

However, it is really not until the seventeenth century, as Spain began to abandon her imperial designs and looked inwards to the home-base, that moves to consolidate Spanish national identity involving language policies take shape. Particularly prominent in the moves to formulate a sense of Spanish, as opposed to Castilian, identity for the monarchy and the state is the Conde Duque de Olivares, whose famous 'secret' memorandum to Philip IV in 1624 exemplifies this awareness that strength can only be found for the king's policies by bringing political and administrative centralisation to Spain. He writes (cited in Linz 1973: 43):

> The most important thing in Your Majesty's Monarchy is for you to become king of Spain, by this I mean, Sir, that Your Majesty should not be content with being king of Portugal, of Aragon, of Valencia, and Count of Barcelona, but should secretly plan and work to reduce these kingdoms of which Spain is composed to the style and laws of Castille, with no difference whatsoever.

Clearly a major obstacle in any such centralising policy would be the existence of different vernaculars (linked with their diverse regional identities) thus bringing the need for one 'national' language onto the agenda.

During the eighteenth century the position of Castilian throughout Spain is strengthened by the increasing use of Castilian by the now very centralised Catholic Church, and the use of Castilian in the education system. To this can also be added the effect of universal male conscription into a Castilian-speaking army, and the establishment in 1713 of the Real Academia de la Lengua Española. The latter with its motto '*limpia, fija, y da espendor*' ('cleanse, fix and give spendour') is an early example of the purifying and standardising influence that Anderson observes in dominant languages.

The 1808 invasion by Napoleon had the effect of uniting, in a sense of solidarity against the common enemy, even those who had previously been in conflict with the central government. A sense of Spanish (rather than Castilian, Catalan, Galician, etc.) patriotism was experienced. However this was followed by a century of deep divisions and internal conflict, unable to build on that moment of national patriotism (see Chapter 5). Whilst many of these conflicts took place on the peripheries where a strong sense of difference was present, it is significant the lack of importance that the different sides in these conflicts paid the role of regional languages.

Nonetheless, the latter half of the nineteenth century saw the resurgence of cultural activities in languages other than Castilian in various parts of the Peninsula, notably in Catalonia, Galicia and the Basque Country. These cultural movements signalled new or increased literary outputs in the minority languages, and required focusing on the written language for the first time in many centuries. This period, therefore, also saw significant work in the area of codification and elaboration of the non-Castilian languages.

These cultural and linguistic 'renaissances', as they are generally called, which flourished in the second half of the nineteenth century, were stimulated by the European-wide nationalism movements, in particular those inspired by the French and German writers discussed above. The Romantic movement emerging from the ideas of Herder and his followers, with their emphasis on cultural and linguistic discreteness and uniqueness, helped revive an interest in hitherto marginalised groups and their cultures (Hobsbawm 1990). Such thinking inevitably influenced the cultural revivals beginning to take shape in Catalonia, Galicia and the Basque Country. However, Romanticism and its ideas about cultural nationalism was also embraced by Castilian intellectuals, such as the group of writers producing work around the turn of the century. The sense of national decadence and inadequacy produced by the final loss of Spain's once great empire was challenged by these writers (some of whom while deliberately choosing to write in Castilian were from the periphery – e.g. the Basque authors Unamuno and Baroja). While these writers sharply criticised the Spain they saw around them, they supported the view that a united Spain could be great and should be regenerated and modernised, and in particular emphasised the greatness of Castile. They were scornful of the splintering effect of the various peripheral nationalist movements. But it is this same frustration with Spain's decadence that was leading the Catalans to formulate their new nationalism and impetus for modernisation based on their local communities and detached from the problems associated with the central state.

As Spain entered the twentieth century, then, its sense of national identity was challenged both by the lingering reaction to the loss of her empire and international prestige and her inability to modernise, and by the impatience from the linguistic minority communities on the periphery with the central state bureaucracy and administrative incompetence. While the imperialist past and Bourbon centralism had ensured Castilian dominance, creating a nation-state similar to others in Europe, the chaotic political situation of the nineteenth century had failed to bring the linguistic minorities entirely to heel, allowing the peripheries' nationalisms to flower in a climate of European Romanticism-inspired cultural nationalism. Before turning to the present-day situation of Spain to discuss the current linguistic context and its relation to national identity, I would like to trace more specifically the history of the non-Castilian communities who have managed to maintain their own particular identity and separate language despite the imposition of Castilian hegemony.

The Resurgence of Nationalist Movements on the Spanish Periphery

This discussion will centre on three communities principally: the Catalans, the Basques and the Galicians. Other regions of the Peninsula can be associated with the nineteenth century's revived interest with separate, non-Castilian, identity (see Chapter 1), but this is to a much lesser degree, and often is also in some way linked with these three. This is not to belittle the importance of the sense of identity that these regions may have, but it recognises the fact that they do not have a claim to a widely spoken discrete language different from Castilian, Catalan, Basque or Galician.

1. Catalan

At its peak, Catalan was the principal language of a large area, including not only present-day Catalonia itself, but also parts of Southern France, Aragon, Valencia, the Balearic Islands, as well as enclaves in Italy, North Africa and Greece. Its prestige during this period (eleventh to fourteenth centuries) was on a par with French and Italian, as well as other languages of the Peninsula like Castilian and Portuguese. It increasingly replaced Latin (and later Provençal) as the language of cultural and literary production. Only in Aragon did it remain merely the spoken variety. Literary and philosophical output flourished, and even as Catalan's political power diminished in the fifteenth century, Catalan can boast a Golden Age in letters, notably in Valencia. From the sixteenth century onwards with the rise in Castile's power, Catalan was on the decline, and parts of the original *Paisos Catalans* (Catalan countries) were lost (as Rousillon to France) or separated. Repressive laws and the increased presence of a Castilian-speaking hierarchy meant Catalan lost its prestige and became largely a spoken language only, suffering therefore dialectalising tendencies (see Valverdú 1984). The process of castilianisation and oppression of the Catalan language continued until the nineteenth century and the *Renaixença* (see, e.g, Valverdú 1984; Ferrer 1985).

The *Renaixença* began as a poetry-centred movement. However, by the second half of the nineteenth century, it had become far more than a cultural expression, inspiring also a political movement. Initially with an important literary output, which reflected the influence of the European Romanticism movement as writers exalted their past, and also particularly highlighted (even mythologised) forgotten groups, traditional cultures with their popular legends and stories, the Catalans achieved an impressive production of lyric poetry and extended this interest to the popular domain with such activities as the *'Jocs Florals'*, which were oral poetry competitions, modelled on the lines of similar medieval contests and later taken up in the Basque Country and Galicia. This cultural movement coincided with the emergence of Catalonia as an industrial society, and some of these new activities reflected new social popular concerns.

Throughout the intellectual development of the ideas of the *Renaixença*, language emerges as the central issue around which the Catalans based their claims to a separate identity. Amongst the first influential Catalanist political thinkers, Valentí Almirall sees language as an essential core value to Catalan identity (see Conversi 1990), which he promotes as a central plank to their political aspirations. This is a theme taken up by the leading nineteenth-century politician Enric Prat de la Riba, whose book *La Nacionalitat Catalana* (1906) is the basis of much of the thinking of modern Catalan nationalism. Prat de la Riba was significantly influenced by the German Romantic writers, including Herder, through the work of the Catalan philosopher Llorens i Barba who introduced their ideas to Catalonia (see Conversi 1993; Siguan 1993). For Prat de la Riba, language, along with culture and territory, forms the spirit that defines the nation (Prat de la Riba 1986 edn: 100–1). As Conversi (1993) notes, referring to Prat de la Riba's work:

> Many passages emphasize language as the more visible expression of the national soul and prime bond of union between the different Catalan-speaking territories. . .. The Herderian link has been repeatedly revived in the Catalan academic world and society, from several perspectives, different political sides and academic milieux. Thus, linguistic theories of the deep existing links between language and thought, have reached far beyond the academic circles. . .to be reflected in many contemporary political pamphlets and programmes.

As president of the *Mancomunitat*, a limited early form of Catalan local government, Prat de la Riba continued to promote the Catalan language, setting up the *Institut d'Estudis Catalans* under whose auspices much codification and elaboration of the Catalan language was carried out by the linguist Pompeu Fabra.

2. Basque

The Basques were forced to retreat further and further into the more inhospitable, and therefore less accessible, of their lands by the constant wars which mapped out the Peninsula from the Roman times to the sixteenth century. Despite these conflicts with invading forces, the Basque language has been only a little influenced by external linguistic groups (see Diez et al. 1977/1980). In return for retaining their cherished *fueros* (rights), the Basques accepted Castilian and eventually Spanish dominance more readily than the Catalans, and were able to maintain a separate but subordinate identity because of this. The Basque language continued to be spoken in much the same way as Catalan, as an oral variety in a diglossic situation, Castilian being the language of power. Unlike the Catalans they did not have a significant medieval literary, written corpus in Basque to serve as a basis for maintaining the unity of the language. Basque, therefore, has suffered from divisions into dialects and subdialects, some almost mutually incomprehensible. To some extent this also reflects the geographical terrain, with many isolated mountain and valley settlements where contact was minimal. This dialectal fragmentation of the language has been an obstacle right up until the present day (see Chapter 12). Politically, too, the Basques were divided, with no one strong kingdom, as the Catalans had had. The communities in Viscaya and Guipuzcoa had no one leader, and were rigidly separate from the Kingdom of Navarra, the latter being still today only partially Basque-speaking. Whereas Barcelona has always served as a brilliant centre for all things Catalan, the Basques have not had such a clearly defined focus.

The nineteenth century saw an increased awareness of Basque culture and eventually a form of Basque nationalism; as in Catalonia, the Basque Country, unlike the rest of Spain, experienced major industrial and economic development parallel with other parts of nineteenth-century Europe. But besides these similarities, there are very many differences between the two regions, as their different histories already suggest. The two most obvious differences between the modern nationalisms that developed in the two regions is, first, the role that language played in constructing their identity, and, second, the very different reactions by the industrial bourgeoisie in the two regions. The contrasting levels of popular involvement in the two regional movements is also significant, with the Basque case being backed by a very small group of committed intellectuals.

While in Catalonia it could be argued that the cultural and political nationalist movements grew out of the industrialisation process taking place, in the Basque Country the opposite is almost the case. The Basque urban bourgeoisie was content to work with Madrid, and in fact the major Spanish banking elites were Basque ones, intricately bound in with the Spanish state's economy and political fortunes. The Basque language was barely spoken in urban areas, or by the middle class, and while it was indeed middle-class intellectuals who wished to revive the Basque identity, they had to rely on the 'pure' Basques of the isolated rural areas as their base.

In both Catalonia and in Galicia, cultural revivals preceded political expressions of regional identity. In the Basque Country it was largely a radical political manifesto which, along with cultural representation, inspired Basque nationalism at the turn of the century. The father of modern Basque nationalism was Sabino Arana (1865–1903). Arana and his followers saw Basque urban society with its modernising industrialisation and influxes of immigration as threatening the essence of Basque identity, which he set out to re-confirm and define (see Chapter 12). Unlike the Catalans, it was unrealistic to place too much importance on the role of language, as Basque was not a widely spoken language, even compared with Catalan or Galician. In fact it was only used as a way of excluding those who were clearly not Basque by birth or descent. In this early nationalist thinking the most important common value for the Basques was to be race. Evangelista de Ibero, a major writer of this Basque movement, wrote in 1906 (cited in Linz 1973: 37) when defining and contrasting the meanings of 'nation' and 'state':

1. Nation

1. What is a nation? The ensemble of men or peoples who have a same origin, a same language, a same character, the same custom, the same fundamental laws, the same glories, the same tendencies and aspirations, and the same destinies.

2. Of all these properties, which constitutes essentially a nationality? In the first place, the blood, race or origin; in the second place, the language. The other qualities are nothing but the consequence of the other two, most specifically of the first.

This emphasis on race ('blood' and 'origin') contrasts significantly with Prat de la Riba writing at the same time about Catalan nationalism (cited in Linz 1973: 37), where the emphasis is above all on the bonding effect of language:

We saw the national spirit, the national character, the national thought; we saw the law, we saw the language; and from the law, the language and the organism; the national thought, the character and the spirit, bring the Nation; that is a society of people who speak a language of their own and have the same spirit that manifests itself or is characteristic for the whole variety of the whole collective life.
. . .we saw that Catalonia had a language, a law, an art of its own, that it had a national spirit, a national character, a national thought: Catalonia was therefore a nation.

The choice of race and not language as the prime core value (see Conversi 1990) in Basque nationalism is a significant difference compared with Catalonia. With the use of the Basque language being less widespread and with little in the way of a literary tradition, it is not surprising that the literary cultural movement in the Basque Country was on a far smaller and less wide-reaching scale than its Catalan counterpart. The nationalist movement, however, did focus its political aspirations with Arana founding and leading the *Partido Nacionalista Vasco* (PNV), which shared many similarities with Prat de la Riba's *Lliga* (see Chapter 1).

3. Galicia

The earlier form of the language spoken in Galicia was Galaico-Portuguese, a Romance variety that emerged from the Roman occupation. Claims that Galician and therefore Portuguese have been strongly influenced by the Celtic languages spoken in this area on the arrival of the Romans are hard to substantiate, although their significance in terms of popular beliefs in the construction of Galician national identity should be noted (see Chapter 1). It is generally considered that the separation of Galician from Portuguese took place around the eleventh century, although this is a very slow and gradual process and it can be said that they shared in the success of Galician lyrical poetry which was widely acclaimed in the Middle Ages (twelfth to fourteenth centuries). Santiago de Compostela's importance as a pilgrimage destination meant that this literary production was known further afield than the Iberian Peninsula and was in turn influenced by the Provençal troubadors.

The nineteenth-century cultural revival in Galicia, her *Rexordimento*, differs significantly from that which took place in Catalonia and the Basque Country in that it was restricted to literary and cultural production. The political awareness which followed these movements in the other two regions was much slower to emerge in Galicia, and we can only really talk of a political articulation of Galician nationalism from well into the twentieth century (see Chapter 14). The principal explanation for this is the economic condition of nineteenth-century Galicia, which was an extremely poor rural society, suffering high levels of emigration to other parts of Spain, Europe, or above all, Latin America. Galicia was a backward and traditional society not experiencing the challenges of modernisation or industrialisation that was taking place in Catalonia and the Basque Country. It was also geographically very isolated, a feature that has always helped shaped Galician history.

Nonetheless European-wide influences such as Romanticism did lead Galician intellectuals to examine their historical and cultural roots and rediscover pride in their region and language. Some important writing was produced in Galician. *Xogos Florais* were held, modelled on the Catalan ones, and the poetry read at these was published. The most famous writer of this movement is Rosalía de Castro, who, however, reverted to publishing only in Castilian towards the end of her life. By the turn of the century a Galician Royal Academy had been established with the aim of standardising and codifying Galician. The need to decide on norms for the written language and to represent Galician identity was important not only, as in the other regions, to overcome too much deviation because of various existing dialects, but, particularly, in the case of Galician, because of its ambiguous position as regards Portuguese.

The Crisis of Nationalism in Twentieth-Century Spain

The beginning of this century found Spain in a very volatile situation, with a traditional, conservative and highly centralised political system which desperately needed to modernise its economy and build up its industries (see also Chapters 6 and 7). The tensions in the regions reflected this economic and social instability, heightened by the newly rediscovered cultural awareness of their different identities. The 1936–9 Civil War was, amongst other things, a bloody manifestation of Spain's multiple identity crises.

With the forces of centralism winning the Civil War, the years that followed saw harsh repression by the Franco dictatorship towards the minorities on Spain's periphery. During this regime the language question was a highly political topic. The use of minority (non-Castilian) languages was seen as anti-patriotic. These languages were therefore proscribed from public use and ridiculed. A situation, once again, of enforced diglossia existed in the regions, such as Catalonia, shutting down the enormous expansion in the use of minority languages which had taken place during the Second Republic. The regime carefully chose to refer to these languages as 'dialects'. It was claimed that the non-Castilian languages were inferior, and they were characterised, along with such 'non-standard' varieties of Castilian as Andalusian, as the speech only of the uneducated and peasantry. All the patriotic rhetoric of the dictatorship centred around the concept of '*lo castellano*' (things Castilian); anything challenging this was considered dangerously subversive.

In the early part of the Franco period infringements against the laws prohibiting the use of languages other than Castilian were heavily punished with fines and imprisonments. But in 1966 the dictatorship relaxed its attitudes a little with the passing of the so-called Freedom of Expression Law, which removed the stricter forms of censorship in favour of prior, self-censorship. As a result, private organisations were now allowed to teach mother-tongue languages other than Castilian, and publishing was once more permitted in these. To some extent this reflects the confidence of the Franco regime, as it judged that it had little to fear from unflattering views published in non-Castilian languages, given the inevitably limited readership. The regime deliberately encouraged a certain type of media coverage in non-Castilian languages of a sort which might in fact seem to trivialise their cultures – reports on dance competitions or local fiestas or how to cook local dishes – leaving 'serious' news and politics to be reported in Castilian.

The 1978 Spanish Constitution

The 1978 Constitution passed after Franco's death is a marvel of compromise and consensus. Not least is this true in the very definition of what Spain is: the ambiguities between the central state and the many regions within this state who cherish first and foremost their own separate cultural identities. The relationship between the central government and the autonomous regions has continued to be uneasy, but it has gone a long way to meeting regionalist demands.

As well as attempting to recognise Spain's plurinational nature in the Constitution, its drafters also set out to acknowledge Spain's multilingual/multicultural configuration with the Article 3 language clause, in which linguistic rights are enshrined. The first clause of Article 3 states: 'Castilian is the official Spanish language of the State.' Significantly this talks about 'state' and not 'nation' as well as 'Castilian' and not 'Spanish', an important statement acknowledging the existence of various 'Spanish' languages. This has been bitterly disputed by many, not only on the political right (e.g. Salvador 1987: 92). This clause, however, goes on to say: 'All Spaniards have the duty to know it [Castilian] and the right to use it.' Few if any national constitutions worldwide prescribe the *duty* to know a language. However, it is not clear what 'know' in this context means. It could refer to an entirely passive skill which does not require production in the language.

The second clause declares: 'The other Spanish languages will also be official in the respective Autonomous Communities in accordance with their statutes.' This enabling definition of Spain's minority languages is, thus, qualified by the highly prescriptive constraint of limiting their official status to their own territorial space. This clear geographical limitation means realistically that the future role of the minority languages will always take second place to Castilian. It could even be argued that it contravenes the spirit of later articles of the Constitution which claim equality for all Spanish citizens. Those Spanish citizens whose mother-tongue is not Castilian could argue that they do not have equal linguistic rights with those who are Castilian mother-tongue speakers. Native Basque speakers cannot expect the Spanish state to provide Basque teaching to their children if they happen to live in, for example, Seville. On the other hand, throughout the Spanish state Castilian may be used and must be provided for (see Mar-Molinero 1994).

The third clause appears to confirm a belief in linguistic plurality when it states: 'The richness of Spain's different linguistic varieties is a cultural heritage which shall be the object of special respect and protection.' The exact meaning of words such as 'respect' or 'protection' needs interpretation. It is probably fair to say that this final clause has permitted a new and imaginative understanding of Spain's linguistic map. It has allowed Autonomous Communities in their statutes to define their local linguistic variety, and even when this is not considered a discrete separate language from Castilian, its own particular features can be recognised and protected. This has inspired work on lexical and phonological features in, for example, Andalusia and the Canary Islands in order to draw up guidelines on what constitutes these regions' respective language varieties. The implications of this for such areas as education and the media are very significant, raising such issues as those of standard versus local language varieties, and forms of acceptable literacy.

Despite these ambiguities in the constitutional framework there is no denying the substantial advances that have taken place since 1978 in the promotion and status of Spain's minority languages and cultures. These efforts are supported not only by Article 3 of the Constitution but also by the relevant Autonomy Statute and, in particular, by the local Linguistic Normalization Laws. The greatest activity in terms of language planning efforts is at present taking place, as would be expected, in those areas which have historically shown the keenest sense of their own identity and nationalist aspirations – that is, Catalonia, the Basque Country and Galicia. However, a more limited degree of minority language protection and promotion has also taken place in Asturias, Aragon, Navarre, Valencia and the Balearic Islands.

By far the most active and apparently successful language promotion programmes are taking place in Catalonia. Today the Autonomous Community of Catalonia has more than six million inhabitants, of whom approximately 90 per cent claim to understand Catalan, whilst over 60 per cent admit to speaking it in some form (EC Commission 1990).[2] Catalan has always been the language of all the Catalan

---

2. For an interesting presentation and discussion of data on the use and knowledge of Spain's minority languages according to a recent sociolinguistic survey, see CIS 1994.

population, including, significantly, the upper and middle classes, and in this sense, it is importantly different from Basque and Galician. This has meant that the language serves as a symbol of social mobility and acceptance with the ensuing favourable attitudes to its use and teaching. This has undoubtedly helped overcome its single greatest obstacle which is the large non-native Catalan speaking immigrant population now resident in Catalonia.

With currently less than two and a half million inhabitants the Basque community is the smallest of the three where a minority language is being promoted. Fewer than 25 per cent of these claim to speak Basque (EC Commission 1990), reflecting the difficulty of access to the language compared with Catalan and Galician. The language has considerably less prestige and status than Catalan within its community.[3] There have, nonetheless, been improvements and successes as Basque is promoted through the education system (see Chapters 12 and 13) and used in local government wherever possible. But the obstacles against the learning of Basque create the sense that its promotion is above all symbolic rather than practical.

Galicia has not been affected by immigration, and therefore a very high percentage speak the language, some 90 per cent of its nearly three million population (EC Commission 1990). However, Galician continues to lack status and therefore is not used for social advancement or for more educated literate purposes, except by a tiny minority of middle-class intellectuals. What changes are now taking place as a result of the new language policies must also be seen in the context of a counter movement by the so-called '*reintegracionistas*', wanting closer identification with Portuguese (see Chapter 14). Neither the *reintegracionisats* nor the *independentistas* (those who see Galician culture and language as separate from either of their larger neighbours) are able to substantially counter the influence and dominance of Castilian.

Conclusion

Clearly issues of national and group identity are present in all these activities to promote and protect minority language rights in Spain, as they are also in the Castilian centre's determination to allow only limited linguistic independence. By restricting the promotion of non-Castilian languages to discrete geographical areas, the continued domination of Castilian as 'national' language is ensured. The minorities'

---

3. However, for discussion of how the Basque language has become a far more potent cultural symbol to the Basque sense of identity in recent years, and its present ethnolinguistic vitality, see Chapters 12 and 13.

cultural identities are only acknowledged when they are linked to territorial identities.

Likely changes in political power structures within the European Union point to the emergence of a Europe of the Regions, where the traditional national state centre might be increasingly bypassed through a relationship between the European supranational centres of power and the local regional centres (see Chapter 15). A major principle of the European Community is the encouragement and right of the freedom of movement of persons within the member states. This policy must have language implications, above all challenging the notion that linguistic and cultural identity can be tied to one geographical space. If Spain is to honour the spirit of the EC's 1977 directive encouraging all member states to provide at least some mother-tongue education for the children of immigrants, this will put a strain on the delicate balance arrived at between the present national language and the indigenous minority ones, a balance by no means viewed by all as ideal.

The Catalans, in particular, are pushing this relationship to its limit with attempts in 1993 to increase the amount of compulsory teaching in Catalan that would be offered in their schools. The ensuing tussle with the Supreme Court in Madrid in order to test the measures' constitutionality is putting in jeopardy the hard-won right to almost complete self-determination in the formulating of educational policies which has allowed the various Autonomous Communities to promote their own sense of identity. This tension, however, is inevitable: given that equal status for the co-official languages is the stated goal of the communities where a second language is spoken, and given the unequal dominance of Castilian, only positive discrimination in favour of the minority language, it could be argued, would ever make this aim possible. The accusations of discrimination that are now being heard from non-Catalans who feel that the language normalisation programme to promote Catalan has gone far enough should come as no surprise (see Mar-Molinero 1995).

Language is indeed the symbol of many of the identity crises throughout Spain's history and also today. And while the most significant arena for this discussion has been in the peripheries where languages other than Castilian are spoken, it should not be forgotten that there are many areas of Spain where a variety of Castilian is spoken, but the cultural identity is not Castilian, such as in Andalusia, Extremadura or Aragon. However, it is likely that precisely the lack of a separate linguistic identity has been the main reason that these regions have been more subordinated to the Spanish-Castilian *patria* than other communities on the periphery. As Linz (1973: 99) writes: 'Spain today is a state for all Spaniards, a nation-state for a large part of the population, and only a state but not a nation for important minorities.'

References

Alter, P. (1985, English translation 1990, 1991), *Nationalism*, London/ New York

Anderson, B. (1983, 1991), *Imagined Communities: Reflection on the Origins and Spread of Nationalism*, London/New York

Barnard, F. (1969), *Herder on Social and Political Culture*, Cambridge

CIS (Centro de Investigaciones Sociológicas) (1994), *Conocimiento y uso de las lenguas en España*, Madrid

Conversi, D. (1990), 'Language or Race? The Choice of Core Values in the Development of Catalan and Basque Nationalisms', *Ethnic and Racial Studies*, vol.13(1), pp.52–70

—— (1993), 'The Influence of Culture on Political Choices. Language Maintenance and its Implications for Basque and Catalan Nationalist Movements', *History of European Ideas*, vol.16(1–3), pp.189–200

Diez, M., Morales, F. and Sabin, A. (1977, 1980 2nd edn), *Las lenguas de España*, Madrid

EC Commission (1990), *EC's Minority Languages: Spain, Portugal and Greece*, Brussels

Ferrer, F. (1985), *La persecució política de la llengua catalana*, Barcelona

Fishman, J. (1972), *Language and Nationalism*, Massachusetts

Gellner, E. (1983, 1992), *Nations and Nationalism*, Oxford

Hobsbawm, E.J. (1990), *Nations and Nationalism since 1780*, Cambridge

Hutchinson, J. and Smith, A. (eds) (1994), *Nationalism*, Oxford

Kedourie, E. (1960, 1993 edn), *Nationalism*, Oxford

Linz, J. (1973), 'Early State-building and Late Peripheral Nationalism against the State: The Case of Spain', in Eisentadt, S.N. and Rokkan, S. (eds), *Building State and Nations*, vol.II, Beverley Hills/London, pp.32–116

Mar-Molinero, C. (1994), 'Linguistic Nationalism and Minority Language Groups in the "New" Europe', *Journal of Multilingual and Multicultural Development*, vol.15(4), pp.319–29

—— (1995), 'Catalan Education Policies: Are Castilian-Speakers Persecuted?', *Journal of the Association of Contemporary Iberian Studies*, vol.8(1), pp.49–56

Prat de la Riba, E. (1906, Castilian translation 1917, 1986 edn), *La nacionalitat catalana*, Barcelona

Salvador, G. (1987), *Lengua española y lenguas de España*, Barcelona

Siguan, M. (1992, English translation 1993), *Multilingual Spain*, Amsterdam

Valverdú, F. (1984), 'A Sociolinguistic History of Catalan', *International Journal of the Sociology of Language*, vol.47, pp.13–29

Williams, C.H. (1984), 'Ideology and the Interpretation of Minority Cultures', *Political Geography Quarterly*, vol.3(2), pp.103–25

5

The Nation-Building Process in Nineteenth-Century Spain
José Alvarez Junco

The Legacy of the Early-Modern Period

At the dawn of the so-called 'Age of Nationalisms', Spain was one of the oldest political units established in a region of Europe, immensely fragile and shifting borders. The territory spanned by the Spanish monarchy had maintained (as it does today) almost identical borders since the early sixteenth century. The dynastic union had a number of specific features. It comprised separate kingdoms with different legislations and autonomous institutions, which even maintained customs borders between them, thus differentiating the confederation from what we would today regard as a nation-state (see Chapter 1). At the same time, however, the subjects of that monarchy shared the same religion, viewed themselves as beset by common enemies with whom they were constantly at war, and there was no shortage of intellectual writings evoking a *Spanish* collective identity (e.g., Mariana 1592–1605), which some authors have described as pre- or proto-national, but which I prefer to term *ethno-patriotic*.[1]

Such expressions were an elitist phenomenon and their importance was seriously diminished by their scarce dissemination among the population as a whole. The rudimentary communications and the absence of a broad cultural marketplace suggests that the bulk of the general population felt much more linked to their local communities than to any 'imaginary community' spanning territory beyond the immediate area. And the Catholic Church's control over educational

---

1. Since *natio*, a word used in the Middle Ages referring to those people sharing the same place of birth and the same language, did not develop its modern political meaning until the appearance of the theory of the sovereignty of the people; *patria*, on the other hand, also a word of Latin origin, was more related to the community to which the individual belonged, and *amor patriae* was mentioned since Roman times as a civic virtue.

institutions and such communications media as did reach the illiterate population (primarily the weekly sermon) again suggests that religious identity held more sway than ethno-patriotic identity among the populace at large. Yet, as the anti-Napoleonic reaction would demonstrate, religion and patriotism were intimately linked. Spanish ethno-patriotic identity, bequeathed by the ancien regime to the age of Napoleonic invasion, can be characterised by the following four traits.

First, there was a fusion of religious and political identity. The subjects of the king of Spain were by definition Catholic, and this was accepted both by the subjects themselves and by their foreign observers. The whole of the ancien regime's legitimising discourse and the vigilant eye of institutions such as the Inquisition had left a seemingly indelible Catholic legacy. Nowhere is this more bluntly expressed than in the 1812 Cádiz Constitution, which stated that 'the Roman Apostolic Catholic religion, the only genuine one, *is and shall perpetually be* the religion of *all* Spaniards'.

A second feature was a deep-rooted xenophobia, primarily anti-English and anti-French. Spain had been isolated from the European world, and particularly the Protestant world, since the times of Philip II; and continual warring and religious clashes had contributed to fostering an averse attitude toward everything foreign. The first and most logical target of this antipathy was England (*la pérfida Albión*), the adversary in almost all the prior centuries' wars and competitors in the American market. Yet, curiously, this xenophobia was also directed, and in almost even greater doses, at the French, closer to home and allies to the Spaniards for one century (due to the family ties between the reigning monarchs). Francophobia was fuelled by the fact that the neighbouring country had provided the administrative-political and cultural model underpinning Spanish elites since the arrival of the Bourbons. No matter that this model had been adopted for 'patriotic' reasons, that is, as a means of buttressing the Spanish State and overcoming the problems associated with the seventeenth-century decline; its adoption had still required the uprooting or overhaul of many inherited traditions ('national' traditions they would later be called) such as clerical influence, disdain for manual labour and the institutional diversity of the old kingdoms. Hence the widespread resentment elicited in conservative circles, and the population in general, by all things considered French.

Eurocentrism was a third notable aspect of this ethno-patriotic identity. So intense was this Eurocentrism that practically all observers postulated the existence of a Spanish decline dating from the mid-seventeenth century (since the loss of the Habsburg hegemony in Europe), heedless of the fact that the Madrid court would for another century and a half continue to impart orders to American dominions that made up the largest empire on earth. In terms of commercial monopoly the metropolis's control was more nominal than real, but Castile's political and cultural influence over the greater part of the New World was enormous. Yet in the Spanish ethno-patriotic rhetoric of the Modern Age, the American empire was regarded as no more than a minor component.

A last trait of this Spanish ethno-patriotism prior to the 'Age of Nationalism' was its defensive, victimised and self-pitying tone. From the early seventeenth century, at a time when her armies were locked in combat on numerous European fronts, Spain was presented by Francisco de Quevedo (*España defendida*, 1609) as the humble long-suffering subject aggrieved by insolent, haughty foes. Particularly after the reign of Philip IV, rarely was mother Spain depicted in triumphant terms comparable to the opulent Serenissima Venezia, the proud Britannia, the pure, audacious and defiant Marianne. Instead, she was portrayed as the *Mater Dolorosa* of Catholic iconolatry.

Spanish Nationalism at the Beginning of the Age of Nationalisms: The 'War of Independence'

Modern times, liberal revolutions, and the 'Age of Nationalisms', entered Spain with the Napoleonic army. This invasion was to cause the country enormous problems, but it certainly did not seem to threaten the existence of the Spanish State or Spanish collective identity. On the contrary, it can be argued that it was an excellent beginning from the point of view of a nation-building process, because the modern period was inaugurated by a conflict labelled as nothing less than a 'war of national independence' – the significance of which was magnified by the fact that the enemy was not only a European power, but the model drawn upon by Spain's reformist elites and which had aroused such great animosity among broad sectors of the Spanish population.

The nationalist interpretation of this war was an enormous simplification, not to say an outright falsification. Napoleon's aim was not to convert the Spanish monarchy into a dependent territory of the French empire, but to change the ruling dynasty. This was a stratagem neither unheard of nor alien to Spanish tradition, given that the same thing had occurred one hundred years earlier, with positive results according to general opinion, and it had by no means given rise to a situation of formal dependence on France. Both the treaties concluded between Charles IV's ministers and Napoleon, and the latter's decree by which his brother Joseph was appointed to the Spanish throne, stated that Spanish territory (including the American empire) would remain united, with the same boundaries as before, and without ties to any other foreign monarchy. Thus, the war which began in May 1808 did not involve the liberation of a territory subjugated by an imperial power and, as such, was not a 'war of independence'.

The conflict initiated in 1808 was, in reality, an enormously complex phenomenon, which can only be understood by distinguishing a number of different levels or coinciding sub-conflicts which fed off each other. First, the war of 1808–14 was undoubtedly an international war, waged between the two great European powers of the time: France and Britain. All the major battles of the war, except for Bailén, consisted of clashes between an almost exclusively French army and another mainly English army commanded by an English general. Second, the conflict contained elements which allow it to be classified as a civil war. The loyalties of Spanish elites, and especially those of the intellectuals who had supported the enlightened reforms of recent decades (such as the count of Cabarrús, Gaspar de Jovellanos, Juan Meléndez Valdés or Manuel Quintana) were deeply and almost evenly split between the two sides.

Also required for an understanding of the conflict is a consideration of its xenophobic, anti-French elements. As already mentioned, throughout the whole of the preceding century such dark sentiments had been fuelled by Gallic influence over the Spanish court, and the May 1808 rising was in this sense the culmination of a century's hate. Another of the stronger sentiments driving many of the combatants was a Manichean, highly personalised view of the political problems of the day, in which prime minister Manuel Godoy, Evil Incarnate, was blamed for all the calamities afflicting the *patria*, while the heir to the crown, Ferdinand VII, the Good Prince, was thought to personify all hope of rectification and redemption. Although Godoy's rule had certainly accumulated numerous disasters in recent years (wars, epidemics, famines, the loss of the fleet at Trafalgar), the truth is that his unpopularity, and the parallel idealisation of Ferdinand, issued more from moral than political judgements. Godoy was believed to be the queen's lover, with Ferdinand seen as the suffering son, maltreated by a feeble father and an invidious mother (Herr 1965). Lastly, the anti-Napoleonic war also featured a political-religiously-inspired anti-revolutionary protest. This aspect has been widely debated throughout the nearly two centuries elapsed since then, and its existence has generally been rejected by liberal historians, who from the beginning associated the patriotic uprising against the French with a desire for reform of the country's institutions, that is, with anti-absolutist protest. But it is difficult to deny the prevalence of calls to defend the inherited religion against the atheistic invaders, emanating most vehemently from the rural clergy.

In spite of all this complexity, the new nationalistic rhetoric was entering Europe, and the Cádiz supporters of Ferdinand of Bourbon very skilfully used it in order to blur all shades of opinion and to present the struggle as a national uprising of the Spanish people against a French attempt to dominate them. Some twenty years later, in the 1830s, after the wars of independence of the Spanish American empire, historians discovered the name which best fitted this nationalist vision, and the 1808–14 war was christened the 'War of Independence' (Alvarez Junco 1994b), a label which has yet to be revised.

From then on the 'War of Independence' would be a pillar of the century's most ambitious effort to construct a Spanish nationalist mythology. Witness the monuments erected to the conflict's 'martyrs', and the conversion of 2 May (but not 12 October, Eurocentrism again prevailing over a nod to American engagements) into a nationalist holiday.[2] This myth-making was generally pursued with more insistence by liberals. To cite but two examples: the republican propagandist Fernando Garrido declared the uprising against the French to have been 'the most important political event in the history of our *patria*' (Garrido 1865: 109), and the greatest novelist of the century, Benito Pérez Galdós, devoted the first of his series, *Episodios nacionales,* to this war.

The populist content of this nationalist mythological elaboration (it was the 'People' who had saved the fatherland, when the elites had abandoned it) gave particular legitimacy to the event with the onset of the period of Romanticism and *volksgeist.* Also important was the prominent role played by Catalans and Aragonese (Gerona and Zaragoza had been the two cities which had suffered the longest and cruellest sieges by the Napoleonic troops) in the heroic deeds of the Spanish nation. Thirdly, the struggle proved the permanent existence of a Spanish identity: since the stubborn resistance against the French troops by most of the Spanish population was interpreted as the re-enactment of the heroic spirit of Numantia and Saguntum, the Celt-Iberian towns which had confronted Carthagenian and Roman might. This behaviour, repeated after two thousand years, was presented as a proof of the unique love of Spaniards for their independence, a national trait which enabled them successively to defeat the best armies in the world ('*que no puede esclavo ser/pueblo que sabe morir*', 'cannot be enslaved/a people who know how to die', as the famous patriotic verses by Bernardo López García, written half a century later, ran).

2. 2 May is the anniversary of the popular insurrection in Madrid against the Napoleonic troops in 1802, and 12 October the anniversary of the so-called discovery of America.

A Shift in the International Image: The Emergence of Romantic Spain

Seen from the outside, and partly because of the anti-Napoleonic war, Spain also underwent a re-evaluation. Lord Byron's idealisation of Spain in 1809 (similar to Victor Hugo's *Orientales* a couple of decades later), and the hundreds of memoirs written by British or French veterans from the Peninsular War (as the 'War of Independence' was referred to in Britain and France), plus the arrival in Paris and London of paintings by Velázquez or Murillo, some as a result of the plundering of Spanish churches by the Napoleonic army, some as presents to Lord Wellington, all led to a sudden discovery of the Spanish Golden Age. Romantic writers beginning with Washington Irving and Théophile Gautier, and the royalist volunteers who travelled to Spain from all over Europe during the Carlist wars, would complete this picture in the mid-nineteenth century.

As a result, Spain's image changed. It is not that the old 'Black Legend' died, but as a product of a shift in the sensibilities of the Europeans it was re-evaluated. To Montesquieu, Spain had only been the country of idle nobility, ignorance, cruelty, arrogance, fanaticism and, as a result of all of that, decay. For the Romantic writers, first influenced by the Spanish performance against the Napoleonic armies, Spain was a country of strong passions, brave people, banditry, blood and sun. Almost all the characters were the same (the conquistador, the inquisitor, the idle aristocrat – now converted into *guerrilleros*, bandits, Carlist friars, proud beggars, bullfighters), but they now represented different things: bravery, pride, dignity, intense religious feelings, closeness to death and scorn for it. All this was epitomised in Mérimée's *Carmen*, later translated into the enormously successful opera by Bizet.

The change, therefore, had little to do with Spain. In reality there had taken place a shift in the moral values and internal demands of European society. Spain began to be positively valued because it offered, on the one hand, an *exoticism* which satisfied the curiosity and the need to consume refined cultural products typical of the new middle classes, who were attaining a considerable degree of well-being. Furthermore, Spain was seen as a *pre-modern society*, and this was a second source of its magnetism. Intellectual elites in post-revolutionary France or industrialised England were not so positive about the effects of 'progress' as enlightened thinkers had been in the previous century. Revolutionary terror, political instability, the empire of mercantile values, all this produced a critical reaction. In artistic and intellectual circles it became fashionable to distance oneself from the moral cynicism and aesthetic mediocrity of the so-called 'bourgeois philistine';

modern society was boring; many were affected by the 'spleen', *le mal du siècle*. Spain, conveniently idealised as a paradise still untouched by industrialisation, urbanisation and capitalism, offered the image of a country 'loyal to its identity': something which was attractive to legitimists who saw Spain as an example of loyalty to the king and religion, as well as to those who felt nostalgia for a less politically developed society, based on personal relations and commitments rather than on the link with an anonymous bureaucratic state; or to those who were afraid of a social explosion due to the crumbling of traditional social hierarchies after the industrial revolution and saw in Spain's lower classes 'dignity' and disdain for material values; or finally to those who lamented the repression, the conventionality, the anonymity, characteristic of urban mass societies and thought they had found spontaneity, joy of living, innate aesthetic sense in Spain (Alvarez Junco 1994a).

None of these travellers and observers were really interested in understanding Spain. Rather, they were guided by the prejudices and concerns that they brought from their countries. The Spain that they were looking for – and which naturally they found – was nothing more than an idealisation, the counter-image to the reality they rejected and left behind. There was an ambivalence about modernity, as proven by the fact that none of these writers seriously adopted Spain as a *model* to imitate, but only as an object to cherish. Hence the unease, even irritation, felt by local elites committed to modernising the country upon hearing this kind of praise from visitors, who enjoyed greater security and a higher standard of living in their countries. The supposedly positive image of romantic Spain has thus infuriated, or at least provoked scepticism amongst, cultivated Spaniards for centuries, the same as the Black Legend image did prior to it.

But there is something in which both Spaniards and non-Spaniards certainly agreed by the middle of the nineteenth century: there was such a thing as a Spanish identity, a Spanish character, a Spanish 'soul' or 'essence', with very definite traits; the Spanish way of being was, in fact, one of the stereotypes most widely accepted among the European collective identities of that period. This international recognition concurred with a similar internal acceptance. Throughout the whole nineteenth century nobody seriously challenged the existence of a Spanish nation, the same as nobody challenged the unity of the Spanish State: certainly not the Carlists in the 1830s and not even the federalists and cantonalists of 1873.

The Liberal Version of Spanish Nationalism

In accordance with developments in other European countries, secular intellectual elites who came from the middle or even ruling classes tried to link their efforts to modernise the country with a nationalist revivalism. After their collaboration with the anti-Napoleonic resistance of 1808–14, Spanish liberals were forced into two successive periods of exiles (1814–20 and 1823–34), where the new Romantic ways of understanding social realities reinforced their initial nationalism. One of the indications of this evolution was their concern for national history, mostly sparked by the publication of histories of Spain written by English and French authors (Durham 1832–33; Romey 1838–51). The nation-building efforts of Spanish elites thus came late in comparison to those of other countries, although by the middle of the century Spanish intellectuals were trying hurriedly to regain the time they had lost in this field. Beginning with Modesto Lafuente's thirty-volume work, published in 1850–66, some dozen other general histories of Spain appeared before the end of the century. The contrast between the lateness of this wave of interest for the national history in the nineteenth century and the precocity of Spanish ethno-patriotism in the early modern period (Lafuente's general history of Spain appeared two and a half centuries later than the work with the same title published by Juan de Mariana, and throughout that period no comprehensive national history was published) is very revealing of the particular course of the Spanish nation-building process.

By the middle of the nineteenth century, not only history books attested to this interest in the construction of the national past. Romantic taste for historical painting was also creating the images of the main historical feats, and it would be these images that were passed on to the twentieth century. Even today, all the illustrations of history schoolbooks come from the period between 1850 and 1900. And, from a more fictional standpoint, Benito Pérez Galdós began in 1882 to publish his highly successful novelistic series of *Episodios nacionales*, which surveyed the nineteenth-century political upheavals, beginning with the 'War of Independence', where the protagonist was the Spanish *pueblo*, portrayed as a suffering and innocent victim of evil rulers and the only possible hope for the country's redemption.

The basic premise of these liberal historians was that Spain embodied an essential national character that, since time immemorial, had survived wave after wave of invaders. This idealised nation had reached its zenith in the Middle Ages, when the 'Spaniards', locked in yet another battle to preserve their identity in the face of a foreign invasion, had instituted a society characterised by popular participation and tolerance, regional and local diversity, and constraints on royal power expressed in *fueros* (local rights). The crown, insofar as it had unified the future nation and counteracted the factious and arbitrary power of the nobility, was generally portrayed in favourable terms by these authors; although the Catholic Monarchs, final architects of 'national unity', were not immune to criticism from the most radical liberals over their creation of the Inquisition and expulsion of the Jews. Criticism of the monarchy sharply increased when judging the two centuries of rule by the 'foreign' Habsburg dynasty. Charles V had abolished Castilian freedom when suppressing the *Comunidades* revolt in 1521, and embarked Spain on dynastic wars that bankrupted the country. Liberal historians tarred Philip II with the same brush as wielded by his avowed Protestant enemies; even the most moderate underscored his severity and religious intolerance, his scorn for the Aragonese *fueros*, and the commercial and intellectual damage caused to the nation by his resolve to isolate the country from the rest of Europe and Protestant contagion. Philip III was blamed for the negative economic effects of his expulsion of the Moors. His son, Philip IV, had blindly surrendered to the despotic ambition of his favourite minister, the Count-Duke of Olivares, and also attacked Catalan *fueros*. The helpless Charles II, the last of the Spanish Habsburgs, had only reaped the sad harvest of the policies of his predecessors (Tapia 1840; Cortada 1845; Terradillos 1848; Castro 1852).

The main aim of these historical products was to lay the foundations of the liberal state, which was going to undertake the programme of political and social modernisation of the country. Their basic idea was that through history one could picture the nation as slowly emerging and asserting itself in the territory of a sovereign state. From history one could also grasp the 'essence' of the nation, the 'nation's spirit', its distinctive civilisation, which is the result of its unique history, culture and geographical profile, from which derived a set of moral prescriptions for individual and collective life. This lesson was intended to be taught in schools so that Spaniards could take pride and participate in all the glories of their country's contribution to humanity. At the same time, the more practical purposes of this national socialising process were: first, the aim to legitimise the construction of a nation-state, supposedly first founded by the Visigoths and then restored by the Catholic Monarchs, but which, in reality, was being built in the nineteenth century itself, while these intellectual products were been fabricated; second, the dissemination and widespread acceptance of the new social values which coincided with the liberal programme.

Obstacles to the Nationalisation of the Country

A number of factors thwarted the success of the nation-building process undertaken by liberal elites. First and foremost, the acute political crisis suffered by the Spanish State throughout most of the nineteenth century. For at least seventy years (1808–75) the legitimacy of the Spanish State was constantly questioned, with fluctuations from liberal revolutions to periods of autocracy, from one dynasty to another, and from monarchy to republic.

From an international perspective, Spain became a third-rate power after the loss of its navy in Trafalgar and the subsequent loss of the American empire. In spite of the prevailing notion that Spain's 'decline' had begun in the mid-seventeenth century, for another one and a half centuries the country had remained an important power, participating in *all* major European wars. It was the loss of the empire in the first quarter of the nineteenth century that marked Spain's exit from the European stage. Since 1814 Spain has participated in *none* of the major European conflicts. The country faced no external threats, no international enemies, and only a few, brief, colonial wars, whose result, it should be noted, could only rarely be mentioned as source of pride. Spain, therefore, did not experience anything similar to the Franco-Prussian war, or to the two World Wars in the twentieth century. Massive numbers of people were never called to arms and instilled with patriotic fervour; whole populations were not offered, in exchange for supporting their respective fatherlands, expanded electoral rights and social welfare. All those processes of 'nationalisation of the masses' (Mosse 1975) did not take place in Spain, simply because the decades before and after 1900, when other European powers were at the peak of their power, expanding and conquering the world, coincided with Spain's constant political crisis and impotence. On the other hand, of course, the same neutrality presented here as a lost nation-building 'opportunity' may well have allowed the weakly integrated Spanish monarchy to survive as a state.

Furthermore, the Spanish State was chronically indebted. Debts had begun to accumulate in the eighteenth century, with the costly wars waged by Charles III and Charles IV against Britain, and the situation was only aggravated by the devastating effects of the Napoleonic War, the loss of the navy in Trafalgar and the subsequent loss of the American empire. In the 1830s the catastrophic First Carlist War also took its toll, and its cost could only partially be financed by desperate recourses such as the disentailment of church lands. By the end of that decade one-third of the public budget was devoted to paying the interest on government bonds, and the Spanish State proved unable to liberate itself from this burden for the rest of the century. As a result, governments were impotent to influence the economy or implement their political measures. The most they could do was to provide for the army payroll, for a few civil servants and for the expenses of the royal house. For its subjects, the state limited itself to the 'extraction-coercion' cycle, typical of the early-modern period in Europe. No wonder then that it did not foster feelings of identification, and that Spain became the country of anarchism.

Apart from the meagre resources the Spanish State could gather in support of a nationalising process, a second crucial obstacle was the rulers' lukewarm approach to this task. Unlike some other pre-existing European states – primarily France during the Third Republic – the Spanish authorities were openly apathetic in relation to the intellectual elites' effort to create a national identity. Patriotism had taken to the stage at the beginning of the century linked to liberal revolution, and for several decades the idea of *patria* seemed to be in open conflict with the monarchy. By mid-century, it continued to be ignored or merely paid lip-service by government officials. Except for very brief periods, governments were linked to an oligarchic coalition of landed nobility and · newly enriched bourgeoisie, and were utterly afraid of a nationalist idea which meant mass mobilisation and participation, and a new civic education which could detach individuals from tradition, from family, province and religion. Hence, rather than opening the Pandora's box of nationalism, Spanish rulers chose to rely on a traditional dynastic-religious legitimation of power.

Little effort was, therefore, made to penetrate into the society and the territory by the state institutions, to build a national identity and update the pre-existing monarchy as representative of that identity (Núñez Seixas 1994; Riquer 1994). Sporadic jingoistic declarations and organised patriotic outbursts could not hide the fact that the spread of nationalism had not taken hold among the population. Obligatory enlistment in the service of the *patria* was met by widespread evasion or desertion by the lower classes, and privileged exemptions among the upper classes. The latter, the initial promoters of nationalist rhetoric, did not rally to their country's call and preferred to keep their money and their children at home. Except for those sectors specifically linked to the military or the central bureaucracy, state service did not occupy an important place in the scale of values of upper- or upper-middle-class Spanish families, contrary to the strong military tradition in Germany or civil service ideal in France. Conversely, in Spain the state was viewed as the patrimony of those called to serve it. The rulers themselves, with their exemption-riddled conscription system, sent the clear message that 'service to the *patria*' was not an honour, but a burden to be borne by the lower classes. And the lower classes, naturally, showed no enthusiasm for this patriotic burden (Sales 1974; Serrano 1987: 285–99).

Besides the lack of truly universal military service, Spanish governments were incapable of creating a state school system until the second half of the century, and then an ineffective and underfunded one at that. The various political forces were not even able to agree on a set of national symbols. Spain had no national flag until 1843, and it was to be challenged by both Carlists and republicans in subsequent civil wars until 1939. Hardly any patriotic monuments were undertaken by the government; nor were national glories exalted in street names or commemorative plaques. As late as the Spanish-American War of 1898 there was no national anthem and the *Marcha de Cádiz*, a lyric-less *pasodoble*, had to be pressed into service as the battle hymn during that conflict. The current anthem, the *Marcha Real*, was only informally adopted in the twentieth century, banished by the Republic and re-established by Franco, albeit modified to include strains from the Carlist *Oriamendi* and from the Falangist *Cara al Sol*.

The Shift of Spanish Nationalism towards Conservatism

During the second half of the nineteenth century traditional Catholic thinkers seemed to understand the importance of the new nationalist rhetoric and began to elaborate a patriotic canon opposed to the liberal version. In the historical field this task was often the work of clerics, and no doubt inherited many features of the old histories of the church, now mixed in with nationalist elements. Its beginnings can be dated in the 1860s, when Víctor Gebhardt produced his *Historia General de España* (1861–4), followed by other less prominent authors (Belmar 1861; Sánchez Casado 1867; Merry y Colón 1873 and 1889, etc.), and culminating with the famous compendium by Marcelino Menéndez y Pelayo in 1882.

The common denominator of these historical versions was Catholicism – or, to be exact, 'Catholic unity' – as the 'foundation' of Spanish nationality and legitimation of the national political institution par excellence: the monarchy. For if, as one of these authors wrote, 'the monarchy and the clergy (are) the two luminaries placed by the Almighty in the firmament', forced to choose between the two heavenly bodies there was no doubt as to which had priority. Nothing was more abrasive to these authors than the intrusion into the ecclesiastic world of civil authorities. The Muslim invasion of Spain, for instance, was seen as a 'divine punishment' for the sins of the last Visigoth kings in their hateful attempts to rein in the powerful bishops: 'thus did vanish the Spanish nation the moment the divine liberty of the church was attacked' (Belmar 1861: 22–31). The zenith of this union of crown and cross was, it was claimed, to be found in the reigns of Reccared (the Visigoth king who switched allegiance from Arianism to Catholicism), of Ferdinand III, the conqueror of Córdoba and Seville (whence Saint Ferdinand), of the Catholic Monarchs, and, above all, of the Habsburg monarchs of Spain, 'kings whose every act was subordinated to religion, to which they submitted social life and who stood before the world as genuine standard-bearers of Catholicism'. Thanks to such kings, Spain reached its political apogee, 'favoured by invisible guardians'. Conversely, 'the Bourbon race', as two authors wrote in the 1880s in clear offence to the reigning dynasty, brought an end to 'genuinely Christian Spanish policies, (because) basing themselves on the sophistic distinction between politics and religion, (they) only pursued worldly interests'. Thus, Charles III, the enlightened regalist king, was seen to have 'recklessly opened the doors of the kingdom to revolution' (Merry y Colón and Merry y Villalba 1889: 146, 181, 190). This conservative animosity towards the Bourbons mirrored the liberals' distaste for the Habsburgs, without doubt one of the fundamental lines of division between liberal and Catholic-conservative historiography.

The best summary of the National-Catholic position was expressed by Menéndez y Pelayo in his well-known comments: 'We were probably not destined to form a Great Nation because of the land we live on, nor because of our race, nor because or our character. . .. Only common religion can provide a people with its own specific life, with the consciousness of a strong unanimity; only religion can legitimate and found the laws. . .. Without a common God, a common altar, common sacrifices, without praying to the same Father and being reborn in a common sacrament, how can a People be great and strong?. . . Christianity gave its unity to Spain. . . Thanks to it, we have been a Nation, even a great Nation, and not a multitude of individuals' (Menéndez y Pelayo 1882, 1967 edn: vol.2, 1036).

The differences between the conservative and the liberal-progressive mythical versions of the national past are summarised in the following table:

Table 5.1.

National Histories of Spain	Golden Age	Decadence	Redemptive Ideal
Liberal-Progressive	Middle Ages: Cortes, *fueros*, democratic town councils Religious tolerance	Habsburg: Foreign absolutism Repression of the *Comunidades* of Castile Suppression of local *fueros*	Freedom, democracy (federalism, in some versions)
National-Catholic	King Reccared Ferdinand III Catholic Kings Philip II Counter-reformation Council of Trent Golden Century mystics and theological plays Anti-Islamic wars European hegemony of the Habsburgs	17th century: 'feebleness' of the last Habsburgs 18th century: 'Anti-Spanish' Bourbon reformism 19th century: revolutions, a-religious drift	Unity 'on all fronts' (political, religious, linguistic, racial) Strong crown (without inter-ference in religious matters)

These competing visions of the national identity finally produced a kind of syncretic version, dominant in the history textbooks at the end of the century. It typically began with self-satisfied *Laudes Hispaniae*, according to which the Iberian Peninsula was the bountiful expression of divine preference for its inhabitants: temperate climate, fertile fields, mighty rivers, grains of all kinds, luscious fruits, exquisite wines. This paradise was home to a people portrayed, as in both liberal and conservative elaborations of the national history, as ever faithful to their traditional identity and zealous defenders of their independence from all foreign contamination. Numantians – or rather 'Spaniards in Numantia' – proved the heroism of the race. Seneca certified the stoicism inherent to the national character. The eight-century-long struggle against the Muslims was the natural reactions of a proud independent people against foreign invasions; with the added meaning of being evidence, the same as other wars against Turks or Protestants, of the Spaniards inherent loyalty to their religion. Their fervent attachment to their true selves had recently been confirmed in Zaragoza and Gerona when Napoleon had dared to arouse the 'fearsome Iberian lion'.

Such portrayals of national identity might be enough to fill school textbooks and 2 May editorials, but in the end led to a conformist political agenda. For independence having been secured, what other major goals were left? This insistent glorification of an already achieved and unthreatened independence revealed the lack of any dynamic national programme. In the international sphere Spanish nationalism was not a mobilising ideology because it was only identified with very limited projects (such as the Tetouan war of 1859–60 in Morocco) which, moreover, the governments made little or no attempt to popularise. Nor were nationalist feelings associated with border disputes or the construction of a unitary Iberian state. Domestically, the link between of nationalism and liberal revolution tended to wane after the defeat of Carlism and the compromise reached with the Catholic Church and the oligarchy by the middle of the century (although a new link between nationalism and internal reform would reappear in post-1898 'regenerationist' movements). By the end of the nineteenth century the most significant role left to Spanish nationalism was the purely reactionary one of serving as the unifying ideology of all those opposed to (liberal or social) revolution and, in the twentieth century, to Catalan and Basque autonomy.

The Refuge of Frustrated Modernising Elites in a Populist, Anticlerical, Eschatological Myth

Frustrated in their efforts to 'nationalise the masses' and modernise the country, Spanish intellectual elites concentrated on a cultural battle, basically waged against the church, portrayed as the inherent enemy of an idealised Spanish people. Following the myths created during the Napoleonic War, and breaking away from the eighteenth-century elitist tradition, the people now came to represent the real physical and moral strength of the nation, the factor that determined its character and habits, quite in accord with the new Romantic notions of the '*Volk*'. In spite of the fact that the Spanish people, and especially the rural masses, did not support the liberal revolution (and even the urban masses, when they did support it, acted in a very irrational and violent way, as in the anticlerical outbursts of 1834–5), political and intellectual elites expected another redeeming intervention similar to that in 1808 against the 'usurpers of the Fatherland's freedom'. All they had to do was to 'wake up' the people, the Hero, asleep under the effects of the friars' and priests' drugs.

Within this populist mythology on which modernising elites based their political programme, the Catholic clergy stood in a role antagonistic to the 'People' (a character without which there would be no possible epic). Among intellectual elites liberalism and anticlericalism were almost automatically linked. The Catholic Church was blamed for all the past and present ills of the country. The clergy was, allegorically, the *Dragon*, which hid in its cave the elixir (science, knowledge) the Hero needed to strengthen himself and to put his Lady, the Republic, on the throne. Descriptions of the clergy emphasised their *strange sexual behaviour* (a topic most dear to the leftist press), or their depiction as a *sect*, with immense and occult powers (in the same way as Jews were seen by the European Right). The critique of the church is thus placed within a global *apocalyptic and nationalistic* framework. The clergy are seen as an obstacle to the sudden, and almost magical, solution to the national problem. The clergy were not only to be blamed for the colonial failure, but were made responsible for *all* national failures. The whole history of Spain would be free of all unhappy memories had the church not existed, because all such memories were related to tyrannical rule and because clerical preachings and clerical power spread femininity and weakness, which undermined patriotic and warlike social values. 'Religious fanaticism never produces heroes'; for this reason Spain is 'debased by its submission to the priest, cowardly in its fear of hell'. 'This explains why through the ages our wealth has been dissipated, our soil depopulated and our character weakened' (Alvarez Junco 1993).

The only known antidote against the stupefying venom spread by the clergy among the people was science and education; the schoolteacher stood as the natural antagonist to the priest. Intellectuals thus portrayed their own role as a kind of Merlin who had the medicine (culture) that would wake up the sleeping Hero (the people) and snatch him from the claws of the Dragon (the church, with its venomous teachings). Of course, in a way this reflected the battle for education and nationalisation of the masses going on in the country, but it lacked realism and displayed instead a strong moral, unreal and populist flavour, not far removed from the Russian *narodniki* model.

This mythical construction revealed its importance in 1898. The disastrous international performance of the Spanish State in 1898 closed the nineteenth century and provoked a dramatic internal reaction. One of the typical complaints of the moment was the relative indifference with which the popular classes lived the national crisis. This was only to be expected given the lack of socialisation of the lower classes in a national identity. The independence of the last colonial territories was only viewed as a personal loss by those intellectual and political elites who had worked so hard in the nation-building process: journalists, writers, politicians, lawyers, professionals. But this was precisely the time when intellectual elites were brandishing their recently acquired opinion-making powers (as the *affaire Dreyfus* was showing so memorably in France), and they managed to convince everybody that 'the country' was in a mortal crisis. The mythical aspects of progressive nationalism also explain the unexpected anticlerical turn of the 1898 crisis. The years 1899–1909 would witness the most important anticlerical wave in modern Spanish history.

Conclusion

The general conclusion to be drawn from this chapter is that processes of 'nationalisation of the masses', usually studied in relation to the new nation-states formed in the nineteenth century, such as Germany or Italy in Europe, or countries of mass immigration, such as Argentina or the USA outside Europe, were also necessary for old traditional European monarchies if they were to survive as modern nation-states. A successful example of these ethnicisation processes was, of course, Republican France (Weber 1976). Well-known failures were the Austro-Hungarian or the Ottoman empires. Spain was a middle-of-the-road case: an old traditional monarchy which survived, but under political and economic circumstances which made its effort at nationalisation of the masses weak and insufficient. In the twentieth century, conservative forces would finally make a determined effort to nationalise – but too late. Elites were already attracted either by social revolution or by alternative nationalisms. And the link between 'Spanishness' and its lateness, and its link to military dictatorships, gave a bitter flavour to the idea and the symbols of Spain. Here, it seems to me, lay the root of present-day problems.

References

Alvarez Junco, José (1993), 'Alle origini dell'anticlericalismo nella Spagna degli anni Trenta', in Giuliana Di Febbo and Claudio Natoli, *Spagna anni Trenta. Società, cultura, istituzioni*, Milan, pp.193–212
—— (1994a), 'España: El peso del estereotipo', *Claves de Razón Práctica*, no.48, pp.2–10
—— (1994b), 'La invención de la Guerra de la Independencia', *Studia Historica*, no.12, pp.75–99
Belmar, Francisco Saturnino (1861), *Reflexiones sobre la España, desde la fundación de la monarquia hasta el fin del reinado de San Fernando*, Madrid
Castro, Fernando de (1850–63), *Resumen de Historia General y de España*, Madrid
Cortada, Juan (1845), *Historia de España, dedicada a la juventud*, Barcelona
Durham, Samuel Ashley (1832–3), *History of Spain and Portugal*, 3

vols, London

Garrido, Fernando (1865), *La España Contemporánea*, Madrid

Gebhardt, Víctor (1861–4), *Historia general de España y de sus Indias, desde los tiempos más remotos hasta nuestros días*, 7 vols, La Habana and Madrid

Herr, Richard (1965), 'Good, Evil, and Spain's Rising against Napoleon', in Herr, R. and Parker, H.T. (eds), *Ideas in History*, Durham, pp.157–81

Mariana, Juan de (1592–1605), *Historia de Rebus Hispaniae*, 30 vols, (Spanish version published in Toledo 1601)

Menéndez y Pelayo, Marcelino (1882, 1967 edn), *Historia de los heterodoxos españoles*, 2 vols, Madrid

Merry y Colón, Manuel (1873), *Elementos de Historia crítica de España*, Seville

Merry y Colón, M. and Merry y Villalba, A. (1889), *Compendio de Historia de España*, Seville

Mosse, George (1975), *The Nationalization of the Masses. Political Symbolism and Mass Movements in Germany from the Napoleonic Wars through the Third Reich*, New York

Núñez Seixas, Xosé M. (1994), 'Questione nazionale e crisi statale: Spagna, 1898–1936', *Ricerche Storiche*, vol.24, no.1, pp.87–117

Riquer, Borja de (1994), 'La débil nacionalización española del siglo XIX', *Historia Social*, no.20, pp.97–114

Romey, Charles (1838–51), *Histoire d'Espagne dépuis les premiers jours jusqu'à nos jours*, Paris

Sales, Nuria (1974), *Sobre esclavos, reclutas y mercaderes de quintos*, Barcelona

Sánchez Casado, Félix (1867), *Prontuario de Historia de España y de la civilización española*, Madrid

Serrano, Carlos (1987), *Le tour du peuple*, Madrid

Tapia, E. de (1840), *Historia de la civilización española*, 4 vols, Madrid

Terradillos, Angel María (1848), *Prontuario de Historia de España*, Madrid

Weber, Eugen (1976), *Peasants into Frenchmen. The Modernization of Rural France, 1870–1914*, Stanford

—6—

'The Lion and the Pig': Nationalism and National Identity in *Fin-de-Siècle* Spain

Sebastian Balfour

Fin-de-siècle Spain was branded by war and defeat. The colonial wars in Cuba and the Philippines and the Disaster of 1898, as a result of which Spain lost the scattered remnants of her old empire in an unequal war with the United States, touched on the lives of almost all Spaniards and shaped the course of politics thereafter. The magnitude of the national disaster can only be fully understood in the context of the era. The last quarter of the nineteenth century was an age of imperialist expansion when the Great Powers vied to establish their spheres of influence over the last untouched markets of the world. In that race, the lesser of those Powers were forced to curtail ambitious projects of expansion or, as in the case of Spain, to cede their old colonies.

Spain's loss of empire, therefore, was not an isolated event but part of a wider process of colonial redistribution which drew the new contours of global power (Pabón 1963; Jover 1979). It was also an age when the possession of colonies was seen as the hallmark of a vigorous nation. The ideology which drove this expansion was social Darwinism which posited that in the forward march of civilisation, the weaker powers had to give way to the stronger. The British Premier, Lord Salisbury, gave voice to this belief in a speech in 1898 in which he made a thinly disguised reference to Spain as a dying nation.[1]

The Disaster of 1898 was also a national catastrophe because it destroyed the fiction maintained throughout the nineteenth century, not only that Spain was a great power with an imperial vocation but that its empire was different. Unlike the 'parvenu' empires of the new powers, it was believed to be based on racial, cultural and spiritual bonds resistant to the lure of commercial considerations. This was also a fiction in that the colonies were organised fundamentally for the economic benefit of the metropolis. Not even the independence of the mainland

---

1. For the effect of this speech in Spain, see Torre del Rio (1985: 163–80).

American empire in the first quarter of the nineteenth century had dented this sense that Spain had a special vocation amongst imperial powers. The loss of this part of the empire had been cushioned by the retention of residual colonies, especially by what was to become for a while the richest colony in the world, Cuba.

The significance of the loss of Spanish America had also been obscured by the domestic conflict which raged on and off during the nineteenth century between liberalism and absolutism and then between liberals, Carlists and republicans. It could be said, therefore, that Spain's post-imperial crisis of identity was postponed for half a century. When it finally emerged, it was all the deeper because of the prevailing orthodoxy of imperial expansionism. We only have to contrast the context of 1898 and that of the early 1950s to understand the anguish which the loss of empire caused many Spaniards and the apparent grace with which Britain handed over her empire.

This special imperial vocation in Spain in the late nineteenth century was part of a greater self-delusion. The Bourbon Restoration of 1875 had ushered in a comparatively long period of stability after the turmoil of the Carlist wars and the chaos of the First Republic. Its political system was based on a consensus among Spain's elites to restore order and to share in the spoils of the colonies. The army had agreed to withdraw to the barracks and the Catalan and Basque bourgeoisie had accepted a subordinate position in the hierarchy of power in exchange for state protection and the privilege of a captive colonial market. On the surface, the political system was based on a democratic model copied from Britain: two parties, Conservatives and Liberals, put themselves up for election and alternated in power, the regent exercising the prerogative to call on them to form or dissolve a government after appropriate consultation.

In reality, the parties were merely assemblies of notables representing two factions of the landed oligarchy, which was the product of a marriage of convenience between the old aristocracy and the landed elite that had emerged through the liberal disentailments of the first half of the nineteenth century. This oligarchy exercised power through a hierarchy of patronage which stretched from Madrid to the smallest town in the country. Aside the pact with the army, the oligarchy's political control depended on a consensus with elites, such as the industrial bourgeoisie, who were not directly represented in the two parties and on the demobilisation of most of the population (see Chapter 7).

The price that was paid for this stability was the weak projection of the liberal state over its citizens and the subordination of the liberal elite to the ideological residue of the ancien regime. Unlike its French equivalent, the Spanish state remained too feeble to establish a common market within its frontiers or to enforce a uniform system of justice based on consensus and not on the repeated use of martial law; it was also too weak to impose a uniform culture and administration or to project modern secular values throughout the nation (see Chapter 5). While Spain remained a largely rural, clerical and unmodernised country with poor communications and low rates of literacy, such a system could function as long as it could satisfy the demands of the elites excluded from direct political power. But as the pace of modernisation quickened on the periphery from the 1880s onwards – in Catalonia and the Basque Country in particular – the consensus and order on which the Restoration system was based was put increasingly under strain.

The Spanish-Cuban War of 1895–8 and the war with the United States in 1898 exposed the fragility of the Restoration Settlement. As the demands of war grew, most of Spanish society was mobilised in support of the war effort. This was both a physical and ideological mobilisation. In the space of four years, over 200,000 troops were sent out to Cuba and the Philippines, drawn mainly from the poorer classes because the better-off could buy exemptions from military service. Most poor families, therefore, suffered the temporary or permanent loss of a young relative, a father, a son, a breadwinner. The mass call-up was justified in terms of the national interest. The colonies were seen as part of Spain so that the recruits were told they were being sent off to defend the motherland overseas. There was a festive spirit as the troops were seen off in stations and ports, with bands playing and bishops blessing. And for the first time in many parts of Spain, national concerns began to vie with local and class identities. Spaniards of all classes and localities were encouraged to internalise images of national identity which were in reality those of the ruling oligarchy.

The components of this nationalism can be discerned in the rhetoric of the press and of popular culture. It should be said that throughout the conflict, there were few signs of opposition to the war. Much has been made of sporadic anti-war protest but this was extremely rare.[2] In the prevailing mood of jingoism, most of those who opposed the government's policy or suffered distress as a result of the war did not make their feelings public. There were many who evaded the call-up, the poor by emigration or flight and the better-off by buying exemption or paying for a substitute (Serrano 1987). Of the political organisations, only the anarchists, the Socialists and the small group of Federalists led by Pi y Margall were against it. Indeed, the public mood of bellicosity grew the closer the war with the United States loomed. The evidence indicates that the approaching conflict aroused the enthusiasm at

2. Such as the famous women's demonstration in Zaragoza in August 1896.

least of the urban classes. In demonstrations, bullfights, circuses, sports events, zarzuelas, popular songs, and in the *género chico* plays in the café theatres, Spaniards celebrated the martial virtues of the Spanish character and the coming victory over the Americans.

This rhetoric of war played on the justice of the Spanish cause: Cuba was Spanish and the Cuban insurrectionists were traitors when they were of Spanish origin, and savages when they were black (though there was grudging admiration for the intrepid black general, Antonio Maceo (Gaziel 1958: 99)).[3] In the imagery of this nationalism, Spanish-ness was based on supposed innate characteristics; Spaniards were a pure, warrior race, valiant, chivalresque and Christian. The historical reference-points which underpinned this view were the siege of Numancia, the Reconquest, the Conquest of the Americas and the battle of Lepanto against the Turks.

One of the commonest images of national identity centred on the bullfight, which was seen as a noble sport expressing the essential valour of the race. Patriotic corridas were held in which the bullfighters and their entourage wore the colours of the Spanish flag and in one case, where the sand of the bullring itself was painted in these colours. Bullfighting correspondents encouraged their readers to see the corrida as a metaphor for war. In one article, the Cuban war is described entirely in bullfighting metaphors; Spain, it concluded, criticised by foreigners for its 'weakness' for bullfights, was the strongest of all the nations.[4] The bulls themselves became imbued with the qualities of the Spanish. A corrida columnist, referring to one of the American generals in an article entitled 'Stupid Pessimisms', exclaimed: 'I'd like to see what General Miles himself and his 50,000 men would do in the open if we let loose on them 50 of Miura's bulls.'[5]

These traditional images of Spanishness were sharpened by contrast with the Other, the Americans. In some of the press and in popular songs and verses, the enemy was portrayed as a mongrel race composed of the scum of the earth. They were seen as cowards, partly because of this racial plurality, and partly because they were supposed to be motivated solely by money. As Protestants or worse still atheists, they represented a threat to the true faith, Catholicism, seen as an essential feature of Spanish identity. The difference between the national stereotypes of Spaniards and Americans was condensed into two contrasting metaphors, the lion and the pig. The lion, the ancient symbol of

3. *Diario de Zaragoza*, 10 December 1896; *Almanaque de las Provincias* (1902). For racist pictures of black Cuban insurrectionists see, for example, 'De Manifesto', *El Cardo*, 11 March 1898.
4. 'Notas Taurinas', *Diario de Zaragoza*, 12 December 1896.
5. Carlos Crouselles, 'Pesimismos estúpidos', *Madrid Taurino*, 1 May 1898.

the kingdom of León, was one of the emblems of the Spanish monarchy and appeared on the national shield. Before and during the war, it was often accompanied in cartoons and illustrations by that of a woman also representing Spain. She was, on different occasions, a matronly mother-figure and a virgin lusted after by a lecherous old Uncle Sam.

While the lion could be said to represent nobility, bravery, generosity and purity, the pig, in contrast, was plebeian, gluttonous, dirty, cowardly and mercenary. A typical cartoon depicted a Spanish soldier bayoneting a pig, which starts vomiting money as the bayonet pierces its belly. Moreover, as the favourite food on Spanish tables, the pig was more respected dead than alive. Indeed, bacon, pork and ham became sub-tropes for the pig metaphor. Translated freely, a typical wartime lyric went:

> If the war lasts a long time
> The price of ham will fall
> Because of the many yankees
> That the Spaniard will kill.[6]

The food image gave rise to unintended ironies. Spanish troops, besieged by the Americans in Santiago de Cuba, celebrated a minor incident in the war favourable to their side by parading through the streets shouting 'Down with bacon'. It was at a moment when their own supply of bacon, the last nutritious food remaining in the city, was about to run out (Corral 1899: 173).

A deconstruction of the lion and pig metaphors would suggest, firstly, that they were ideal compensations for a real inferiority. The official symbol of the United States, the eagle, was too powerful an image for Spanish jingoism to contemplate and, in several cities, the crowds tore it down from the entrance to American consulates in Spain.[7] Secondly, it could be argued that the values expressed by the image of the lion were those of the ancien regime, of traditional, rural, aristo-cratic Spain represented by the ruling landed oligarchy. As compared with the supposed values of American society, they stood for a rejection of modernisation and a celebration of an unchanging utopia, a mythical Spain united to her empire by the sacred bonds of Hispanism.

In this view, the defeat of Spain by the United States is thus seen also as a defeat for a traditional civilisation by the burgeoning forces of

6. 'Si la guerra dura mucho/se abaratará el jamón/por los muchísimos yankees/que matará el español' (*La Publicidad*, 24 April 1898). For other examples of the pig theme, see *Blanco y Negro*, 19 February and 5 March 1898.

7. For example in Madrid on the 24 April, 1898: *El Imparcial*, 25 April.

capitalism. After the disaster in the Bay of Manila, a popular illustrated magazine, plumbing the depths of pathos, described 'the healthy, greasy pig trampling on the dying lion.'[8] Behind this image of defeat lies another encoded meaning: the healthiness of the pig represents the global triumph of commercialism while the dying lion symbolises the defeat of values associated with the ancien regime.

These images of nationalism and national identity were shared by all those who supported the war effort. Even those republicans who rejected the Restoration state entered into a sort of patriotic contest whereby they sought to prove that they were truer patriots, upholders of the imperial tradition which the ruling classes had failed. The paradox was that one of the models they had looked to for inspiration was precisely Republican America. This contradiction at the heart of Spanish republicanism was a token of its ideological subordination to the values of Restoration society (Alvarez Junco 1994: 285–90).

The spectacular failure of the Restoration state to hold on to the colonies broke the spell that held the political system together. The elder statesmen of the regime were now seen as magicians without wands, their wartime rhetoric as empty as the state's coffers at the end of the war. The contrast between the triumphalism of nationalist discourse during the war and the pathos of defeat in its wake weakened even further the state's capacity to mobilise the population for national causes. The Disaster undermined the incipient growth of popular imperial sentiments, in marked contrast to the surge of enthusiasm for imperialism in many other parts of Europe in the same period (Baumgart 1982). The Spanish state was no longer able so easily to draw upon traditional images of national identity to re-establish its authority or to create a popular base for a new nationalism based on military and commercial penetration into Africa.

This became clear in the events of the Tragic Week of July 1909. They were precipitated by a minor military campaign in northern Morocco in an area policed by Spain in accordance with international agreements. A decree on 11 July ordered the mobilisation of reservists who had thought themselves free of any further obligation to do military service.[9] The call-up provoked virulent protests which in Barcelona in particular, partly because it was the port of embarkation, turned into a violent and prolonged confrontation with the authorities.

The circumstances in which the reservists were mobilised could not fail to evoke bitter memories of the war of 1895–8. The company responsible for the shipment of the troops was the same, the policy of

8. 'Crónica General', *La Ilustración Española y Americana*, 8 May 1898, p. 262.
9. See a statement to *Le Journal* in Brissa (1910: 8).

selling call-up exemptions was still in force, the same or similar notables were sending off the recruits with patriotic speeches to the accom-
paniment of bands playing popular marches, and as in many send-offs
during the previous colonial war, devout middle-class ladies were distributing religious medals and free cigarettes to the soldiers (Connelly
Ullman 1968: 135). While there had been a genuine display of patriotic
enthusiasm amongst the troops in the war against the United States, the
conflict in Morocco was seen in terms of class interests; that is, it was
perceived as a war that was solely for the benefit of Spanish investors
whose financial interests were threatened by the upheaval in Morocco.
As the band played the Royal March in the port at Barcelona, the
crowds whistled in derision and many conscripts threw the medals over-
board.[10]

The crisis of legitimacy in the wake of the Disaster was also a crisis
of identity. The defeat and the loss of empire encouraged centrifugal
tendencies in conceptions of national identity. Spain's precarious unity
among its different regions had been constructed around a common
endeavour to extend its dominion and its religion to the Empire and to
extract the wealth contained therein. With the loss of the last colonies,
the already fragile ideological ties binding the regions to the centre from
which that Empire had been run were put under even greater strain; this
was particularly true of Catalonia because the ruling order had failed to
retain the colonial markets which had absorbed so many of the region's
exports. More importantly, rapid modernisation especially in Catalonia
and the Basque region in the second half of the nineteenth century had
widened the socio-economic and cultural gap between the centre and
the periphery. The sense of alienation towards the dominant oligarchic
order felt by many Basques and their more outward-looking and
cosmopolitan middle-class counterparts in Catalonia was merely heightened by the Disaster.

The crisis caused by the Disaster therefore flowed into a longer-term
crisis generated by modernisation. In many parts of Spain, industrialisation, urbanisation, migration and the spread of communications
networks were undermining the social and ideological structures of the
Restoration system. The change in values that ensued was quickened by
the effects of the wars. As the new century progressed, there grew a
plurality of identities in more developed parts of Spain, replacing
traditional self-images with new perceptions of regional and class
identities. The barely articulated divisions within Spanish society rose
to the surface and multiplied. And in the aftermath of the Disaster three
broadly defined visions of the nation-state and Spanish nationalism

10. 'Lo que haya de caer, caerá', *El Progreso*, 19 July 1909.

could be said to emerge as alternative models to those represented by the Restoration system.

The first was articulated by the Catalan bourgeoisie. Despite their close association with the Catalan nationalist movement, they were in fact proposing to transform the Spanish state rather than merely to assert Catalonia's autonomy. The wealth of the Catalan industrialists had derived from their almost exclusive access to a lucrative colonial market and from the protective tariff barriers erected by their patrons in the state behind which they could exploit the domestic market. The loss of the colonies was a devastating blow and although a severe economic crisis was averted, the Catalan bourgeoisie were forced to reconsider their relationship with the Spanish state. New foreign markets had to be found and the domestic market needed urgently to expand to replace the colonial trade. Both these demands required a policy of neo-colonial expansion and a programme of internal modernisation which the Restoration state was clearly unable to deliver in its existing form.

What they aimed to do, in league with the Catalan nationalist movement, was to sweep aside the corrupt electoral system in Catalonia and from their new power base take over the Spanish state and reconstruct it (Prat de la Riba 1906, 1910 edn: 140–1). Their model for a revived nation-state was modernising but also conservative, paternalist and neo-colonialist. It was devolutionary, as well, firmly rooted in the belief in the reinvigorating effects on Spain of regional autonomy. There was no room in this model for the unitary vision of traditional Spanish nationalism. The new state they envisaged would embrace different ethnicities and languages.

The second vision of a reformed nation-state was also modernising but, in contrast to the Catalan model, centralist. It was propounded in the aftermath of the Disaster by the regenerationist movement, led by Joaquín Costa and the glass manufacturer, Basilio Paraíso. This movement embraced disaffected sections of the middle classes hit by the post-war rise in taxes imposed to finance the state deficit. The regenerationist programme was also largely backed by the republicans. Republican nationalism, somewhat chastened and tempered by the Disaster, sought to give a populist dimension to traditional nationalism, stressing the innate virtues of the Spanish masses in contrast to the decadence of their rulers. Both regenerationists and republicans remained deeply hostile to regionalism, which they saw as both elitist and divisive. The national interest, in republican eyes, lay in the construction of a progressive, modern, lay state, whose model was the France of Waldeck-Rousseau. This ambition was shared by the Socialists who saw the development of a modern bourgeois state as an essential stage on the path towards socialism (Robles Egea 1994: 293–312).

The third current of opinion seeking to remodel the nation-state emerged amongst professional officers in the first decade of the new century. It could be defined as an effort to reconcile the needs of modernisation and traditional nationalism. Whilst there had existed a wide range of political tendencies among officers in the nineteenth century, including revolutionary republicanism, military opinion moved rapidly rightwards in the early part of the twentieth century. This ideological shift was partly a response to the growth of anti-militarism in the wake of the Disaster; it was also a result of the officers' own alienation from the political system and of the use of the army to quell the increasing volume of social unrest. In the absence of any class or political force with which the officers could identify, the military elite rediscovered a sense of historical mission to uphold the national interest. This current of opinion within the army sought to sweep away the ineffectual two-party system of the Restoration regime and modernise the nation through an authoritarian state; by creating a strong economy and a disciplined society, Spain could rebuild its military strength and recover greatness through imperialist expansion into Africa.

Military nationalism, however, as it emerged in the early twentieth century, shared some of the features of traditional nationalism. It outlawed divisions of class and region, both of which were seen as a threat to the nation whose integrity it was the duty of the army to defend. The growing alienation between centre and periphery found expression in chauvinist and even racist stereotypes on both sides which merely served to reinforce their divisions and, amongst the army and other ideologically conservative sections of society, to strengthen a conception of national identity constructed on a supposedly archetypal Castilian character.

Indeed, the Disaster and the challenges of modernisation encouraged a renewal of traditional views about Spanish history and the nature of Spanishness. One such view, as I have argued, saw Spain's role as champion of the spiritual world against the invasion of materialism. Accordingly, it was believed that the source of Spain's future resurgence lay in the Hispanic traditions of its former empire; by increasing trade and cultural contacts with the ex-colonies, Spain could create a new cultural empire as a counterbalance to the Anglo-Saxon world. Beside the lion, two icons were commonly wielded in defence of this supposed vocation: Ariel, the symbol of the spirit as opposed to the capitalist Caliban, and Quixote, now ready to sally forth on a third voyage to bring spiritual values to a world losing its way.

A distorted and partial view of Spanish history, renovated by the historian Menéndez y Pelayo in the latter part of the nineteenth century, was also mobilised to defend tradition against the inroads of modernisation (Menéndez y Pelayo 1882; Alvarez Junco 1994). The 'true' Spain was seen to lie in the spirit of the Counter-Reformation and in the Second of May 1808 uprising against the French invaders. The ancestral Castile of the Reconquest also became a model for a renewed Spain. Indeed, Castile exerted a fascination even among those regenerationist writers most critical of the supposed decadence of Spain. Their nostalgic musings over the medieval ruins and the harsh landscape of the meseta helped to nourish this conservative myth of national identity.

This celebration of medieval Spain and of traditional rural life was perhaps a flight from the dilemmas of modernisation which increasingly threatened the autonomy of the petty bourgeoisie, caught between the revolt of the lower classes and the spread of capitalism (Balfour 1994: 1–19). For more conservative sectors, such as the Carlists, the familiar social structures of the countryside, its rituals and the old paternalism of landlord and priest, were seen as bulwarks against the corrosive moral effects of industrialisation and urbanisation. It should be clear, however, that there was no monolithic conception of nationalism and national identity on the Right. In contrast to the utopian, rural and clerical currents I have just outlined, military nationalism was modernising and expansionist. This contradiction would remain a fundamental component of the Right in the decades that followed.

The three different visions of nationalism and the nation-state defined in this chapter were sharpened by the rise of popular discontent in the first decade of the century. This was mainly the consequence of the surge of industrialisation that had taken place since the 1890s, which filled the industrial centres with new layers of workers. In the climate of disaffection of the post-Disaster period, these masses were mobilised by populist republicans such as Lerroux in Barcelona and Blasco Ibañez in Valencia and by the socialist and anarchist movements. The rise of social tension – city riots, strikes, terrorism – reinforced military authoritarianism while inhibiting the emergence of the two other models of nation-state.

Thus the political system of the Restoration regime survived for a while because neither Catalans, nor the parliamentary Left nor the army were able to impose their alternative and conflicting models for a new nation-state (Balfour 1995). But as the twin challenge of regionalism and working-class agitation grew, the army combined with more traditional sectors to impose their own solutions on Spanish society, firstly in 1923 and then in 1936. The military rebellion against the Second Republic sought to mobilise in its favour the right wing myth of national identity and imperial vocation which had been reshaped by the Disaster of 1898 and the tensions thrown up by modernisation.

References

Alvarez Junco, J. (1994), '"Los amantes de la libertad": la cultura republicana española a principios del siglo XX', in Townson, N. (ed.), *El republicanismo en España (1830–1977)*, Madrid, pp.265–92

Balfour, S. (1994), 'The Solitary Peak and the Dense Valley: Intellectuals and Masses in *Fin de Siècle* Spain', *Tesserae*, no.1, pp.1–19

—— (1995), 'Riot, Regeneration and Reaction. Spain in the Aftermath of the 1898 Disaster', *The Historical Journal*, vol.38, no.2, pp.405–23

Baumgart, W. (1982), *Imperialism. The Idea and Reality of British and French Colonial Expansion 1880–1914,* Oxford

Brissa, J. (1910), *La Revolución de julio en Barcelona*, Barcelona

Connelly Ullman, J. (1968), *The Tragic Week. A Study of Anticlericalism in Spain, 1875–1912*, Cambridge, Mass.

Corral, M. (1899), *¡El Desastre! Memorias de un voluntario en la campaña de Cuba*, Barcelona

Gaziel (1958), *Tots els camins duen a Roma. Història d'un destí, 1893–1914*, Barcelona

Jover Zamora, J.M. (1979), *1898, Teoría y práctica de la redistribución colonial*, Madrid

Menéndez y Pelayo, M. (1882), *Historia de los heteredoxos españoles*, Madrid

Pabon, J. (1963), 'El 98, acontecimiento internacional', in *Días de Ayer*, Barcelona, pp.139–95

Prat de la Riba, E. (1906, 1910 edn), *La nacionalitat catalana*, Barcelona

Robles Egea, A. (1994), 'Republicanismo y horizonte europeo', in Townson, N. (ed.), *El republicanismo en España (1830–1977)*, Madrid, pp.293–312

Serrano, C. (1987), *Le tour du peuple. Crise nationale, mouvements populaires et populisme en Espagne (1890–1910)*, Madrid

Torre del Río, R. de la (1985), 'La prensa madrileña y el discurso de Lord Salisbury sobre "las naciones moribundas" (Londres, Albert Hall, 4 mayo 1898)', *Cuadernos de Historia Moderna y Contemporánea*, no.6, pp.163–80

7

The Failure of the Liberal Project of the Spanish Nation-State, 1909–1923

Francisco J. Romero Salvadó

It is important, first of all, to underline the relative extent of the word failure. The liberal project failed in the sense that it did not manage to create a modern nation-state based on solid foundations. The liberal governing elites never accomplished the successful transition of Spain from a sluggish, largely rural economy, whose social and political life was still marked by localism and elitism, into a modern, democratic and centralised state. However, the liberal State remains to the present day the most successful and long-lasting era of social peace and political stability in modern Spanish history. It was established in December 1874 and did not collapse until September 1923.

During this period a nation-state began to emerge: a system of mass education was developed, mass communications and newspaper circulation expanded, urbanisation proceeded, and the economy became more integrated in a consolidated national market (Fusi 1989: 35, 37). Yet it was an artificial nation-state, created from above and which paid no attention to regionalism and pre-existing local and economic realities (Riquer 1990: 120). The constitution of 1876 conceded freedom of expression and association, political parties and trade unions were allowed to exist, and in 1890, universal male suffrage was introduced. Despite all these constitutional trappings, the liberal state was far from democratic. In fact, it was an oligarchic system which by its very nature, conserving important remnants of the ancien regime, obstructed and delayed the birth of a modern nation-state. Real power was monopolised by two monarchist or dynastic parties, Conservatives and Liberals. They were not modern political formations but groups of notables and professional politicians who guaranteed the political supremacy of the financial and landowning oligarchies of the country (Tuñón de Lara 1992: 108–19, 190–4, 202–11). Most of these political barons did not have a proper national view, let alone a coherent project of a modern nation-state which could appeal to a majority of the population. These liberal politicians' main concern was *vivir de la política* ('to enjoy the profits of politics'), retain the support of their local clienteles and *ir tirando* ('live from day to day').

The foundation of the whole system was the so-called *'turno pacífico'* or the systematic rotation in power of both dynastic parties. The *turno* of parties in office served to maintain a fiction of political competition as well as providing the governing elites with a safe mechanism by which they could share the spoils of administrative graft. The dynastic parties did not even bother to campaign to win popular votes as their power was based on electoral falsification, patronage and the widespread apathy of the masses. Elections were just part of the constitutional fiction as, in practice, the Interior Minister (*Ministro de la Gobernación*) manipulated the results so that the governments always obtained a working majority (Varela: 1973).

The governing classes had to pay a heavy price for their monopoly of political power. In order to keep the system functioning smoothly, they depended on the goodwill of extra-constitutional groups. Their parliamentary majorities rested on the activities of the local bigwigs or *caciques*. Helped by the reality of cultural and socio-economic backwardness, the *caciques* delivered the votes of their areas and in return they were allowed to run their localities as private fiefdoms. *Caciquismo* was deeply rooted in the patron–client network of a traditional society and precluded the development of a modern nation-state (Romero Maura 1973; Kern 1974; Varela 1977). The result was the ruralisation of political life and a remarkable contrast between legal centralism and real localism (Fusi 1989: 34).

Furthermore, the liberal state was affected by the exceptional position enjoyed by Crown and army. The regime was not created from below but by a military *pronunciamiento* in December 1874, which brought about the restoration of the Bourbon dynasty. Both dynasty and army occupied central positions in the new order. The military were the guarantors of its existence. The *Ley de Constitución del Ejército* of November 1878 not only granted the army control of its own internal affairs but also confirmed that its primary function was the defence of the nation from its internal enemies. With a still very rudimentary police force, public order was under its competence.[1] Popular upheavals were immediately followed by the suspension of the constitution and the declaration of martial law which gave the army total control of public

---

1. The first steps were taken during these years to create a national police force. In 1907, the *Ley de Creación de la Policía* (law to establish a national police force) was approved; and in 1912, the *Dirección General de Seguridad del Estado* (National Security Council) was created.

life (Ballbé 1985: 227–8, 233–4; Lleixà 1986: 60–1). The king was at the top of the political system. Authority did not derive from popular consent through elections but from royal support. As head of the state, the monarch was the one who made possible the *turno pacífico*. The king and not public opinion produced political change. When he considered that the party in power was 'spent' he granted the leader of the other dynastic group a decree of dissolution of Cortes which enabled him to make the new elections (Fernández Almagro 1977: 15–18).[2]

The failure of the liberal elites to generate a cohesive national identity and a modern state became apparent with the colonial disaster of 1898. This moment initiated the crisis of legitimacy of the Restoration system. The essayist Joaquín Costa declared that Spain was a country which although viewed historically as grandiose and imperial, was actually one of the most ruined and troublesome outskirts of the planet – a place which could only produce *caciques*. As late as 1920, the influential philosopher, José Ortega y Gasset, criticised the artificiality of Spain as a nation in his celebrated *España Invertebrada* (*Invertebrate Spain*). Together with the colonial disaster, as society and economy modernised, new perceptions of regional and class identities emerged which could not be absorbed or co-opted by the rigid structures of the Restoration system. In turn, this failure led to political protest and fostered the slow growth of rival socialist, regionalist and democratic projects supported by the rising organised labour movement, the Basque, the Catalan and the republican-leaning middle classes. They all sought to regenerate and modernise Spain. As the working classes and Catalan and Basque nationalists grew bolder, the liberal politicians were gradually displaced by Crown and armed forces. King and army cast away liberal principles and instead coined a new type of nationalism which was aggressive, belligerent, uncompromising, intolerant and highly critical of the corruption and *caciquismo* of the ruling liberal system. The colonial defeat had the effect of alienating the army from the liberal state. Officers began to feel that maintenance of social order and unity of the fatherland was their sacred duty. Thus they resented the existing constitutional practices as inadequate to crush the pernicious effects of regionalism and class conflict.

Having begun to reign in 1902, Alfonso XIII not only sided with his officers in their disputes with the politicians but also took advantage of his constitutional prerogatives to appoint prime ministers and thus

---

2. During the liberal Monarchy, most political crises were known as '*Orientales*' as they were made and solved at the *Palacio de Oriente*, residence of the king. It is also true to say that the king many times merely ratified a change of government brought about by the peculiar mechanics of the *turno* system.

further party factionalism. Incidents like the officers' assaults on Cat-alanist journals in 1905, the passing of the *Ley de Jurisdicciones* the following year and the brutal suppression of the anti-militarist riots in Barcelona in July 1909 (Tragic Week) revealed in full the shallow foundations of the liberal regime and the emergence of the alliance of Crown and army as the symbol of a new nationalism prepared to bypass constitutional practices in order to destroy what they regarded as threats to national unity and social order (Ballbé 1985: 273–8).[3]

The Tragic Week in 1909 cut short the career of the most dis-tinguished dynastic politician of the era, Antonio Maura. Unlike the other monarchist leaders, Maura realised that the liberal order had to be reformed. As leader of the Conservative Party, he tried to carry out what he termed 'revolution from above', the only coherent project emanating from one of the dynastic politicians.[4] His aim was to cleanse and reform the system by attracting and mobilising the support of part of the electorate – the Catholic middle classes – to replace the artificial *caciquista* foundations of his party. However, Maura's clerical leanings and authoritarian style won him the outright opposition of republicans and Socialists. In the summer of 1909, the call-up of reservists to undertake a new colonial adventure in Morocco, when memories of the ordeals suffered by soldiers in Cuba and the Philippines were still fresh, brought about his downfall. The Catalan proletariat revolted and was only subdued with brutal repression and high casualties. A campaign ensued under the slogan *Maura No!* in which members of the Liberal Party took part. The King, who initially had promised Maura his total support, changed his mind and on 21 October 1909 accepted a resig-nation that Maura never submitted nor constitutionally was forced to with an overwhelming majority in the Cortes (Maura and Fernán-dez Almagro 1948: 154–5; Cierva 1955: 148, 155, 162; Cambó 1987: 169–71).

The short-term consequences of the Tragic Week proved crucial. The Socialist Party (PSOE) abandoned its sectarian position and formed an alliance or *conjunción* with the middle-class republican groups. They

3. In 1905, alleging that a cartoon had offended the honour of the army, a group of army officers attacked the offices of the satirical Catalanist magazine *Cu-Cut*. The king took an active role in the affair. The Montero Ríos administration was dismissed and replaced by another Liberal cabinet led by Segismundo Moret more willing to placate the army. On 20 March 1906 it passed the so-called *Ley de Jurisdicciones*. Henceforth, any offence against the fatherland, the monarchy or the armed forces was to be tried by military jurisdiction. The best analysis of the Tragic Week can be found in Connelly Ullman (1968).

4. The only initiative undertaken by a Liberal leader, José Canalejas's attempt to extend support for the regime to the Left, was cut short when he was assassinated by an anarchist in 1912.

endorsed a programme based on defence of public liberties, radical democracy and social reforms (progressive taxation, labour legislation, pension schemes, accident and sickness insurance, reduction of working hours, etc.) (Gómez Llorente 1976: 126–9). However, a significant part of the proletariat rejected parliamentary practices and found a home in the anarcho-syndicalist movement, *Confederación Nacional del Trabajo* (CNT) founded in October 1910 (Bar 1981: 176–207).

Maura never forgave the role played by the Liberals and refused to alternate with them in power. In October 1913, the bulk of the Conservative Party abandoned its leader and under the leadership of the ex-minister and wealthy lawyer, Eduardo Dato, accepted the continuity of the *turno* formula. The result was the first serious and lasting split in one of the two dynastic parties when a minority of young Conservatives followed the dismissed leader and created the *Maurista* movement (Gutiérrez Ravé 1944: 129–30; González 1990: 39–40). The *Mauristas* constituted the first modern right-wing Spanish nationalist group. In fact, *Maurismo* always remained a movement rather than a party. There were 'left-wing' *Mauristas* who advocated political renovation and were committed to deepening democracy and reform and 'right-wing' *Mauristas* who pursued the construction of an authoritarian state. They all had in common the fact that they were basically young and energetic Conservatives who opposed the status quo represented by the *turno*. They felt a loyal and total devotion to the ousted leader, Maura. Being strongly Catholic and defenders of the Monarchy, the *Mauristas* regarded Maura's calls for mobilisation and education as the best weapons to prevent a revolution from below. They denounced the *turno* as a sham that in the long term was going to lead to the end of the Monarchy. The main target of their campaign was the *turno* ministers and deputies, dubbed court lackeys, mediocrities and men without principles. They considered them all the same, professional politicians merely bent on exalting the personal authority of the king and on preserving their corrupt practices (Romero Salvadó 1994: 18–19).

It was the First World War that finally accelerated the decline of the liberal regime. Ironically, a war in which Spain did not intervene was to alter decisively its contemporary history (Tuñón de Lara 1992: 187). Spain did not enter the war, but the war entered Spain and its ideological and socio-economic impact underlined the failure of oligarchic liberalism and hastened its collapse.

From day one, Prime Minister Eduardo Dato declared the official neutrality of the country. Since 1875 the dynastic politicians had followed a foreign policy of *recogimiento internacional* (international isolation) refusing to join either of the two rival blocs being created in Europe. A distant conflict in the Balkans was no reason to break with a tradition of almost forty years. Furthermore, there was a general awareness of the economic and military inability of the nation to wage a modern war as well as the hope that by maintaining an impartial position Spain could play a leading role in the peace negotiations.[5]

During the war years, most dynastic politicians behaved as if nothing was occurring, ignoring the intensity of the conflict raging beyond the Spanish borders. There was a tacit agreement to avoid the issue of the war. They felt that the Restoration system would not be able to withstand the impact of such a devastating conflict. Yet they could not prevent the country from splitting between Francophiles and Germanophiles. The quarrel between the partisans of the Allies and the Central Powers generated a violent debate, as the war was perceived as an ideological clash in which each of the warring factions came to symbolise certain transcendent ideas and values (Meaker 1988: 1–2, 6–7). Unlike the *inmobilismo* of the ruling liberal politicians, social classes and political groups, depending on their ideal of Spain as a nation, came to identify with the ideologies represented by the two sides. The main Germanophile voices in the country were those of the privileged social groups – the clergy, the aristocracy, the court, the upper bourgeoisie, the army, the landowning oligarchy – and those of right-wing parties such as the Carlists and the *Mauristas*. They regarded a German victory as the triumph of the concept of nation based on traditional values such as monarchism, discipline, religion and a hierarchical social order. On the other hand, the intellectuals, the professional middle classes and those political groups against the existing status quo – republicans, Socialists and regionalists – admired and wished to follow the model represented by France. They believed that the triumph of the Allies would bring about democracy and political freedom throughout Europe. For them, the war in Europe offered the golden opportunity for the creation of a modern nation.[6]

After 1916 national polarisation reached dramatic levels. After the entry of Italy and Portugal into the war, it was evident even to the most rabid Germanophiles that with Spain surrounded by the Allies, to join forces with Germany would be military suicide. Hence they became champions of strict neutrality since this was seen as the best way to support the German cause. In contrast, the Francophiles described strict neutrality as a sham and switched to positions ranging from benevolent

5. See letter from Prime Minister Dato to Antonio Maura (25 August 1914) in Maura and Fernández Almagro (1948: 472–3).

6. There is abundant literature on the division in Spain between Germanophiles and Francophiles during the war. See among others, Cenamor Val (1916), Ballesteros (1917), Posada (1923). Also see Public Record Office, *Foreign Office Papers*, 371–2471/73.963. Secret Report (29 July 1915).

neutrality towards the Allies to diplomatic rupture with the Central Powers and even open intervention.

As the indiscriminate activity of German submarines began to take its toll of the Spanish merchant fleet and some of the operations of Germany's spy network revealed its utter contempt for the principles of neutrality, the Liberal Prime Minister, Count Romanones, began to contemplate in early 1917 the possibility of getting closer to the Allied camp. Unlike the other dynastic leaders, Romanones believed that Spain should abandon strict neutrality. As early as August 1914, the Count had shocked the governing class when he had openly stated his pro-Allied views in a famous editorial called 'Fatal Neutralities'. According to Romanones, the war offered Spain a golden opportunity to expand her Empire in North Africa and strengthen her economy through closer collaboration with the Allies. Although he did not advocate diplomatic rupture with the Central Powers, he made clear that Spain should abandon isolation and move towards the Entente. Romanones' sympathy for the Allied cause was certainly reinforced by his economic links with France. He was one of the largest shareholders of mining concerns in Andalusia and Northern Morocco, partly exploited with French capital, and the production of his companies in Asturias went mainly to France to support her war effort.

Foreign events brought the argument around the neutrality issue almost to boiling point. In March 1917, the Tsarist autocracy was overthrown and one month later the United States abandoned its traditional isolationism and intervened in the conflict. The Francophiles regarded developments in the international arena as the confirmation that the Allies represented the cause of democracy and progress. By demanding that Spain should join that camp they were opting for a future Europeanised, secular and democratic Spain. The intensification of the German submarine offensive against neutral shipping in February 1917 and the subsequent interventionist attitude adopted by the United States, followed by several Latin American republics, persuaded Romanones that the time had come to break off diplomatic relations with Germany. The German sinking of the *San Fulgencio*, a vessel carrying a much needed cargo of British coal, torpedoed outside forbidden waters despite having a German safe conduct pass and heading towards Spain, seemed to the Liberal leader the right psychological moment to exploit popular opinion and take the final step against the Central Powers. However, the Count met the opposition of the neutralist section of his party led by the lacklustre Marquis of Alhucemas and of the King himself. In April 1917 Romanones, the leading dynastic politician committed to more active intervention, was dismissed by the King and the Marquis of Alhucemas, leader of a rival Liberal faction, appointed

Prime Minister. From that time, the Liberal Party was irretrievably divided.[7] Again in the summer of 1918, as the campaign of German outrages continued unabated, the Spanish government planned to take stern measures.[8] Yet once again the government faced the royal veto and had to back down.[9] Fearing that he could follow the fate of the Tsar Nicholas II, Alfonso XIII vetoed the entry of Spain into what he regarded as a dangerous adventure with probably the wrong friends (the Western democracies).

Parallel to that process of ideological polarisation, the impact of the war on the economy and society was crucial in bringing about the disintegration of the liberal state. As an immediate consequence of the conflict, Spain experienced its first real industrial take-off. Spain benefited from her neutral status to supply both camps, foreign competition was almost eliminated in the domestic market, and new outlets, which had to be abandoned by the belligerent nations, were taken over. This was an era of unexpected economic expansion in which a dramatic drop in imports together with a rise in the volume and prices of exports meant that the balance of trade went from a situation of chronic deficit to one registering huge surpluses. However, the economic boom benefited only certain regions and certain social classes. Industrial regions entered a period of feverish activity while other agrarian areas of the Peninsula were devastated by shortages and unemployment. Furthermore, the precarious transport system virtually collapsed under the new pressures, and the explosion in external demand, the difficulty in importing basic products and the increase of money in circulation brought about a galloping inflation (Bernís 1923; Instituto de Reformas Sociales 1923; García Delgado, Roldán and Muñoz 1973; Cabrera, Comín and García Delgado 1989). Different dynastic administrations proved impotent to deal with the new situation. In fact, they were unable or unwilling to intervene forcefully against those who were benefiting from the exceptional circumstances provided by the war. This was scarcely surprising, as those profiting were most often the very same *caciques* to whom the governing elites owed their votes.

7. For the crisis of April 1917 see Real Academia de La Historia, *Archivo Romanones* (hereafter A.R.), File 63, dossier 46 (April 1917); for the division of the Liberal Party see A.R., File 1 (June–July 1917); also see Soldevilla (1917: 268–79).

8. See for instance the campaigns carried out by the journals *El Parlamentario* (January–February 1918) and *El Sol* (March 1918) delivering evidence that Germany was behind many of the terrorist activities in the country.

9. Fundación Antonio Maura, *Archivo Antonio Maura* (hereafter A.M.) File 272; letter from Dato to Maura (3 September 1918).

Failure of the Liberal Project

Both the Catalan industrial bourgeoisie and the organised labour movement saw their position strengthened by the structural changes in the economy in relation to that of the ruling landowning oligarchy. The failure of an *inmobilista* and centralist state to carry through a modernising programme which recognised the Catalan question and could meet the urgent demands of the proletariat increased their determination to seek a new political realignment of forces in the country.

The objective of the *Lliga Regionalista*, the party of the Catalan industrial bourgeoisie, was to put an end to the political monopoly enjoyed by the centralist landowning oligarchy in Madrid and to establish a new decentralised system which would promote the growth of a modern capitalist economy based on the Catalan model. Aware of its recently gained economic strength, the *Lliga* sought to translate the new reality into political terms. In May 1916, it initiated a campaign to obtain Home Rule for Catalonia. This was followed by an obstructionist strategy in parliament which blocked all the economic initiatives of the Minister of Economy, Santiago Alba. At the same time, the hardships, shortages and inflation produced by the war resulted in the conclusion of the historic labour pact of July 1916. For the first time in history, the two traditionally rival workers' movements – the Socialist UGT-PSOE and the anarcho-syndicalist CNT – agreed to join forces and collaborate to force the governments to implement measures which could alleviate the distress and misery of the working classes. Both organisations subscribed in March 1917 to a manifesto in which the ruling system was accused of being the cause of the widespread distress of the population and threatened its overthrow by means of a general strike.

It was, however, the attitude of the army which precipitated the all-out revolt against the ruling system. Inflation and shortages eroded the living standards of the officers. The conflict on the continent revealed the incapacity of the Spanish military to engage in a modern war. This encouraged the dynastic governments to break a tradition of non-intervention in military matters and to introduce a comprehensive programme of reform and modernisation. In 1916 a Bill of Military Reform was passed in an attempt to deal with the sensitive question of reducing the vastly overmanned officers corps by introducing tests of physical and intellectual ability (Boyd 1979: 51–2). Deeply disturbed by their increasing economic hardship and incensed by the government reforms, the officers responded by creating from the second half of 1916, *Juntas Militares de Defensa*, a military version of trade unions. These *Juntas* quickly counterattacked denouncing the corruption and nepotism which characterised the *turno* politicians. Attempts to dissolve them were met with the refusal and then the open insurrection of the officers.[10] Their attitude provoked in June 1917 the fall of the existing administration and opened a period of constitutional crisis which encouraged the Catalan bourgeoisie and the labour movement to make their bid for renovation.[11]

The *Juntas'* movement was above all an outburst in defence of the corporate interests of the army and a direct challenge to civilian supremacy. Yet the failure and hollowness of the liberal order was amply displayed when leading forces of civil society – trade unions, industrial bourgeoisie, the bureaucracy – did not rally to its defence. On the contrary, they regarded the officers' rebellion as a golden opportunity to bring about a political revolution. The organisation of an Assembly of Parliamentarians in Barcelona on 19 July 1917 represented the most important attempt during the liberal Monarchy to create a modern and progressive state founded on the principles of genuine democracy and federalism (Soldevilla 1917: 325–39; Simarro 1918: 365–79). Hopes in the Assembly were short-lived. It failed to obtain the support of the dynamic Right represented by the *Mauristas* (Romero Salvadó 1994: 22).[12] Without the presence of Maura, an initiative endorsed by Catalans, Socialists and republicans could never appeal to the officers.[13] Hence the revolutionary strike organised in August 1917 by the labour movement in order to implement the principles defended by the Assembly was brutally crushed by the army.[14]

The collapse of the general strike ended any hopes of establishing a democratic and modern state which could appeal to different social classes in the nation. Yet the liberal state was living on borrowed time. On the night of 26 October an ultimatum signed by all the corps of the army was delivered to the King demanding the dismissal of the existing cabinet (Márquez and Capó 1923: 216–22). The structural crisis of the

10. It was Alfonso XIII who, terrified that the Russian events could be repeated in Spain, ordered the War Minister, General Aguilera, to disband the *Juntas de Defensa.* See Romanones (1947: 135–7).
11. Fernando Soldevilla (1918: 63–5), argues that a military coup had been organised for 2 June if the government had tried to crush the officers' rebellion.
12. Despite the opinion of some leading *Mauristas,* Maura refused to participate in any political manoeuvre which might endanger the throne. See A.M. File 397; Dossier 7, letter of Antonio Maura to Angel Ossorio (12 July 1917).
13. The *Juntas de Defensa* sought in vain to obtain the political leadership of Maura. See A.R. File 389; Dossier 10. Correspondence from Gustavo Peyrá (Catalan *Maurista* in close contact with the *Juntas*) to Maura (20, 25 and 28 June 1917).
14. In fact, the revolutionary strike was provoked by the government in order to scare the bourgeoisie and compromise the officers in the crushing of the disturbances. Then the government could claim to be the saviour of social order. On the events of August 1917 see among others Soldevilla (1917: 363–404); Saborit (1967: 67–74); Lacomba (1970: 213–84); Serrallonga (1991: 169–94).

liberal state had become a reality that was only to increase in the following years. In October 1917 constitutional practices were preserved but the political order was in tatters. From then onwards, increasingly divided into rival factions, the dynastic parties entered a period of irreversible decay. The *turno pacifico,* foundation of the established order since 1875, had been destroyed. Henceforth officers and King behaved increasingly as an anti-constitutional party with power of veto to make and topple cabinets.

After the Bolshevik Revolution in Russia, Spain was caught in the spiral of social violence and ideological militancy which swept across the continent. After 1918 the social and economic situation worsened dramatically. The kind of artificial protection which had existed during the war years disappeared and the country's traditional deficit in trade was again revealed. Prices continued to increase, reaching a peak in 1920, while salaries lagged far behind (Instituto de Reformas Sociales 1923: 10–11). News of the Allied victory and the Bolshevik triumph in Russia as well as the post-war economic recession intensified the separatist feeling in Catalonia and the class struggle in the nation at large. The difference was that now more intransigent elements led the offensive. The *Lliga Regionalista,* the conservative regionalist party of the Catalan industrial bourgeoisie, gradually lost the hegemony of Catalan politics to more radical groups. Also within the labour movement, the anarcho-syndicalist CNT took advantage of the widespread discontent and popular militancy to become the main force of the organised working class. The result was growing social conflict, political instability, and in the end, the destruction of the liberal state (Carnero 1989: 79).

Frightened by the growing power of the CNT, the Spanish bourgeoisie in general, and the Catalan in particular, dropped any reformist intentions that they might have harboured in the past and sought to defend their economic interests. Industrialists saw an imminent economic recession on the horizon which they planned to counter by massive lay-offs of workers and cuts in production. But first, the anarcho-syndicalist movement had to be crushed. Hence industrialists turned to the army for protection and together sealed an alliance which not only operated behind the back of the central government but even behaved as an anti-state, forcing the fall of those cabinets opposed to their plans. Between 1918 and 1923, the authority of the short-lived governments hardly went beyond the capital. Parliament became more than ever a talking-shop with no real power. Politicians were unable to put an end to the terror which reigned in the country. The endless spiral of violence spread from Catalonia to other regions. Industrialists hired gangs of thugs and in coordination with the army sponsored paramilitary groups. Leading syndicalists were killed and thousands of militants arrested. Anarchist groups responded in kind, assassinating employers, overseers and strike-breakers (Farré Morego 1922; Calderón 1932; Ignacio 1981).

Between 1919 and 1923 the calls for a new authoritarian, centralist and anti-liberal state became deafening. More than ever before, demands for a new order which could save the fatherland from separatism and social disorder became an integral part of the modern nationalist discourse.[15] The King lambasted the constitutional system in May 1921 and then in the summer of 1923 toyed with the idea of taking on himself the role of national saviour.[16] Alfonso XIII, if not the inspiration, at least knew of and did not oppose the military coup staged by the Captain General of Barcelona, Miguel Primo de Rivera, in September 1923. In seizing power, the army confirmed its tradition of intervention in politics. Yet with his *pronunciamiento* in 1923, Primo de Rivera was breaking with the past. The army did not represent a particular political group but claimed to be above politics and just defending the sacred values of the nation. The army had thus become both the symbol and the pillar of national unity. In line with the anti-parliamentarian tendencies rising at the time in Europe, its objective was the establishment of a strong, authoritarian and centralised state which by destroying both the inefficient liberal system and the threat of the organised labour movement and separatism offered the road to economic modernisation from above.

References

Ballbé, Manuel (1985), *Orden público y militarismo en la España constitucional, 1812–1983*, Madrid

Ballesteros, Lorenzo (1917), *La guerra europea y la neutralidad española*, Madrid

Bar, Antonio (1981), *La CNT en los años rojos: del sindicalismo revolucionario al anarcosindicalismo, 1910–1926*, Madrid

Bernís, Ignacio (1923), *Consecuencias económicas de la guerra*, Madrid

15. As early as 8 March 1919, *La Acción*, the *Maurista* journal, had called for a dictatorship. This kind of rhetoric increased among right-wing newspapers following the successful seizure of power by Mussolini in Italy in October 1922.

16. In a speech in Córdoba on 23 May 1921, Alfonso XIII called for the support of the nation to bypass parliament where vital legislation was never approved. See Fernández Almagro (1977: 301). In the summer of 1923 the King was persuaded to drop the idea of trying to establish his own personal dictatorship by Antonio Maura. See Maura and Fernández Almagro (1948: 533).

Failure of the Liberal Project

Boyd, Carolyn P. (1979), *Praetorian Politics in Liberal Spain*, Chapel Hill

Cabrera, M., Comín, F. and García Delgado, J.L. (1989), *Santiago Alba: un programa de reforma económica en la España del primer tercio del siglo XX*, Madrid

Calderón, Fernando (1932), *La verdad sobre el terrorismo. Datos, fechas, nombres y estadísticas*, Barcelona

Cambó, Francesc (1987), *Memorias*, Madrid

Carnero, Teresa (1989), 'Modernització, desenvolupament polític i canvi social: Espanya (1874–1931)', *Recerques*, no.23, pp.73–89

Cenamor Val, Hermógenes (1916), *Los españoles y la guerra: neutralidad o intervención*, Madrid

Cierva, Juan de la (1955), *Notas de mi vida*, Madrid

Connelly Ullman, Joan (1968), *The Tragic Week: Anticlericalism in Spain, 1875–1912*, Harvard

Farré Morego, José María (1922), *Los atentados sociales en España*, Madrid

Fernández Almagro, Melchor (1977), *Historia del reinado de Alfonso XIII*, 4th edn, Barcelona

Fusi, Juan Pablo (1989), 'Centre and Periphery 1900–1936: National Integration and Regional Nationalisms Reconsidered', in Preston, Paul and Lannon, Frances (eds), *Elites and Power in Twentieth-Century Spain*, Oxford, pp.33–44

García Delgado, J.L., Roldán, S. and Muñoz, J. (1973), *La formación de la sociedad capitalista en España*, Madrid

Gómez Llorente, José Luis (1976), *Aproximación a la historia del socialismo español*, Madrid

González, María Jesús (1990), *Ciudadanía y acción: el conservadurismo maurista, 1907–1923*, Madrid

Gutiérrez Ravé, José *(1944), Yo fui un joven maurista*, Madrid

Ignacio, León (1981), *Los años del pistolerismo. Ensayo para una guerra civil*, Madrid

Instituto de Reformas Sociales (1923), *Movimientos de precios al por menor durante la guerra*, Madrid

Kern, Robert W. (1974), *Liberals, Reformers and Caciques in Restoration Spain*, Albuquerque

Lacomba, Juan Antonio (1970), *La crisis española de 1917*, Málaga

Lleixá, Joaquim (1986), *Cien años de militarismo en España*, Barcelona

Márquez, B. and Capó, J. (1923), *Las juntas militares de defensa*, La Habana

Maura, Gabriel and Fernández Almagro, Melchor (1948), *Por qué cayó Alfonso XIII*, Madrid

Meaker, Gerald (1988), 'A Civil War of Words', in Schmitt, Hans A. (ed.), *Neutral Europe between War and Revolution, 1917–1923*, Virginia

Posada, Adolfo (1923), *Actitud ética ante la guerra y la paz*, Madrid

Riquer, Borja de (1990), 'Sobre el lugar de los nacionalismos-regionalismos en la historia de España', *Historia Social*, no.7, pp. 105–26

Romanones, Count (1947), *Notas de mi vida, 1912–1931*, Madrid

Romero Maura, Joaquín (1973), 'El caciquismo: tentativa de conceptualización', in *Revista de Occidente*, no.127, pp.15–44

Romero Salvadó, Francisco J. (1994), 'Maura, Maurismo and the Crisis of 1917', *Journal of the Association for Contemporary Iberian Studies*, vol.7, no.1, pp.16–26

Saborit, Andrés (1967), *La huelga de agosto de 1917*, Mexico City

Serrallonga, Joan (1991), 'Motines y revolución. España en 1917', in Bonamusa, Francesc (ed.), *La huelga general, Ayer*, no.4, pp.169–91

Simarro, Luis (1918), *Los sucesos de agosto en el parlamento*, Madrid

Soldevilla, Fernando (1917), *El año político de 1917*, Madrid

—— (1918), *Tres Revoluciones (Apuntes y notas)*, Madrid

Tuñón de Lara, Manuel (1992), *Poder y sociedad en España, 1900–1931*, Madrid

Varela Ortega, José (1973), 'Los amigos políticos: funcionamiento del sistema caciquista', *Revista de Occidente*, no.127, pp.45–74

—— (1977), *Los amigos políticos: partidos, elecciones y caciquismo en la España de la Restauración, 1875–1900*, Madrid

8

Community, Nation and State in Republican Spain, 1931–1938

Helen Graham

The military coup launched on 17–18 July 1936 against the Second Spanish Republic failed in its own terms. But although it did not achieve complete political and territorial control of Spain, the coup was remarkably successful in precipitating a state crisis of unprecedented proportions. Most obviously, the rebellion shattered crucial state instruments – the army itself and the police forces as well as the state administration. The extremeness of the ensuing fragmentation is only explicable, however, if we take into account that there were already major 'fault lines' within the Republican project itself.

By Republican project we mean the entirety of the counter-hegemonic project (i.e. one constructed against elite interests) which apparently brought together sectors of the labour Left with progressive republican groupings in an attempt to realise political, economic, social and cultural reforms to modernise and pluralise – in short, Europeanise – Spain as a polity and society. This integral reform programme, whose implementation was first attempted by the republican-Socialist coalition of 1931–3, would, so the theory went, sweep away the remains of the ancien regime both by renovating the state and by making the Republican nation.

But these attempts to implement reform were unsuccessful. This failure is usually attributed to increasing polarisation between 1934 and 1936 which caused the collapse of the political middle ground and ended in the military coup. But one could argue that in Spain – as elsewhere (Luebbert 1991)[1] – polarisation was a consequence rather than a cause: in other words, it was the *prior* failure of the inter-class Republican project between 1931 and 1933 which itself produced the symptoms we term 'polarisation'. For by 1933 not only had the counter-

---

1. Italy 1918–22, Weimar Germany and the Austrian Republic as the major contemporary European examples.

hegemonic project disintegrated into its labour and republican components – neither of which was strong enough on its own – but both were also internally highly fragmented. This disintegration was partly the result of intense pressures arising from the impact of the 1930s economic crisis. But there were also longer-term structural factors operating: Spain's particular historical experience of uneven development had already produced social and class formations which were highly *internally* fragmented.

Extrapolating from this, it could be argued that to understand why the Republican state and war effort came to be reconstructed at the beginning of 1937 (Graham 1991: 74–5) on the basis of an inter-class Popular Front alliance, we need to look beyond the specific, conscious ideological or political agendas of the Spanish parties (Graham 1991)[2] to a particular configuration of social forces. In other words, the reconstruction of the Popular Front was necessary precisely because of the high degree of internal social and cultural fragmentation obtaining among non-elite classes and constituencies in Spain in the 1930s.

But the immediate effect of the military coup was to increase the already severe fragmentation of counter-hegemonic political constituencies[3] and social/cultural identities. The Left had to seek with even greater urgency to re-integrate as many of the fragments of its now reduced potential support base into an inter-class 'popular' project (Juliá 1988: 256)[4] – the 'least weak' option – in an attempt to create a viable resistance to the military rebellion and also to have a minimally sufficient social base to be able to institutionalise the Republican order after winning the war. But reaching beyond the fragments was to prove a far from easy task and in some ways the coup would permanently alter the political landscape of the Left.

2. For example, the alliance's instrumentalisation in the Socialist movement's internecine war or the Communist Party's bid to become a mass party.

3. The intense fragmentation of these non-elite groups is not surprising when one considers that in the 1930s Spain's elites were themselves unable to come together to forge a coherent class project – either as a means of moving forward out of economic stagnation or in order to relegitimate their own rule after the fall of the monarchy in 1931. Indeed the integral crisis which underlay the decade in Spain was as much about this dual elite crisis as it was about the challenge posed by the Left and the excluded social constituencies it represented. In the 1940s Francoism itself was made as the military dictatorship mediated between the different sectors of capital in order to weld a new elite project together (Richards 1995).

4. 'The rise of a language of popular revolution in the 1930s, the return to a new popular front in 1935, the constitution of unitary committees in the summer of 1936, the definition of the war as a national/popular struggle in 1937; all of these phenomena, over and above the political leaders, must be understood in relation to a specific social structure and process of construction of the social classes.'

The first victim of the blast triggered by the July 1936 military rebellion was progressive republicanism itself. It suffered what was to prove a permanent political eclipse as a substantial part of its social base – smallholders, tenant farmers, provincial businessmen and some sectors of the professional clas̨es too – sided with the rebels. But if we return to our initial point, the military coup which crystallised this ꞓrocess was not so much the cause as an extreme consequence of reꞓ̨olicanism's prior failure to elaborate a strategy to sec̨re an adequate social support base for its reforming political project.

Essentially the pre-war Republican yc̨ars – and crucially 1931–3 – saw the exposure of republicanism's inability to deliver social or economic reform. As always, progressive republican groups claimed these as policy objectives, but as always they lacked policy *strategies* (Macarro Vera 1989). Their in practice largely laissez-faire approach to social and economic matters in the 1930s[5] was rooted in a fear of alienating their middle-class base (Juliá, 1994). Their concomitant strident anticlericalism was at some level undoubtedly perceived as a way of attracting a working-class base *without* running the political risks of other sorts of reform. Of course this plan was a non-starter given the severity of the economic crisis. And not only was strident anticlericalism an insufficient appeal to win them significant working-class support, but it also lost centrist and progressive republican groupings a significant part of their potential middle-class constituency to a clerical party of dubious democratic credentials (CEDA) whose agenda was driven at least in part by elite landed interests irreducibly antagonistic to the Republican project. By being both anticlerical and in practice not delivering on social or economic reform, the republicans ensured the atomisation of any potential counter-hegemonic project.

The republicans had little grasp of material politics. From the beginning they confused idea and reality, taking the *de jure* declaration of Republican liberties for their realisation – as if the mere existence of 'the Republic' would pacify marginalised social sectors (particularly those identified with the anarcho-syndicalist labour union, the CNT). But these sectors did not experience the Republic as the historic republican ideal of social and political inclusion but as continued legal, civil and economic exclusion – in the form of repressive legislation, violent state action, poverty and unemployment (Ealham 1993; Graham forthcoming).

1930s republicans, just like their nineteenth-century predecessors,

---

5. The republicans lacked an overall fiscal strategy in the 1930s, yet this was the essential precondition of viable social reform.

also tended to assume that the republican nation already existed. Blind to the multiple local frames of meaning which underlay the popular celebrations of the fall of the monarchy in April 1931, they failed to understand the need actively to take on the political and cultural task of 'making the nation', as a dynamic project *vis-a-vis* the future. In consequence, Republicans *only talked about the nation to each other* – that is, inside the Cortes [Spanish parliament] – and even then it was a rather ossified discourse: '1492 and all that.'[6] There was little sense of the political need to invent new traditions or revivify old ones. And we should remember too that there was no significant orchestrated public political dialogue until as late as 1935 – when Manuel Azaña, the pre-eminent leader of Spanish republicanism (and Republican President from May 1936), made his famous open air speeches (Preston 1987: 99–100). By then, of course, after two years of a conservative government blocking or reversing reform, the popular mood was distinctly radical which only increased the republicans' underlying ambivalence about popular mobilisation *per se* – as something dangerous and ultimately uncontrollable. And this growing unease would in turn expose yet more of republicanism's internal political contradictions.[7] These fears no doubt also reinforced the republicans' tendency to focus on 'top-down' state-building (although not necessarily very successfully so) – Azaña once commenting that the Republic began and ended with the state. But state renovation – encapsulating his own implicit conception of the Republic as an abstract intellectual challenge – was just not enough. At their peril the republicans ignored the need actively to engage in building a social base, to articulate a pro-active, over-arching state nationalism which could mobilise across specific social constituencies and regional allegiances. In the end the republicans Left behind too many fragments of their potential social base – both popular catholic and proletarian – and the ultimate cost of so doing was political eclipse by military coup.

But in the wake of that military coup, nor could the labour Left provide a sufficiently coherent alternative counter-hegemonic project. For, as we shall see, as with republicanism, similarly with the Left, the coup exposed and exacerbated all the underlying social, political and cultural contradictions and cleavages within it.

---

6. All of these problems are evident even in Azaña's parliamentary interventions, see for example those on Arnedo events, p.126; on the Sanjurjada (debate 10–11 August 1932), pp.358–60; on Catalanism, pp.262–304 (especially pp.271–2) and on Catalan statute, pp.288–9; on Casas Viejas (debate 2 February 1933), p.482; on amnesty (11 July 1933), p.718; and on the Popular Front (15 April 1936), in Manuel Azaña (1992).

7. See discussion of the concept 'pueblo', pp.11–12 below.

The heady days of popular resistance did, we know, produce radical experiments. But the essential precondition of these was the *abeyance* of the state. Under the impact of the coup the collapse of national political-administrative structures, whether those of the state or of parties and labour organisations, created the opportunity (and indeed the necessity) for what we have called the popular revolution: that is, the locally focused, social transformation of productive and distributive infrastructure in some parts of Republican territory. This took the form of industrial collectivisation, above all in urban Barcelona, and of agrarian collectives and co-operatives particularly in Aragón, the Levante and the Republican south (Jaén province, Ciudad Real and part of Córdoba).

But the abeyance of the state is not the same as its destruction. Simultaneously with these radical social developments whose protagonists were focused on local change, on community goals – whether in terms of a factory, urban neighbourhood or village – the political remnants of the Popular Front coalition were looking for ways to begin rebuilding a liberal-democratic Republican state. This weak state impulse was borne by the Socialist party and union leaderships (PSOE/ UGT), somewhat ambiguously backed up by centre and centre-Left regional nationalist forces in Catalonia and the Basque Country (the *Esquerra* (Catalan republican Left) and PNV (Basque Nationalist Party) respectively).

To these forces was added the newly-ascendant Spanish Communist Party (PCE). In the second half of 1936 the party was rapidly picking up a new base from centre-Left republicanism's old one – both urban and rural, and notably among professional sectors, especially those with ties to state employment. Even more importantly the PCE was functioning as a conduit, bringing previously unmobilised sectors of the population – both working and middle class – to the state by encadring them either in the PCE itself[8] or in one of a wide range of Popular Front organisations (*Guerra y Revolución*, vol.2, 1966: 267; Claudín 1975: 711–12). This 'nationalisation' of the population was part of a wider modernisation process which the war had speeded up. The scale and rapidity of the PCE's mobilisation of youth in the JSU (United Socialist Youth) and its associate organisations is particularly noteworthy

8. PCE membership was recorded (at the plenary session of the party's central committee) in March 1937 at 249,140 of whom over half (an estimated 131,600) were at the front. Recruitment was notably from among those of no previous political affiliation and, linked to this, particularly from among the conscripted young (see note 9). Wartime membership figures for Madrid (capital and province) for the period up to May 1938 also reinforce this picture, PCE archive (Madrid) microfilm XVII (214), frames 108–13.

(Claudín 1975: 230–1; Graham 1991: 73).[9] As the PCE's critics were only too ready to point out, the party was less concerned to attract a politically conscious vanguard than it was the Republican masses. And in the case of previously unmobilised young Spaniards of various social backgrounds it did so by appealing to a mix of the necessary (an efficient military defence), the novel/modern (Montero 1995: 131–2)[10] and (in some cases) the patriotic (Claudín 1975: 230–1).[11] The PCE was crucial to the viability of the new Frontist alliance for two reasons. First, because of the ambivalent attitude of bourgeois regional nationalists who saw the undermining of the central state as 'positive' insofar as it increased their own *de facto* power, even though they realised that state fracturing had in more general terms administered a shock to the socio-economic status quo they wished to see protected. Second, the PCE was important because the military rebellion had dislocated the national structures of the social democratic movement (PSOE and UGT) whose functioning was already seriously impaired by internal factional strife (Graham 1990, 1991).

In the aftermath of the July 1936 coup, these slowly gathering statist forces were opposed by the radical Left, comprising anti-state purist sectors of the libertarian movement (CNT-FAI-FIJL),[12] some sectors of the UGT, and the small, dissident marxist party, the POUM – whose base was essentially confined to Catalonia. If the radical Left wanted to protect and consolidate the social transformations which the force of the centrifugal blast rather than their own theoretical or strategic and organisational resources had facilitated, then they had to channel that social mobilisation into a *political* project which could articulate power throughout the Republican zone. In other words, the radical Left had actively to defeat Popular Frontist currents in the battle for state power.

9. As the name United Socialist Youth suggests, the Socialist and Communist youth organisations merged (in April 1936) having then a combined membership of between 40,000 and 50,000 (the vast majority of whom were Young Socialists). The fact that by January 1937 the JSU was estimated to have some 250,000 members incorporated into military units – this amounting to 70 per cent of the total membership – indicates the scale and rate of mobilisation in the Republican zone.

10. Russia together with other expressions of modernity such as 'aviation, the radio, the telephone gave life great interest'. Montero is discussing how in the 1920s the idea/image of revolutionary Russia was incorporated into the concept of modernity held by contemporary Spanish youth.

11. '. . .they were attracted by the party's military virtues and by a simplified ideology in which the idea of revolution was identified with anti-fascism mingled with patriotism.'

12. The libertarian movement was composed of the anarchosyndicalist trade union (CNT), the purist anarchist group (FAI) and the libertarian youth organisation (FIJL).

But they could not compete politically because the radical Left was even more internally fragmented than the Front. The fear that a political alliance might materialise between the CNT and UGT, as the heavy-weights of the Left, obsessed the Popular Frontists – as reports in the Socialist and Communist Party press during the second half of 1936 make clear. But they were mistaking (as others have since) union pro-tagonism in the *ad hoc* structures of the early weeks and months of the conflict – necessary to cover essential functions (defence, distribution, supply, etc.) in the face of *state* crisis – for an articulated political strategy that could challenge the Popular Front in its bid to reconstruct the liberal democratic order and bourgeois state power.

The internal fragmentation and weakness of the Left had many facets. Partly it was determined by the loss of the most radical sectors of the Republican base – the landless proletariat – when large areas of the rural south fell to the military rebels in the early months of the war. In addition, both the UGT and the CNT had serious structural limitations as organisations. Both were 'invertebrate': each lacked the necessary organisational articulation which could have allowed them to operate as an alternative political power in place of the bourgeois state. As the unions lacked the organisational means to channel political power, then the social radicalism of the July Days had no future. More-over, there were ideological contradictions within the CNT (between pro-Frontists and anti-state purists) as well as significant, debilitating divisions between the CNT and the UGT. Apart from more narrowly organisational rivalries, these divisions stemmed from the antagonistic relations between sectors of their respective social constituencies and memberships. (In general terms the UGT tended to unionise relatively privileged sectors of the working class – artisans, skilled workers, etc. – while the CNT's constituency was poorer, unskilled, migrant labour or the unemployed, in short, the dispossessed and the marginal.) The crisis conditions of the 1930s exacerbated these tensions between UGT and CNT sectors, particularly in relation to strike policy, and the ensuing legacy of bitterness was a significant obstacle to wartime alli-ance.

As a result of these factors, which I have examined in greater detail elsewhere (Graham forthcoming), we get the rearticulation of the Pop-ular Front as the least weak option. Above and beyond the specific political agendas of the Socialists and the PCE, this option had the potential to resume the maximum possible number of fragments of the counter-hegemonic project. These fragments ranged from the organised urban working class (in the PSOE and UGT and to a lesser extent in the PCE), to the old republican middle classes now in the PCE and to a certain degree in the Catalan PSUC and also in the new white-collar unions (often PCE-led) of the UGT (especially in Catalonia), all the way to the post-18 July influx of the newly encadred of various social provenance (and particularly the young as we have mentioned) mainly to the PCE and/or to the many parallel Popular Front organisations it promoted (the anti-fascist women's alliance, girls' and boys' associations, a variety of organisations connected with rearguard social/welfare services, the soldiers' clubs, etc.). Also forming an important part of this Republican alliance were the regional nationalist groupings of *Esquerra* in Catalonia (which included the small Catalan peasantry or *Rabassaires*) and, more problematically, the PNV in the Republican Basque Country (Vizcaya).

The Front's proponents saw it as offering the best basis for the Republican war effort (and for national reconstruction beyond that) precisely because Popular Front was about reconstructing state power. This was certainly achieved to a considerable extent – in terms of the army (militarisation), police cadres, control of frontiers, economic control (the centralisation of industrial/trade control, customs and exports, etc. in ministerial hands). But then the Popular Front faced the problem of the claims of its Catalan and Basque nationalist constituents to what were effectively 'pieces of the state'. The issue here was not the socio-economic basis of state power *per se* – those battles died with the social revolution in 1936. Both Basque and Catalan nationalists represented broadly the same kind of political and social class forces as their Popular Front counterparts of the central Republican government. For it was not only the Basque Country's big industrial bourgeoisie but *also Catalonia's* that was 'in emigration' (often in fact in Nationalist, i.e. rebel-held, San Sebastián) waiting on Republican defeat and discussing future economic plans.

Regional nationalist claims in Catalonia and the Basque Country to a piece of the state were legitimised by reference to a particular historical experience, the cultural specificity deriving from it, and in relation to the Republic's commitment to the principle of a democratic, plural system. But the problem here was the war itself. The Republican state, struggling to consolidate itself in order to fight the war, could not afford the practical consequences of the autonomy statutes – in terms of the lack of co-ordination, the time and energy spent on disputes over the respective political and economic jurisdiction of central and autonomous governments, the waste of human energy and (to some extent) material resources this involved and the inefficiency and demoralisation which resulted. 1937–8 saw this jurisdictional battle within the Republican camp undermine the Popular Front alliance. But my intention here is not to cast nationalist agendas in the Republican zone as the 'enemy', but rather to suggest that the situation points us back to the longstanding problem with the Republican project: the absence of an overarching, mobilising state nationalism.

The weakness of the Popular Front strategy (as of its predecessor, the Republican project of 1931–6) lay in its privileging state construction virtually to the exclusion of building the Republican nation. This tendency was of course massively boosted by the fact that the war was being fought in desperate and ever-deteriorating conditions of material shortage, as a result of the operation of Non-Intervention which amounted to an embargo on the Republic alone. (Its impact over time, the increasing material deprivation, especially hunger, as the war progressed and the burgeoning black market, seriously undermined the Popular Front – all of which means that we must construct the social history of the Republic at war if we are properly to understand its political failure.) But precisely because of this situation the Popular Front war effort needed a national discourse even more acutely, in order to hold the fragments together in spite of savage material disadvantage and to mobilise and infuse morale into the vital civilian front.

Ironically of course the rapid political eclipse of the libertarian movement (CNT-FAI-FIJL) removed the force which more than any other on the Left had a discourse and practice of community. Its great strength – contrasting with its political weakness (the lack of an articulating political project) – was its superior appreciation of the dynamics of popular mobilisation. The libertarians understood its basis in local imperatives and community goals, in the possibility of changing the immediate lived environment in all its aspects, social, economic and cultural as well as political. They also understood the value of mobilisation as a liberating, socially and culturally transformative *process*, as compared with the Popular Frontist concentration on end result – the mobilisation/nationalisation of the Republican population for the state/ war effort. And even though the libertarians did not articulate it as such, this underlines for us the crucial missing link: a 'bottom-up' linkage between the fragmented popular constituencies of Republican Spain and the Republican state.

The wartime Popular Front's lack of an adequate 'national' discourse, its failure to build languages or elaborate policies to make the nation was in part due to the pressure of other tasks. But the concentration on the state also had a lot to do with the longstanding perspectives and preoccupations of Spanish social democracy. Its cultural project had always been a much lower priority and was therefore significantly less developed[13] than either the republicans' or anarchists' (Cobb 1995: 134). That wartime premier Juan Negrín and his Socialist colleagues seemingly thought it appropriate to use the same abstract, universalist Enlightenment discourse of national liberation when addressing the disparate domestic constituencies of the Republic as its statesmen and diplomats used in international forums such as the League of Nations, indicates a serious failure of political imagination and strategy. Negrín's comment that the Republic represents the legitimate government and state, which is why Burgos (the rebel capital) clings to 'tradition', was obviously meant in an upbeat way. But the problem was that the Republic was sorely in need of some 'traditions' which it should have invented years ago.

But at root the PSOE was uncertain about how to handle mass popular mobilisation in the war, which recalls the republicans' deep unease about it the pre-war period (Graham forthcoming).[14] For all that the 'pueblo' (people) was the great rhetorical invocation of historic republicanism in Spain – its liberty and improvement justifying the movement's very existence – the republicans had no means of handling the transformation of an objectified, passive 'pueblo' into an historical subject in its own right (Graham and Labanyi 1995: 6, 15–16). This transformation, occurring in Spain as part of a wider process of social and economic change (i.e. modernisation) but speeded up by the war, exposed the political contradictions and insufficiencies which finally precipitated republican eclipse in July 1936.

The PSOE's similar difficulties here are perhaps unsurprising in view of both its closeness to the political culture of republicanism in many respects (Montero 1995: 131)[15] and given the heterogeneity of the fragments of 'pueblo' which the wartime Republic was called upon to hold together in an alliance. But when the eclipse of republicanism meant the axis of the Popular Front had to be reconstructed, this created an opportunity for the ascendancy of the Spanish Communist Party which

13. It was not until c.1915–20 that the Socialist movement's union centres and *casas del pueblo* seriously began to develop educational and cultural activities; see Pamela Radcliff (forthcoming), p.344, n.3 and p.355, n.29 (page references to ms copy). It is also true that in the Spanish Socialist movement – as in many European social democratic movements – ironically, culture was implicitly understood as *bourgeois* culture (workers should be encouraged to appreciate the 'great' works of art/ literature) (Gruber 1991).

14. For their disquiet in February 1936 when the Popular Front alliance was showing signs of extending beyond parliament to become a movement of mass mobilisation and even direct action in local community spaces.

15. 'By the time the Socialists had joined the republicans in the Conjunción Republicano-Socialista of 1909 there was already a predominant current supportive of a reformist republican vision. As Araquistain remarked, they had given up their ideal Socialist city for that of the republicans.'

proved a good deal more able to confront the vital task of mass mobilisation. As a 'new' party the PCE was not weighed down by the sense
of organisational patrimony which so paralysed the Spanish Socialist
movement (although much more so the veteran UGT leaders than the
parliamentary Socialists associated with the PSOE's wartime executive). But, even so, the PCE had a much more instrumental conception
of party organisation and was consequently more prepared to take risks
in the formidable and erosive task of mobilising and holding together
(via the many 'umbrella' organisations of the Popular Front (see
above)) the disparate and antagonistic fragments of a 'pueblo' which
could only constitute a viable counter-hegemonic project insofar as it
could be held together in a single alliance (Graham 1996).

As we have seen, the Civil War saw the PCE undergo a process of
'republicanisation' whereby it acquired a social base from among both
urban and rural middle-class sectors formerly encadred by republicanism. At the same time the party retained and indeed increased its
working-class base, thus creating a basis for the inter-class, *popular*
initiative of Popular Front within itself. As a hybrid party, it reunited
the fragments of the counter-hegemonic strategy. Its democratic centralist structure, and resulting 'iron discipline', allowed it to maintain an
inter-class line in spite of the enormous tensions arising from the acute
political, economic and social contradictions present in a fragmented
Republican zone. There was no way in which the conflicting demands
these produced could be reconciled in the short term or medium term.
What is being argued here is that keeping the Republican coalition
together for the duration of the war required a party that had a better
grasp of strategic politics than did the 'old republicans' and which,
unlike the PSOE, could be populist and bear the contradictions.[16] The
fact that the PCE could is what one might term the 'functionality of
democratic centralism' in the context of 1930s Spain.

The PCE was central to the task of state reconstruction as we have
seen, but it also had some awareness of the need to make the nation, to
reach out to the Republic's varied social constituencies and begin the
task of assimilating them. The PSOE's response was in general very
disdainful: it disapproved of the PCE's 'lowest common denominator'
approach to popular mobilisation. For example, in Almería the local
Socialists wrote to the PSOE executive deprecating the PCE's 'exces-
sive publicity, dramatic gestures, [its] vulgar and ornate ritual'. But the

---

16. Benefit of hindsight is in operation here, of course, since I am implicitly arguing that the PCE's populism – the essential (if not necessarily sufficient) precondition
of a viable Republican alliance – was the only alternative to the state model/
authoritarian modernisation which was shaped by the Nationalist victors/Francoism.

same letter admits the results of PCE activity: 'the people here are uneducated and impressionable. . .until very recently in thrall to religion. . .which though distorted met a certain need in them. Communist propaganda, full of puerile flourishes, peppered with clichés and accompanied by impressive gestures, has filled the void. . ... The Socialist Party resolves [therefore] to take part in each and every initiative, event, meeting etc. *however ridiculous these appear to us to be*'(Graham 1991: 119; my italics). The Socialists habitually criticised the PCE for its 'hypocritical' pursuit of contradictory policies under the slogan of Popular Front, attributing this to outright political opportunism. But we need to see it as more than this. Even if the PCE's policy line derived from the standard Popular Front 'package' after the Soviet Union and Comintern had begun promoting inter-class anti-fascist alliances in 1935 (Graham and Preston 1987: 1–19) – and the PCE's key slogan/strategy for blurring class distinctions, the 'pueblo laborioso' (labouring nation), introduced around February 1936, certainly did so derive – it still leaves wide open questions about what these policies meant in the Spanish context, why they were appropriate or not, how they operated and with what consequences (Graham 1996).

Indeed our definition of the PCE in the Civil War period is in need of some rethinking. The party's allegiance, via democratic centralism, to a supranational authority – namely the Communist Party of the Soviet Union (CPSU) – has produced some rather simplistic assessments of the PCE's dynamic, to this day not much revised in Anglo-Saxon historiography (Bolloten 1961, 1991),[17] as being somehow reducible to the CPSU's agenda: or, to put it another way, that democratic centralism makes it meaningless to examine the PCE's evolution in relation to the political (and structural) imperatives of the Republic. But at the end of the day the PCE was a *national* party: we need to examine its evolution in the context of the long-term development of the Spanish Left and in the framework of domestic imperatives and conflicts (not least those of the Spanish state) which the Civil War provoked or exacerbated.

Certainly what one could term the 'dysfunctionality of Stalinism' is a factor in the picture: PCE sectarianism, the witchhunts against and assassinations of Trotskyists and other dissidents (most notoriously in the case of the POUM (Munis 1948; Broué & Témime 1972; Suárez

---

17. Bolloten's work – republished in various revised and augmented forms (see References) – has been most influential in this respect. Although it has been implicitly superseded by the research of the last decade, the lack of an up-to-date overview analysis of the Spanish Left in the 1930s or of the Republican state at war has meant that beyond Spain, and above all among an Anglo-American readership, Bolloten's views still have a greater currency than they merit.

1974; *Revolutionary History* 1992)), the specific influence of Comintern advisors, external tensions (often to do with vagaries of the supply of war materials)[18] – all these things meant that in the long run the Spanish Communist Party undermined its own objectives, contributing significantly to the erosion of the Popular Front by mid-1938.

But none of this diminishes the basic argument here, that something else was working through the PCE as the strategic key to an integrated Popular Front strategy, something that went well beyond specific party/ organisational agendas and certainly beyond the Comintern's. I would argue that this has to do with trying to overcome certain structural deficits – that is, of highly internally fragmented social and class forms – which derived from Spain's particular experience of uneven development over the long term.

References

Alpert, Michael (1994), *A New International History of the Spanish Civil War*, London

Azaña, Manuel (1992), *Discursos parlamentarios*, ed. J. Paniagua Fuentes, Congreso de Diputados, Madrid

Bolloten, Burnett (1961), *The Grand Camouflage. The Communist Conspiracy in the Civil War*, New York

—— (1991), *The Spanish Civil War. Revolution and Counterrevolution*, Hemel Hempstead

Broué, Pierre and Témime, Emile (1972), *The Revolution and the Civil War in Spain*, London

Claudín, Fernando (1975), *The Communist Movement. From Comintern to Cominform*, Harmondsworth

Cobb, Christopher (1995), 'The Republican State and Mass Educational-Cultural Initiatives', in Graham, Helen and Labanyi, Jo (eds), *Spanish Cultural Studies, An Introduction. The Struggle for Modernity*, Oxford, pp.133–8

18. Because of the arms embargo imposed on the Republic by the largely British-inspired policy of Non-Intervention (Little 1985, 1988; Moradiellos 1990, 1991; Alpert 1994), Soviet procurement of war materials was what allowed it to survive/wage war against the rebels and their Axis backers. This material dependence – the product of Non-Intervention itself – gave the Soviet Union leverage in wartime Republican Spain it would not otherwise have had. We must, however, distinguish between the conflicts produced by this *external* pressure and those conflicts rooted in *domestic* political, socio-economic, class and cultural divisions. The failure to distinguish has led to some distorted analyses of key events – most notably the May rebellion (Barcelona 1937). This article is part of a larger project on the Republican state at war which attempts to redress this balance.

Ealham, Chris (1993), 'Crime and Punishment in 1930s Barcelona', in *History Today*, vol.43, October, pp.31–7

Graham, Helen (1990), 'The Eclipse of the Socialist Left: 1934–1937', in Lannon, Frances and Preston, Paul (eds), *Elites and Power in Twentieth-Century Spain. Essays in Honour of Sir Raymond Carr*, Oxford, pp.127–51

—— (1991), *Socialism and War. The Spanish Socialist Party in Power and Crisis 1936–1939*, Cambridge

—— (1996) 'War, Modernity and Reform: the Premiership of Juan Negrín 1937–1939', in Preston, Paul and Mackenzie, Ann L., *The Republic Besieged: Civil War in Spain, 1936–1939*, Edinburgh, pp. 163–96

—— (forthcoming), 'Spain 1936. Resistance and Revolution: the Flaws in the Front', in Kirk, Tim and McElligott, Tony (eds), *Community, Authority and Resistance to Fascism in Europe*, Cambridge

Graham, Helen and Labanyi, Jo (1995), 'Culture and Modernity: The Case of Spain', in Graham, Helen and Labanyi, Jo (eds), *Spanish Cultural Studies, An Introduction. The Struggle for Modernity*, Oxford, pp.1–19

Graham, Helen and Preston, Paul (eds) (1987), *The Popular Front in Europe*, London

Gruber, Helmut (1991), *Red Vienna. Experiment in Working Class Culture 1919–1934*, Oxford

Guerra y revolución en España 1936–1939, (vol.2) (1966), Moscow

Juliá, Santos (1988), 'Socialismo en los años treinta: recientes tendencias de investigación', in Juliá, Santos (ed.), *El socialismo en las naciones y regiones*, Madrid, pp.247–56

—— (1994), 'La experiencia del poder: la izquierda republicana 1931–1933', in Townson, Nigel (ed.), *El republicanismo en España (1830–1977)*, Madrid, pp.165–92

Little, Douglas (1985), *Malevolent Neutrality. The United States, Great Britain and the Origins of the Spanish Civil War*, Ithaca

—— (1988), 'Red-Scare, 1936: Anti-Bolshevism and the Origins of British Non-Intervention in the Spanish Civil War', in *Journal of Contemporary History*, vol.23, no.2, pp.291–311

Luebbert, G.M. (1991), *Liberalism, Fascism or Social Democracy: Social Classes and the Political Origins of Regimes in Inter-War Europe*, Oxford

Macarro Vera, José Manuel (1989),'Social and Economic Policies of the Spanish Left in Theory and in Practice', in Alexander, Martin S. and Graham, Helen (eds), *The French and Spanish Popular Fronts. Comparative Perspectives*, Cambridge, pp.171–84

Montero, Enrique (1995), 'Reform Idealized: the Intellectual and Ideological Origins of the Second Republic', in Graham, Helen and Labanyi, Jo (eds), *Spanish Cultural Studies, An Introduction. The Struggle for Modernity*, Oxford, pp.124–33

Moradiellos, Enrique (1990), *Neutralidad benévola: el gobierno británico y la insurrección militar española de 1936*, Oviedo

—— (1991), 'The Origins of British Non-Intervention in the Spanish Civil War: Anglo-Spanish Relations in early 1936', *European History Quarterly*, vol.21, no.3, pp.441–64

Munis, Grandizo (1948), *Jalones de derrota, promesa de victoria*, Mexico City

Preston, Paul (1987),'The Creation of the Popular Front in Spain', in Graham, Helen, and Preston, Paul (eds), *The Popular Front in Europe*, London, pp.84–105

Radcliff, Pamela (forthcoming), *Politics, Culture and Collective Action in a Spanish City: Gijón 1900–1937*, Cambridge

Revolutionary History (1992), *The Spanish Civil War: the View from the Left*, vol.4, nos.1/2, London

Richards, Mike (1995), '"Terror and Progress": Industrialisation, Modernity and the Making of Francoism', in Graham, Helen and Labanyi, Jo (eds), *Spanish Cultural Studies, An Introduction. The Struggle for Modernity*, Oxford, pp.173–82

Suárez, Andrés (1974), *El proceso contra el POUM*, Paris

–9–

Constructing the Nationalist State: Self-Sufficiency and Regeneration in the Early Franco Years[1]

Michael Richards

The decade following the formal ending of the Spanish Civil War in 1939 was a period of extreme violence in Spain. In social, economic and political terms the 1940s witnessed the continuation of the conflict fought with all the forces that the nascent Francoist State could muster. Franco's victory was to be institutionalised principally through the use of physical terror, but also through the legislative actions of the state, through the day-to-day regulation of economic activity and through the construction of a coherent ideology of nationalism. These instruments of repression were not mutually exclusive. They were all related to what the leaders and ideologues of the dictatorship saw as the 'resurgence of the *Patria*'. It was in the interests of this that Francoism's bleak vision of modernity – the confirmation of its victory over democracy, as represented by the Second Republic of the 1930s, and industrialisation at any cost – was pursued.

The purpose of this chapter is to suggest how *autarky*, the state's strategy of economic self-sufficiency, can be explained by the particular conception of *the nation* which the regime sought to foster. Although this vision of the nation in Spain after 1939 was often contradictory, there were a limited number of features which were a constant part of the ideological framework around which the 'New Spain' was to be constructed (Viver Pi-Sunyer 1980). These were, first, an 'organicist' understanding of the *Patria* itself; that is, Spain had to be a 'natural' entity, a 'living organism', composed of a collectivity which shared this particular understanding of the Fatherland. This organicist conception

1. The research on which this chapter is based was partly facilitated by financial assistance from the British Academy and the Cañada Blanch Foundation for which I am grateful. Intellectually, it owes a good deal to discussions over several years with Helen Graham. For its weaknesses, though, the author is wholly culpable.

was foreshadowed in the 'organic determinism' of Regenerationist thinkers around the turn-of-the-century (Ramsden 1974), and organicism was central to the belief-system of Francoist military officers (Losada Malvárez 1990: 28–30). Second, the notion of *unity* was central to this Francoist ideology. The *Patria*, according to Franco himself, was 'spiritual unity, social unity, historic unity'. Catholicism was to be 'the crucible of nationality'.[2] In this pursuit of unity the state was to be central. It was through organised power that the nation would be remade and the people disciplined. This unity, imposed by the state, entailed an iron centralism which denied the existence of regional cultural difference. Finally, unity based upon the idea of the *Patria* was to be reflected in economic and social relations. Autarky was, above all else, the economic manifestation of this extreme nationalism. The 'harmonisation' of capital and labour, 'united' through state corporativism, in 'the interests of the nation', was the rhetoric designed to deny the perpetuation of extreme exploitation in the Spanish post war.

Thus autarky both originated with and provoked effects in not only the economic sphere but also the political and cultural realms.[3] In the pursuit of this re-organisation of the *Patria*, the country, or, more specifically, the people, were consciously divided by the regime, with the aid of its ideologues, into 'Spain' and 'anti-Spain'. The only legitimate collective identity, according to Francoists, was the *Patria*, composed of those who had contributed to the victory of Franco. The country was to be 're-made' in the image of the myth of Franco's 'Crusade' to 'save Christian civilisation' as represented by Catholic Spain. Accordingly, the symbols utilised by Francoism were borrowed from the fifteenth-century era of Ferdinand and Isabella when Spain had previously triumphed over 'malignant foreign powers'. The notion of *expulsion* was once again to be extremely important, at several levels, during the Franco era.[4]

This was the point of departure both for the regime's systematic purge of society and its intervention in economic relations. The obvious brutalities of 'economic self-sufficiency', which contributed to the devastating scarcities of the 1940s, derived from this determination

2. Franco's speech on 24 June 1938.

3. Although this is not meant to suggest that these 'spheres' are ever completely distinct. However, this 'overlap' needs to be shown through analysis and this is the purpose of this chapter.

4. The fifteenth-century *Reconquista* saw the defeat and expulsion of Islam and the Jews. Franco, after 1939, enforced both the physical expulsion of hundreds of thousands of Republicans, as well as a kind of expulsion of free thought through the proscription of 'foreign ideas'.

to punish, while the pursuit of autarky itself facilitated the intervention of the state at all levels in society. In other words, the subject of this chapter is the way in which autarky lent a particularly repressive nature to the centralising nationalism of the Francoism of the 1940s.

Autarky, then, is about nationalism. It has most often been associated with preparations for war or imperial conquest and national industrialisation through the substitution of imports. Both of these influences were significant in Spain in the 1940s (Buesa Blanco et al. 1984; Viñas 1984).

However, the purpose of this chapter is to argue that autarky under the Spanish dictatorship can only be more fully explained by looking at the will of the Franco regime to shape society very brutally through the imposition of a particular view of Spanishness. Indeed, autarky in Spain, as a key element of Francoism's negation of liberalism, came to be, in practice, more consistently applied politically and culturally than economically. While economic elites had relative freedom of manoeuvre, the ideological control of the rest of society was much more rigidly enforced (Richards 1995).

Therefore, in Spain, in the 1940s, *ideology, violence* and *industrialisation* came together in both the theory and practice of autarky. These three elements strongly conditioned, and were strongly conditioned by, a particular kind of nationalism. This chapter, then, will address the question of how these factors influenced the particular form of extreme nationalism represented by autarky in the 1940s.

Ideology

The ideological roots of Francoism lie in a blending of the ideas of specifically Spanish movements with those of European fascist movements and regimes. 'Spanishness' (or *Hispanidad*), the nationalist ideological doctrine around which the Catholic unity of the *Patria* was to be built (González Calleja and Limón Nevado 1988; Escudero 1994), was conceptualised through the influences of integrist Catholicism, regenerationism, authoritarian Carlist monarchism (or *Tradicionalismo*), authoritarian Alfonsine monarchism (via *Acción Española* and *Renovación Española*), and the 26-point programme of the fascist Falange. These influences overlapped to a considerable degree although there were also contradictions particularly in attitudes towards tradition and modernisation.

The main ingredients of this nationalist ideological brew were the eulogising of the Spanish peasantry as the embodiment of national virtues; the maintenance of private property; a revaluation of violence as 'creative' and 'purifying' (Redondo 1939: 27–9);[5] militarism and martial values; and the idea of a national unity and a spiritual and material resurgence based upon the development of myths of empire, Reconquest and Counter-Reformation (Losada Malvárez 1990: 35–44).

The verification of a 'common past' was seen as essential in achieving unity in the present and a 'positive' image for the future. This was to be pursued by the elaboration of a set of ideas based on the notion of Spain's historic destiny as a people (or, more strictly, as a 'living entity') chosen by providence as a source of 'good' (Escudero 1994). An appropriate set of symbols was manufactured in accord with this conceptualisation of Spain's history – a conception which appropriated time itself in acknowledging no distinctions between past, present and future. The 'glorious triumph' of Franco was directly compared to the exploits of the great warrior heroes and empire-builders of Spain's past, like Philip II or El Cid. Indeed, the ceremonies of triumph staged by the regime consistently re-enacted the victory parades of the heroic figures of the Middle Ages, like El Cid, and school textbooks made explicit reference to a continuity in Spanish resurgence between the warrior rulers of the past and the Caudillo himself. Christopher Columbus, an Italian, born in Genoa, was fully appropriated by the regime as a 'Spaniard' since his *enterprises* were 'Spanish'. Indeed, the anniversary of the discovery of America, The Day of the Race (*Día de la Raza*), was also appropriated for the glorification of the dictatorship and was celebrated with great magnificence (Preston 1993: xvii, 329–30, 582–3). The conquistadors of the fifteenth century were portrayed as the ideal of Spanishness against which various 'others' – indigenous peoples, republicans, the Spanish working class – were to be measured (Escudero 1994: 138–263).

In the post-1939 period these concepts were built upon the various meanings of the traditional dichotomy in Spain of degeneration and regeneration.[6] In many ways this way of conceiving of the nation was enunciated in the professed determination to 'purify' or 'purge' Spain (or its people) in the aftermath of the Civil War. Redemption, both in

5. See, also, for example, Ramiro Ledesma Ramos, 'La legitimidad y la fecundidad de la violencia', *Conquista del Estado*, 23 May 1931; José Antonio Primo de Rivera, interview, *La Voz*, 14 February 1936.

6. The fears and concerns in Spanish society about moral and racial degeneration in Spain have not been written of in very extensively historical terms (Pérez Ledesma 1993). However, the novels of Spanish writers around the turn of the century, like Pío Baroja, seem often concerned with ideas of degeneration. Despite this relative lack, it is interesting that 'the problem of Spain' is so often 'diagnosed' in pathological terms by regenerationist philosophers and political thinkers. The obvious example, although there are countless others, might be José Ortega y Gasset, *España invertebrada*, originally published in 1921.

individual and national terms, was seen as only coming through suffering and sacrifice. This was perceived as a way of proving allegiance to the *Patria* as defined by the victors. Franco himself considered that '. . .the suffering of a nation at a particular point of its history is no caprice; it is spiritual punishment, the punishment which God imposes upon a distorted life, upon an unclean history'.[7] It was the task of the 'New Spain' to develop a 'purified' nation. This desire to 'purify' appears to have its origins both in the idea of redemption and the expiation of sin associated with Catholicism, and in the strand of regenerationist thought and *casticismo*,[8] linked to European social-Darwinist theories exemplified or perpetuated by such writers as Joaquín Costa, Miguel de Unamuno, Angel Ganivet, Azorín, Ramiro de Maeztu or José Antonio Primo de Rivera, in the period from the 1890s to the 1930s.

The tradition of regenerationist thought in Spain, which so influenced Francoist ideology, revolved around several related ideas: first, it was believed that a particular Spanish essence existed which could be defined and perpetuated; second, the natural sciences, particularly Darwinist biology, were highly influential and were seen as determining the future development of Spain; third, the evaluation of constitutional politics was marked by a belief that they could only lead to national degeneration and decline; an 'Iron Surgeon' was to be repeatedly called for to cure the ills of the country; fourth, the notion of economic self-sufficiency was reinforced; fifth, the loss of the country's last American colonies, through military defeat in 1898, was seen as symbolic of this national malaise (Tuñón de Lara 1986). Regenerationism did not necessarily separate Francoism from other fascist regimes and movements in the Europe of the 1920s, 1930s and 1940s. The notion of some kind of 'national re-birth' was common to all fascisms (Griffin 1991). Indeed, regenerationism could be seen as Spain's own 'pre-fascism', analogous to the radical-nationalist ideologies of political movements in Italy around the time of the defeat at Adowa in 1896.

Often a concomitant preoccupation for the 'mental health' of Spain implied a shunning of outside or foreign influences. In political terms, liberalism, for example, was seen by Catholic traditionalists as a 'foreign disease', a 'virus' which had infected Spain in the nineteenth century and caused its decline (Blinkhorn 1979: 15–68). According to this philosophy, some sense of order needed to be imposed upon Spanish society which was made up of 'disjointed fragments of different colours, like a beggar's clothing' (Ganivet 1897, 1961 edn: 267).

---

7. Franco's speech, Jaén, 18 March 1940.
8. *Casticismo* has been defined as the search for the essence of Spain in a pure caste or race and the exclusion of foreign elements.

One of the principal concerns of Ganivet's work was *abulia*, originally a medical-psychological term signifying spinelessness, apathy or 'paralysis of the will'. He concluded that Spain suffered from this condition on a national scale. *Abulia* was frequently referred to in Spanish literary works too at this time.

Often, for those who preached regenerationism, Castile was seen as having, necessarily, to be centralising too. Indeed, it was claimed that Castile was possessed of a conquering and imperious 'personality' which would not be denied (Ramsden 1974: 20–1; Losada Malvárez 1990: 25–8). Unity could be achieved by drawing on what Angel Ganivet saw as the particular characteristics of the Iberian people: '. . .we withdraw ourselves. . .to labour so that an original conception might become formed upon our soil. . ... I have faith in the creative virtue of our land.' For him, the restoration of national life required '. . .the concentration of all our energies within our national territory. All the doors through which the Spanish spirit has escaped must be closed with bolts and locks. . .' (Ganivet 1943: 39). The works of Ganivet were reprinted by the state party publishing house in the early 1940s. Fresh interest was aroused in these publications since they were resurrected in order to coincide with the very public transfer of the author's mortal remains to Spain from abroad where he had committed suicide four months after the loss of Cuba in 1898.

The essence of the Spanish character was usually seen as being embodied in the virtues of the Spanish small-holding peasantry of Castile: hard-working, thrifty, selfless, stoical and with an allegiance to the spiritual concept of Spain. The ultimate element in the idealistic foundation of Spain was the 'natural, human stoicism of Seneca'. These virtues, it was believed, could be broadened to encompass Spanish society generally. Miguel de Unamuno's 'nucleus' of the 'eternal Spain' was to be found in the peasantry of Castile: 'There in the interior lives a race of dry complexion, hard and wiry, toasted by the sun and cut down by the cold, a race of sober men, the product of a long selection by the frosts of the cruellest winters and a series of periodic penuries, suited to the inclemencies of the climate and the poverty of life.' The essences of Spanishness were deposited in men, according to Unamuno, like 'sediments' left by a flowing river over centuries. Tradition or 'national character' was to be found in the 'silent lives of millions of men without history' (Unamuno 1895, 1986 edn).

Although the philosophical tradition was vulgarised by political leaders and ideologues in the pursuit of social and political objectives, regenerationism was a constant reference point in the 1930s and 1940s. Around the turn of the century, the social, political and intellectual atmosphere of decline permeated everyday life, at least for the middle classes. Indeed, it might be argued that the particular kind of social development overseen by the Franco dictatorship, initiated in the immediate post-Civil War years, constituted the final achievement of the provincial middle-class aspirations which had been denied during the first third of the century.

This sense of decline was an important component of the climate during the formative years of Franco and his leading ministers such as Juan Antonio Suanzes, the Caudillo's first Minister of Industry and the architect of autarky and industrialisation in the 1940s and 1950s, whose policy and personality were encapsulated in his belief in 'industrial regenerationism, Catholic corporativism and the traditional mentality of the engineer' (Schwarz and González 1978: 22–37), and Luis Carrero Blanco, the dictator's most faithful lieutenant throughout the long duration of the dictatorship. Franco was five-and-a-half years old in 1898 when the remnants of the defeated Spanish fleet limped back to port after the war with the United States. The effect was considerable (Vázquez Montalbán 1978: 10–11, 47–51; Payne 1987: 248). In 1943 the Caudillo made a revealing speech in which he recalled his childhood in Ferrol, on the Galician coast, where he frequently visited the shipyards and saw painted on many of the walls the despairing legend: 'Ships, ships, ships, days of grandeur of the Fatherland' (*'Barcos, barcos, barcos, días de grandeza de la Patria'*), while lamenting the fact that the yards were in silence and nothing was being produced.[9] He would come to see his greatest achievement as wiping out the shame of this catastrophe (Preston 1993: 6). The 'Disaster' of 1898 and the development of regenerationism also influenced wider society – the Catalan bourgeoisie, in particular, was traumatised by the loss of the colonies (Harrison 1990).

The so-called 'problem of Spain' was resurrected as a focus of political and philosophical thought as the economic and social crisis of the 1930s polarised society into two broad antagonistic camps. The ideological formulations produced by the political Right, in response to continued social change and the reforms of the Second Republic, as exemplified in Maeztu's *Defensa de la Hispanidad* (1934) or Ernesto Giménez Caballero's *Genio de España* (1932), were heavily influenced by the regenerationist tradition. In this last work the 'Disaster' of 1898 is used as a symbol of national historic degeneration. According to Giménez, there had been thirteen '1898s'. The first 1898 was the peace signed in Munster in 1648 by which Spain lost its first imperial territories. The sixth 1898 was in 1713 when Gibraltar was lost. The twelfth was 1898 itself. The thirteenth was in 1930 when republicans

9. *Información*, August 1943, p.408. The re-establishing of Spanish naval power was a priority of Franco, Suanzes and Carrero Blanco.

and the Left agreed in the Pact of San Sebastián to concede the statute of autonomy to Catalonia.[10]

Unsurprisingly, then, the central precepts of regenerationist thought continued to form the cultural basis and practical guidelines to Francoist ideology, since the regime saw as its basic task the institutionalisation of the interests of the Right as pursued in the 1930s. Suspicion of that which was not 'organic' to Spain; eulogisation of the peasantry which, during the Civil War, had given proof of its 'great Christian and patriotic fervour'; the authoritarian (or 'surgical') statist organisation of society and labour through the blending of Catholic and fascist corporative ideas and structures; these were the fundaments of the Francoist 'New State' (Montero 1939). The reality of life for Spanish peasants under Francoism belied this constructed image (Castillo 1979). In terms of economic development the notion of the existence of essential Spanish characteristics would become vital in justifying the extracting of huge sacrifices from the working population (París 1942; Robert 1943). Working-class Spaniards, it seemed, had an 'inbred' ability to work long hours with hardly any material sustenance. According to an informant of the state party's investigation bureau, writing in 1946, '(the people) will always be able to be asked for sacrifices since they have already been making them for so many years. . .'.[11] Poverty was elevated into a positive national virtue, an idea with Catholic roots (Losada Malvárez 1990: 67–70). Industrialisation, it was believed, could take place on the backs of the lower orders, avoiding the necessity of importing machinery or finance. Autarky enforced an industrialising process which relied principally on cheap labour rather than modernisation. It was as though those who had sinned against the nation in adhering to 'foreign ideas' during the Civil War had to pay for their political ideology (González Duro 1992: 247). In the 1940s a kind of nationalistic work ethic was imposed through the forcing of double or treble employment and internal migration in search of work (Miguel 1985). Thousands of workers also re-entered the labour market after the end of the Civil War via a period of nationalistic tutelage in a labour camp (Súarez/Colectivo '36 1976). In October 1938, in the midst of the conflict, the Nationalist authorities created the *Patronato Central de Redención de Penas por el Trabajo* (The Central Association for the Redemption of Punishment Through Labour). This body was to oversee the forced labour of prisoners. Its task, according to the propaganda,

10. *Genio de España* appeared in later editions in 1934 and 1938, and two more in 1939, and was subtitled, *exaltaciones a una resurrección nacional*. See Southworth (1978: 34).

11. *Parte Oficial*, FET-JONS, August 1946, Archivo General de Administración (AGA), Alcalá de Henares.

was not only to impose 'a strict juridical order' but also to express 'Spain's mercy'. The 'Christian missionary state' could grant such mercy once 'spiritual atonement and repentance had been demonstrated through the physical effort of labour'. Attendance at mass was rigidly enforced as was the singing of patriotic songs each day as well as the ritualistic learning of the Falangist '26 points' and the articles of the regime's 'Labour Charter', the *Fuero del Trabajo*. Indeed, it was a condition of release that the rudiments of Christian doctrine be shown to have been learnt (El Patronato 1941; Torrent García 1942). The reality in Francoist prisons and camps, in fact, was shaped by an extreme physical brutality which was far more draconian than this ideological indoctrination.

Therefore, in the 1940s, the regenerationist tradition blended with the influence of fascist concepts to produce a pathological 'diagnosis' of the Spanish 'sickness', prescribing certain courses of extreme 'treatment'. There was a strongly isolationist component to the ideology. This 'treatment' was to be administered while 'the patient' – Spain – was kept in a state of 'quarantine' through the practices of autarky. The cracks created by the contradictions between tradition and modernity in Spain were apparently to be papered over by the imposition of an integral Castilian nationalism. However, it was also partly the relative weakness of these symbols of Castilian nationalism as forces of integration which gave a particularly violent tone to the 1940s.

Violence

Although the magnitude of the post-Civil War repression is still the subject of controversy the evidence points to it being massive. Many studies have appeared in the last ten years which tell us a good deal about the repression in particular localities (and allow us to identify some of the individual victims, a necessary remembering which had previously been denied), but which, often, say little about the social and ideological context of the brutality. We certainly know for sure that thousands of executions took place which were never recorded and have, therefore, not been accounted for in quantitative studies. We will never know the true figure. However, although many of these studies calculate a lower figure, it seems quite possible that as many as 200,000 died as the result of Nationalist (Francoist) executions.[12] Again, there is controversy over the scale of the incarceration in prisons and labour camps of workers and other republicans. But the official figures are

12. For the debate about the quantification and nature of Francoist repression see Reig Tapia (1984), Michael Richards (1996).

dramatic enough: 270,000 in 1940. The regime admitted that there were still 40,000 political prisoners in 1945, although, again, the actual figure was probably considerably greater.[13]

What were the objectives of the repression? Franco himself summarised the purposes of the repression in 1939: only those 'capable of loving the Fatherland, of working and struggling for it, of adding their grain of sand to the common effort' would be tolerated. The others could not be allowed back into 'social circulation. . .. Wicked, deviant, politically and morally poisoned elements. . .those without possible redemption within the human order. . ..' Redemption, when it was offered, could only come through labour.[14] He insisted that no amnesty could be granted until the 'murders' of the Civil War had been 'expiated'.[15]

Effectively, Spain was to be a society 'in quarantine', undergoing intensive treatment in isolation. Social 'purification', in the language of the regime, was part and parcel of development and could, it was believed, be most efficiently carried out within a closed society. Political and cultural autarky reinforced this. 'Internalisation' was enforced at both a national and a personal level, at least for 'the defeated'. The tranquility which, according to Franco, Spain needed in the aftermath of the war was to be punctuated daily by the sound of firing squads in the 1940s. In other words, 'national reconstruction' always meant more than the material rebuilding of Spain's infrastructure. Franco's first Minister of the Interior, Ramón Serrano Suñer, gave his view on the situation in Barcelona after its fall in January 1939 to a German journalist: 'The city is completely bolshevised. The task of decomposition absolute. . .. In Barcelona the Reds have stifled the Spanish spirit. The people. . .are morally and politically sick. Barcelona will be treated by us with the care with which one tends to an invalid' (*Catalunya sota* 1973: 229). He was unambiguous in his views about Catalonia. The region's local nationalism was 'a sickness'; 'secessionism' had 'lived as a parasite' from what he viewed as a false patriotism. This 'secessionist virus' had to be treated: 'Today we have Catalonia on the points of our bayonets. Material domination will take little time. I am sure that the moral incorporation of Catalonia into Spain will be achieved as quickly as its military incorporation. . .' (Abella 1991: 59–60). The objective was the eradication of Catalan nationalism and culture: 'Of Catalonia we only want the ground (*el solar*)' (Solé i Sabaté 1993: 88).

From the first moment the task of disciplining the population was

13. Bowker to Eden, 12 December 1944, PRO/FO371/49575/Z89/89/41.
14. *La Vanguardia Española*, 4 April 1939.
15. *Mensaje del Caudillo a los españoles, discurso pronunciado por S.E. el Jefe del Estado la noche del 31 de diciembre de 1939*, Madrid, 1939.

associated with the sealing off of the 'New Spain' from the outside world. The head of the forces of occupation in Barcelona, General Eliseo Álvarez Arenas, promised that the economy of the city, 'so important to the economic future of Spain', would be swiftly reconstructed, but only after a 'period of transition' in which a 'strong principle of authority' backed by an 'iron discipline' had created the conditions for a return to 'normality'. According to Álvarez, the 'New Spain' would be 'autarkic' and 'independent': '. . .from the Pyrenees to the dividing line of Gibraltar, Spain will be Spain and Spain only'. In other words, isolation would facilitate an enforced national and social unity imposed at the point of a gun.[16]

This pathology of national unity as the basis for development was also illustrated by Franco's first Civil Governor in the city in announcing the priorities in resolving the country's crisis: 'While the state remains unconstructed (and in Spain, until now, this has not been achieved for a century) any regional political concept, however cautious and moderate. . .will lead to a fatal continuation of the process of putrefaction which we have just surgically eradicated. . .' (*Catalunya sota* 1973: 292). In other words, violence was seen as being central to the construction of the Nationalist State and autarky — economic, political and cultural self-sufficiency — was seen as being a central part of this process.

Autarky also implied economic nationalism *and* economic violence. The economic priority of the Franco regime after 1939 was the protection of the interests of the powerful *latifundista* landowners of central and southern Spain (Sevilla Guzmán and González de Molina 1989). At the same time, although Spain's elites dreaded the social consequences of continued industrialisation, there was a well-articulated desire to modernise Spain though an enforced industrial policy directed by the state through an anti-import strategy (Miguel 1986: 173–6; Payne 1987: 623–8, 635–6). There was a perceived need for isolation in order to break out of the international system of uneven economic relations. It was claimed that there was national resentment that Spain, as an essentially agrarian economy, was condemned to become ever poorer as the industrialised world simply used her as a source of cheap food while, at the same time depriving the country of her raw materials.[17] Industrialisation had a 'strong ethical sense'. Just as men needed 'upright standards' (*rectas normas*) which 'incorporate them into society,

16. Rodgers to Halifax, 13 February 1939, PRO/FO371/24127/W3036/8/41.
17. See Franco's speech, for example, in Burgos, 5 June 1939 (Franco 1943: p.20). There was, in fact, a good deal of truth in this analysis, as many on the Left in Spain in the 1930s had recognised. However, self-sufficiency in a system dominated by existing elites, with no agrarian reform was not the solution.

nations require equality of opportunities. . . and justice'. 'The creation of industries, which only at the cost of a protectionism *that – and why not say it? – for the moment can partially sacrifice the comforts of a generation, is indispensable*' (Fuentes Irurózqui 1943).[18]

Both of these priorities together – the protection of agriculture and industrialisation – had repressive implications in an atmosphere of a refusal to countenance national reconciliation. The economic strategy of autarky was, in itself, repressive: it expressed the regime's willingness to risk the lives of the working-class population. Autarky was able to be imposed partly because the regime possessed unlimited power to do so. More specifically, the protection of the privileges of the landed elite meant that industrialisation would depend, above all, on the labour of the defeated. The threatening social consequences of such a profound deepening of economic exploitation could be 'neutralised' by the authoritarian state (*Enciclopedia universal* 1939: 768–9; Gay de Montellà 1940).

Autarky and state industrialisation meant a devastating driving down of private consumption levels. The state directed funds to industrial projects and only belatedly imported sufficient food to compensate for its neglect of agricultural modernisation. Total Spanish imports fell by about 60 per cent from 876,140 pesetas in 1935 to 342,754 in 1939. Priorities were arranged into groups; fertilisers had, it was claimed, to be produced nationally so as to diminish the country's trade deficit (Viñas 1984: 213).[19]

This probably had a more destructive effect upon agricultural production than did the Civil War itself. Imports of certain industrial goods had to be reduced so that they might be 'substituted' by national production. Imports of a whole array of foodstuffs would be prevented. Feeding the population appeared to be a low priority of the 'New State'. Indeed, a considerable amount of food was exported by Spain in the 1940s, particularly to Germany, Italy and Britain, in order to earn foreign exchange while whole sections of the population were starving.[20]

---

18. Fuentes was the influential Inspector General of Trade in the Ministry of Trade and Industry in the 1940s, and wrote an introduction to the Spanish edition of an extremely well-received book by Mihael Manoilescu, the Rumanian Minister of Trade and Industry in the early 1930s, which argued the case for authoritarian industrialisation (Fuentes Irurózqui 1943). Manoilescu also wrote a book celebrating authoritarianism (Manoilescu 1938), which was prologued by Raimundo Fernández Cuesta, Franco's first, and disastrous, agriculture minister.

19. Franco's obsession with the trade balance was a reflection both of the protectionist tradition upon which elites depended and upon the crude notion of national prestige shared by the Francoist political class generally.

20. FET-JONS, *Delegación Nacional de Información e Investigación*, Boletín 871, 15 August 1942, AGA, Presidencia, caja 16.

In the period 1940–5 the yearly average decrease of the figure for private consumption, compared with 1935, was 8 per cent. Public consumption, meanwhile rose by an average of 19.4 per cent. This represented a huge and catastrophic shift in the consumption of resources (Carreras 1989).

Intervention by the repressive state was all-pervasive in internal economic relations as well as in foreign trade. The state participated in the construction of a black economy which dominated economic relations in the 1940s (Barciela 1989). It has been estimated that 'legal' supplies covered less than 25 per cent of the barest necessities of the working class. The state authorities were heavily implicated in the illegal economy. In Vizcaya, for example, the black market was run by the head of the Civil Guard, while in Málaga it was run by the Civil Governor for a period.[21] In Barcelona, and indeed in most of the towns and cities of Spain, the local party hierarchy was implicated particularly since the local party chief was normally also the head of the local food distributing authority. The necessary resort to buy (and sometimes sell) on the black market created both a brutal dependency and a situation where much of the population found itself breaking the law and thereby vulnerable to the attention of the state authorities.

The control of food became one of the ways by which Franco's victory was reproduced day-by-day in the post-war period. Official rationing was hopelessly inadequate. Moreover, the supply of the barest necessities was influenced by political considerations (Alburquerque 1981). The provision of 'supplementary rations', which could mean the difference between life and death, was controlled by a local board made up of the mayor (usually a local industrialist or landowner), the parish priest and the local head of the party. Acceptable behaviour would be required before extra rations were dished out.

Autarky and the division of society into victors and vanquished made the economic crisis appallingly more acute. In the five years following the Civil War there were at least 200,000 deaths from malnutrition and diseases related to food shortage over and above the pre-war death rate (Payne 1987: 252). This was part of the economic violence of autarky. There were 25,000 deaths per year from tuberculosis alone; registered deaths from diarrhoea and enteritis in 1941 were 53,307; officially 4,168 died from typhoid fever and 1,644 from typhus in the same year (Sueiro and Díaz Nosty, vol.I, 1985: 135).

Autarky and its concomitant, state intervention, reinforced a determination to regiment labour too. If autarkic development was to work, it was believed that the state would need to direct not only goods but

21. Málaga dispatch, 22 December 1939, PRO/FO371/24507/C40/40/41.

work. The nationalistic mysticism consciously represented by autarky allowed all threats to production, like strikes, to be considered as acts of treason, since they threatened the 'national resurgence', and, were therefore made punishable by execution. Thus corporativism, articulated in the *Fuero de Trabajo*, and autarky, became two sides of the same authoritarian coin. The so-called 'spiritual' elements of autarky – what was described as 'the will and discipline of producers and consumers' as well as the 'patriotic consciousness' of employers, both weakly formulated concepts – were inevitably bound up with the practical ideological and economic requirements of the state. The Rome correspondent of the principal Barcelona daily newspaper suggested this function of self-sufficiency in Italian society under Mussolini: '. . .that vague concept of autarky was translated into a graphic image which was inserted into the senses of the people. . .sublimating it, even converting it into a true catechism, a true guide to politico-social perfection; in a word: into a mysticism'.[22] However, this process of mystification was relatively ineffective in concealing the fact that autarky did not simply require the lower classes to *display* discipline but was actually used as a way of *imposing* discipline.

'Patriotism' was a form of cover for the perpetuation of many of the pre-existing features of economic and social relations in Spain. Doubtless it did not convince the working class, nor many regionalists in Catalonia and the Basque Country. However, the ideology of the *Patria Católica*, which influenced economic and social policy, provided a basis for unity within a previously fractious elite society, whilst the burden of the crisis was laid upon the shoulders of the lower orders. The control of material necessities, based upon the re-establishing of the social status-quo, ensured a necessarily obsessive concentration upon sheer survival. Hunger and the denial of a collective identity to half of Spain, those who had supported the Republican cause, ensured a retreat into the domestic sphere. The state's economic policy atomised society, breaking down social solidarities and forcing the populace to interact with authority always and only as individuals.

Epilogue: Industrialisation

It was in the aftermath of the Civil War that the social basis for industrialisation in Spain was laid. However, in this chapter space only

22. *La Vanguardia Española*, 17 September 1939. In *El mañana económico de Europa*, Virginio Gayola suggested that 'autarky is deep internal conquest. . .displayed in Italy as an expression of the dynamism and the creative will of Italians, as not only an economic phenomenon but also a political and spiritual one' (Clavera et al. 1978: 86).

permits a brief delineation of this process. Despite the emphasis on the condition of the Spanish peasantry in the ideology of the Falange, the Francoist State was from the very first possessed of a will to industrialise: 'conscious and hindering resistance (to industrialisation) ha(d) to be swept away', according to Suanzes (Instituto Nacional de Industria 1941). As we have seen, this was central to the concept of national regeneration. The setting up of the *Instituto Nacional de Industria* (INI), a state holding company, in 1941, designed to boost industrial capitalist development, was justified on the grounds that Spain's 'racial values' would be strengthened through the 'indispensable support of a powerful industrial sector'. This national resurgence was necessary if the country was to realise its 'historic destiny'.[23] The regime particularly determined upon the industrialisation of 'neglected' rural areas in a crude attempt to overcome the effects of uneven economic development. Although its discrimination against Barcelona and Bilbao industry, based on its 'cultural totalitarianism', has probably been overstated, industrial growth was very slow in the early decades of Francoism. At the same time, however, the process of capital accumulation was enormously deepened in the 1940s, largely as a direct result of the actions of the regime.

The nationalistic myth of industrial resurgence for the common good[24] was developed upon a reality of the enrichment of existing elites. The collective sacrifice which was called for in the name of national resurgence was, in reality, enforced in the interests of the concentration of economic power. The context was both repression of the defeated and virtually complete economic protectionism through autarky. During the early decades of Francoism Spanish agriculture performed one of the functions necessary to give impetus to economic development in enormously boosting capital accumulation in the countryside, ultimately allowing for the financing of industrialisation (Barciela 1986).

Despite the evident hollowness of the rhetoric of Empire, autarky did, in fact, allow a kind of *internal* colonisation to take place. Huge profits were extracted by the driving down of agricultural wages. The basis of 'national economic resurgence' was a return to the punishing living conditions and production techniques of the nineteenth century. In the south labourers typically worked for a maximum of 180 days a year. The 1940s saw a return of working from six in the morning until ten at night for an official wage of 4 pesetas; although in some places it was only 3. Women were paid 1.25 pesetas. Landowners controlled the agricultural syndicates which workers did not join unless threatened

23. *Boletin del Estado*, 30 September 1941.

24. Nationalism has often played a central role in industrialisation. See, for example, Garruccio (1969).

with dismissal (Bernal 1993: 151–3).[25] The *latifundistas* also benefited enormously from the black market. The prices of such items as bread and oil reached levels in the 1940s which were not to be repeated until 1975 (Leal et al. 1975: 81–2). The biggest landowners were able to increase their capital by two or three times.[26]

The growth of the holdings of the six main private banks, all closely associated with agricultural interests, reflected this accumulation. Capital increased seven-fold in the 1940s alone. It was these institutions that invested most heavily in industrial development in the early decades of the regime (Múñoz 1969; Esteban 1978: 164).

The suggestion here has not been that Spain experienced industrial 'take-off' in the early post-Civil War years. However, the basis of social and economic development *was* laid in this period. Autarky, in terms of economic 'rationality', was a devastating failure with huge human costs. However, self-sufficiency did both serve particular economic interests and perform certain social and cultural functions. The nature of Spanish nationalism in the immediate post-Civil War period can be discerned by a broad understanding of what autarky and regeneration meant in the context of complete social and political domination. Economic protectionism, integrist Catholicism and a bastardised form of regenerationism combined with fascistic and militaristic ideas about punishment and social engineering to produce a nationalist creed which was above all violent and repressive.

The symbolism of 'crusading' nationalism, sacrifice and purification, combined with massively deepened capital accumulation, also facilitated a relative rapprochement of Spain's economic elites which had been traumatised in the 1930s. Autarky, then, cannot be divorced from ideology and class oppression. Autarkic nationalism contributed to the reconstruction of authority after the Civil War; in this sense, autarky was an extremely violent alternative to an equitable, pluralistic, progressive and *modern* Spanish nationalism.

References

Abella, Rafael (1991), *Finales de enero de 1939: Barcelona cambia del piel*, Barcelona

Alburquerque, Francisco (1981), 'Métodos de control político de la población civil: el sistema de racionamiento de alimentos y productos básicos impuesto en España tras la última guerra civil', in

25. PRO/FO371/26890/C3986/3/41, March 1941.
26. FET-JONS, DNII, Boletín 324, Córdoba, 2 January 1942, AGA, Presidencia, caja 16.

Estudios sobre la historia de España: homenaje a M.Tuñón de Lara, vol.2, Madrid, pp.407–32

Barciela, Carlos (1986), 'Introducción' to *Historia agraria de la España contemporánea*, vol.3, part 2, Barcelona, pp.383–413

—— (1989), 'La España del "estraperlo"', in García Delgado, J.L. (ed.), *El primer franquismo*, Madrid, pp.105–22

Bernal, Antonio-Miguel (1993), 'Resignación de los campesinos andaluces: la resistencia pasiva durante el franquismo', in *España franquista: causa general y actitudes sociales ante la dictadura*, Castilla-La Mancha, pp.145–60

Blinkhorn, Martin (1979), *Carlismo y contrarrevolución en España, 1931–1939*, Barcelona

Buesa Blanco, Miguel, Braña, Javier and Molero, José (1984), *El estado y el cambio tecnológico en la industrialización tardía*, Madrid

Carreras, Albert (1989), 'Depresión económica y cambio estructural durante el decenio bélico (1936–1945)', in García Delgado, J.L. (ed.), *El primer franquismo*, Madrid, pp.3–33

Castillo, Juan José (1979), *Propietarios muy pobres. Sobre la subordinación política del pequeño campesino*, Madrid

Catalunya sota el règim franquista: Informe sobre la persecució de la llengua i la cultura de Catalunya pel règim del General Franco (1973), Paris

Clavera, Joan et al. (1978), *Capitalismo español; de la autarquía a la estabilización, (1939–1959)*, Madrid

Enciclopedia universal (1939), 1936–1939, Madrid

Escudero, María (1994), 'The Image of Latin America Disseminated in Spain by the Franco Regime: Repercussions in the Configuration of a National Identity', unpublished thesis, University of California

Esteban, Joan (1978), 'La política económica del franquismo: una interpretación', in Preston, Paul (ed.), *España en crisis*, Madrid, pp.147–80

Franco, Francisco (1943), *Palabras del Caudillo*, Madrid

Fuentes Irurózqui, Manuel (1943), 'Prefacio' to Manoilescu, Mihail, *Teoría del proteccionismo y del comercio internacional*, Madrid

Ganivet, Angel (1943), *Antología*, Madrid

—— (1897, 1961 edn), *Idearium español*, in *Obras completas*, Madrid, pp.147–305

Garruccio, Ludovico (1969), *L'Industrializzazione tra nazionalismo e rivoluzione: la ideología política dei paesi in via di sviluppo*, Bologna

Gay de Montellá, Rafael (1940), *Autarquía. Nuevas orientaciones de la economía*, Barcelona

González Calleja, Eduardo and Limón Nevado, Fredes (1988), *La Hispanidad como instrumento de combate*, Madrid

González Duro, Enrique (1992), *Franco: una biografía psicológica*, Madrid

Griffin, Roger (1991), *The Nature of Fascism*, London

Harrison, Joseph (1990), 'The Catalan Industrial Elite, 1898–1923', in Lannon, Frances and Preston, Paul (eds), *Elites and Power in Twentieth Century Spain. Essays in Honour of Sir Raymond Carr*, Oxford

Instituto Nacional de Industria (1941), *Notas en relación con la creación y desenvolvimiento de este Instituto*, Consejo de Administración del INI, Madrid

Leal, José Luis et al. (1975), *La agricultura en el desarrollo capitalista español, 1940–1970*, Madrid

Losada Malvárez, Juan Carlos (1990), *Ideología del ejército franquista, 1939–1959*, Madrid

Manoilescu, Mihail (1938), *El Partido Único: Institución política de los nuevos regímenes*, Zaragoza

Miguel, Amando de (1985), 'La autarquía en esta tierra de secano', in Diario 16, *Historia del franquismo*, Madrid, pp.322–9

—— (1986), *España cíclica: ciclos económicos y generaciones demográficas en la sociedad española contemporánea*, Madrid

Montero, Eloy (1939), *Los estados modernos y la nueva España*, Vitoria

Múñoz, Juan (1969), *Poder de la Banca en España*, Madrid

París, Higinio (1942), *Un nuevo orden económico*, Madrid

Patronato Central para la Redención de las Penas por el Trabajo, El (1941), *La obra de la redención de penas – la doctrina, la práctica, la legislación*, Madrid

Payne, Stanley (1987), *The Franco Regime, 1936–1975*, Wisconsin

Pérez Ledesma, Manuel (1993), 'El miedo de los acomodados y la moral de los obreros', in Folguera, Pilar (ed.), *Otras visiones de España*, Madrid, pp.27–63

Preston, Paul (1993), *Franco*, London

Ramsden, H. (1974), *The 1898 Movement in Spain*, Manchester

Redondo, Onésimo (1939), *El Estado Nacional*, Madrid

Reig Tapia, Alberto (1984), *Ideología e historia: sobre la represión franquista y la guerra civil*, Madrid

Richards, Michael (1995), 'Autarky and the Franco Dictatorship in Spain, 1936–1945', unpublished PhD, Queen Mary and Westfield College, University of London

—— (1996), 'Civil War, Violence, and the Construction of Francoism', in Preston, Paul and Mackenzie, Ann L., *The Republic Besieged: Civil War in Spain, 1936–39*, Edinburgh, pp.193–234

Robert, Antonio (1943), *Un problema nacional. La industrialización necesaria*, Madrid

Schwarz, Pedro and González, Manuel-Jesús (1978), *Una historia del Instituto Nacional de Industria, (1941–1976)*, Madrid

Sevilla Guzmán, Eduardo and González de Molina, Manuel (1989), 'Política social agraria del primer franquismo', in García Delgado, José Luis, *El primer franquismo: España durante la se anda guerra mundial*, Madrid, pp.135–87

Solé i Sabaté, Josep María (1993), 'La justicia catalana franquista y sus fuentes', in *España franquista: causa general y actitudes sociales ante la dictadura*, Castilla La Mancha, pp.87–92

Southworth, Herbert (1978), 'La Falange: un análisis de la herencia fascista española', in Preston, Paul (ed.), *España en crisis*, Madrid, pp.29–60

Súarez, A/Colectivo '36 (1976), *El libro blanco sobre las cárceles franquistas, 1939–1976*, Paris

Sueiro, Daniel and Díaz Nosty, Bernardo (1985), *Historia del franquismo*, 2 vols, Madrid

Torrent García, Martín (1942), *¿Qué me dice Usted de los presos?*, Alcalá de Henares

Tuñón de Lara, Manuel (1986), *España: la quiebra de 1898*, Madrid

Unamuno, Miguel de (1895, 1986 edn), *En torno al casticismo*, Madrid

Vázquez Montalbán, Manuel (1978), *Los demonios familiares de Franco*, Barcelona

Viñas, Angel (1984), *Guerra, dinero, dictadura. Ayuda fascista y autarquía en la España de Franco*, Barcelona

Viver Pi-Sunyer, Carles (1980), 'Aproximació a la ideología del franquisme en l'etapa fundacional del règim', in *Papers: Revista de Sociología*, no.14, pp.11–47

Part II

The Nationalist and Regionalist Counter-Consciousness: Competing and Conflicting Identities

–10–

Sardana, Zarzuela or Cake Walk?
Nationalism and Internationalism in the
Discourse, Practice and Culture of the
Early Twentieth-Century Barcelona
Labour Movement
Angel Smith

The study of national identity in early twentieth-century Barcelona is both complex and potentially rewarding for there were two antagonistic nationalist discourses in circulation together with a strong internationalist current within the labour movement. This in a society which, on the one hand, was deeply antagonistic towards the Spanish State but which, at the same time, was racked by bitter internal social divisions. Hence, an analysis of this period can provide insights into the nature of the imbrication between nationalism, culture and social class.

In this chapter I intend to focus on a key aspect of this problematic, the relationship between labour, nationalism and national identity. This is a subject steeped in polemic. In large measure this is a result of the great upsurge in Catalanist mobilisation during the transition to democracy in Spain in the 1970s. This, of course, stimulated the search for the origins of Catalan nationalism or Catalanism, but it was very much linked to present political concerns. These could, on the one hand, provide the stimulus to analyse historical problems from a new perspective, but also entailed the danger of anachronism. One school of thought stressed the 'bourgeois' origins of Catalanism and the failure of the party of the Catalan Right, the *Lliga Regionalista* (1901–33), to achieve any lasting devolution of power to Catalonia (Solé Tura 1974). According to taste this could either be used to reject the leadership of conservative forces over the new politics of nationalism, or anathematise Catalanism as a 'bourgeois' phenomenon. On the contrary, other authors emphasised the coalescence of a popular, interclass, Catalanist tradition in the nineteenth century, which was to prove the most authentic mouthpiece for the Catalan people's demands for autonomy and democracy (Termes 1974). From a leftist perspective it was extremely tempting to adopt such a stance, first because of the experience of the anti-colonialist struggles in the 1960s, and second because such a reading gave historical justification to, at the same time as it was easy to draw parallels with, the struggle for democracy and home rule (usually seen as synonymous) being waged against the Francoist State.

However, both interpretations suffered from serious deficiencies. The linking of Catalanism and 'the bourgeoisie' (effectively the Catalan industrialists) too closely together resulted in a crude identification of ideology and social class and blurred the necessarily interclass nature of any nationalist movement. The defence of a strong popular interclass Catalanist tradition, which supposedly took in both workers and the petty bourgeoisie, and which stretched from the 1850s to the 1930s, also entailed considerable theoretical and practical problems. In the first place, ironically from a leftist perspective, it engendered a certain tendency to minimise class divisions, which could cut through the inter-class block. Hence it became common to talk of 'popular classes' rather than working class, lower middle class and middle class (Ucelay da Cal 1982). Certainly this theoretical construct was useful in warning against too rigid a division between the social strata in the analysis of interclass movements such as republicanism and Catalanism. On the other hand, from the turn of the century in particular, social conflict attained on occasion dramatic levels, and the militant anarchists or anarcho-syndicalists became the leading force within the organised labour movement. Historians who adopted a populist interpretation of Catalanism, I would argue, found it difficult to come to terms with this fact, and, indeed, like the Catalanists of the early twentieth century, tended to a large degree to look outside Catalonia to the policies of the Spanish State to explain tensions within Catalonia.[1] Moreover, the possibility that sections of the Left were hostile to Catalanism was also difficult for this tradition to take on board. Hence the elaboration of singularly unconvincing claims that because of their opposition to the Madrid government and belief in the total decentralisation of power the anarchists could in some way be seen as *de facto* Catalanists (Olivé Serret 1977: 624–6).

1. Hence the fact that from the turn of the century, when the state became somewhat more open, Catalan industrialists were often to the Right of the politicians of the Res-toration system sits uneasily with some Catalan historians' vision of a democratising Catalonia encorseted within an authoritarian Spanish state. The reactionary policies pursued by the Catalan industrial elite is amply demonstrated in Bengoechea (1994).

Sardana, Zarzuela *or Cake Walk?*

Republicanism, Catalanism and Labour in Nineteenth-Century Catalonia

In the nineteenth century, as José Alvarez Junco points out in Chapter 5, the Spanish State made little effort to nationalise the people. The instruments of cultural assimilation and social integration were weak, with the state having frequent recourse to repression. Thus, for example, no adequate education system was set up, with the result Barcelona workers continued to speak Catalan, not necessarily because they were Catalanists but because they had been taught Castilian so poorly.

In these circumstances it seems that some links developed between the emerging labour movement and particularist and regionalist currents which grew up from the 1870s. In the first place, a strong federal republican movement burst on the scene in Catalonia in the years which followed the Glorious Revolution of 1868, gaining strong backing in urban milieux amongst workers, artisans, shopkeepers and small-scale employers. The federalists maintained that a key element in the democratisation of Spanish life was a decentralisation of power to the provinces and municipalities (see Chapter 1), and, Josep Termes has argued, the practice of the most radical of these republicans, known as Intransigents, was steeped in allusions to Catalonia's rights and freedoms (Termes 1972). Secondly, some contacts could be observed between labour and the new left-of-centre Catalanist movement which took shape from the early 1880s. During the 1880s Catalanism widened its social base, especially amongst the urban middle and lower-middle classes, in the heat of campaigns for further protectionist measures for Catalan industry and against rises in taxes on commerce. These protectionist campaigns were launched by textile industrialists and supported by the increasingly class collaborationist textile federation, the *Tres Clases de Vapor* (TCV), the largest trade union in Barcelona at the time (Smith 1991: 346–8). In the demonstrations Catalanist symbols could be observed, such as workers wearing the typical hat, the *barretina* (Izard 1973: 143–4; Cucurull 1978: 246).[2] It has also been pointed out that in the early 1880s leaders of the anarchist wing of the Catalan labour movement showed some sympathy for Catalanist demands. Men like Rafael Farga Pellicer and Josep Llunas i Pujals, despite their ascription as anarchists, were not particularly radical. They showed an understanding of the plight of small-scale commerce and established contacts with Catalanists (Olivé Serret 1984; Gabriel 1986).

2. The patriarch of Catalan anarchism, Anselmo Lorenzo (1974), also indicated a link between reformist sectors of the labour movement and Catalanism from the mid-1870s.

More work is needed on this phase of Catalan labour history. It may be speculated that the more reformist labour representatives were looking to build up an interclass coalition for reform, and that the weakness of Spanish nationalism could mean that it could begin to coalesce around Catalanist demands. Nevertheless, these contacts were, it seems, tentative, while, at the same time, there were other tendencies at hand which were looking to structure alternative identities. In the first place, alongside federal republicanism there developed a Spanish republican tradition rooted in the legacy of French Jacobinism, which equated progress with the democratisation of the established nation state (see Chapter 1). Second, the Spanish Socialist Workers' Party (PSOE), founded in 1879, declared itself to be internationalist and theoretically contrasted proletarian solidarity with bourgeois nationalism, but at the same time it viewed the consolidation of the established nation states as desirable and 'regional particularisms' as reactionary. This position can again be traced back both to Jacobin republicanism and liberal mid-nineteenth-century nationalism, which both saw the European nation states as breaking down feudal barriers, facilitating capitalist development and, thereby, laying the groundwork for human progress (Hobsbawm 1992: 18–21, 88–9, 124–6). Thirdly, within the anarchist movement there was also a more radical, passionately internationalist strand, which regarded any compromises with nationalism as heresy (Alvarez Junco 1976: 333–5).

Class and Nation in *Fin-de-Siècle* Barcelona

From the late 1880s two factors were to give these forces a considerable fillip. First, from these years social tensions and divisions within urban Catalonia became increasingly exacerbated, with the result that politics would in the future to a greater extent than ever before be conditioned by class interests. Second, in the 1890s a fully fledged nationalist movement developed in Catalonia, which, probably in part as a reflection of the widening social divide, was significantly to the Right of the Catalanism of the 1880s, and which began to mobilise an important middle-class base (Marfany 1995: 24–43).

The growth of conservative, middle-class Catalanism was given a great boost by Spain's defeat in the Spanish–American War of 1898 and the resulting loss of her remaining colonies in the Pacific and the Americas. The defeat had serious implications in Catalonia. Cuba in particular had become a key market for Catalan exports. Furthermore, the government's decision in 1899 to raise taxes on commerce and industry to cover the enormous budget deficit which had been run up during the attempt to quell the Cuban uprising led to wide-ranging discontent. The result was a vehement campaign of protest which took in industrials and the commercial middle and lower-middle classes. It climaxed between June and November 1899 with a taxpayers strike of Barcelona shopkeepers known as the *Tancament de Caixes* (literally shutting of the tills). Two years later, after the failure by the central state to integrate representatives of the Catalan middle classes into central government, a new party was born called the *Lliga Regionalista*. Over the following decade it was rapidly to acquire a mass base through much of Catalonia. It called for Catalan autonomy along with other measures designed to boost Catalan industrial and commercial interests. The party was quick to use Catalanism as a tool to mobilise the population. Yet its politics were very much on the Right of the political spectrum. In its early years the party did have a minority liberal-republican wing, but conservatives were dominant. This could be seen in its identification with the Catalan Catholic Church, its support for corporatist rather than universal suffrage, and attacks on strikes and labour organisation (Riquer 1977: 155–211).

Yet while the *Lliga* tried to juxtapose the unity of the Catalan population in the face of the external enemy represented by Madrid government, the reality was that social conflict in Catalonia itself was escalating and at times acquired dramatic levels. The labour movement had largely been undermined by state and employers' offensives in the second half of the 1880s, and in the 1890s had at times to suffer blanket repression. Repression eased from 1898 and subsequent years were to witness a rapid escalation of industrial strife and the emergence of an aggressive anarcho-syndicalist labour movement. This culminated in 1910 within the foundation in Barcelona of the anarcho-syndicalist CNT (Smith 1997).

The effects of this consolidation of conservative middle-class Catalanism combined with the deepening class divisions are very much open to debate. Defenders of the 'popular interclass block' theory of Catalanism have argued that the genesis of the *Lliga* did not lead the lower orders to reject Catalan nationalism. On the contrary, even though leftist groups might say that they did not support Catalanism because they identified it with the Right, the defence of 'Catalan liberties' remained a central element of their programmes (Cucurull 1978: 246; Olivé Serret 1987). This seems, however, to be based more on preconceptions than on detailed empirical research. This becomes clear on studying the evolution of republicanism and anarchism during these years. Over much of urban Spain Spanish nationalist republican groupings were dominant and they had indeed acquired some influence in Catalonia from the 1880s. In the 1890s, in order to mobilise more effectively against the Restoration, elements within these parties moved to the Left, going so far as to declare themselves 'labour' or 'socialist' in order to attract a wider working-class base (Alvarez Junco 1990). A similar pattern could, at the same time, be observed in Catalonia where, in reaction to the growing success of the Catalanists in capturing middle-class votes, sectors of republicanism adopted an increasingly radical tone and image (Duarte 1993). Furthermore, the conservatism of the new Catalan nationalist movement led to the growth of a specifically anti-Catalanist current precisely on the Left of Catalan federalism (Duarte 1987: 99–119). This was possible because, as noted in Chapter 1, Spanish republicanism had structured its own progressive nationalist tradition, which stressed the inherently democratic nature of the Spanish people – the authentic mouthpiece of Spanish nationalism – who had throughout the ages been locked in struggle against Spain's elites. As we shall see, it would be a relatively easy operation to include the Catalan nationalists in this definition of the reactionary elite.

A similar pattern of development could in some respects also be seen amongst specifically working-class bodies. In the late 1880s and early 1890s, in reaction to the undermining of the major Catalan workers' organisations by the state and employers, a new generation of anarchists came to the fore. They were more radical than the old leadership, taking on board syndicalist calls for general strikes. They were also more notably anti-Catalanist than their predecessors, identifying in their press a confluence between Catalanism and 'bourgeois interests' (Reventòs 1925: 143).

This new constellation of political and social forces came dramatically to the fore during the *Tancament de Caixes*. Because of its conservative connotations the republicans were, in general, hostile, and the Barcelona working class was largely absent from the campaign. Protest against the new taxes seems only to have generated some support amongst shop assistants and amongst the most reformist sectors of the labour movement. The only working-class institutions clearly to back the protest were the *Ateneos Obreros* (Workers' Athenaeums). These *Ateneos* were educational establishments which educated the children of the working class. In 1904 there were over 30 such *Ateneos* in Catalonia, which taught about 16,000 students. A study of their politics and internal composition shows that they had become the foremost representatives on the reformist wing of the labour movement, which had been at its height in the early 1880s. The most important of these *Ateneos*, the *Ateneo Obrero de Barcelona*, was founded in 1882 by a number of figures with contacts with the TCV, and, from the late 1890s, supported all the protest movements involving the industrialists and middle classes which led up to the foundation of the *Lliga* in 1901 (Riquer 1977: 96). The *Ateneos'* reformism and, indeed, class collabo-

Sardana, Zarzuela *or Cake Walk?*

rationism was highlighted by their internal structure. They accepted honorary members, who were persons of high social standing who gave donations. They also received government subsidies, and were quick to invite the civil and military authorities to the prize-giving ceremonies they held at the beginning of each academic year. Furthermore, their publications emphasised the importance of self-betterment through saving, and encouraged their working-class readership to try and set up as small-scale industrialists.[3] Though, therefore, one can agree with Josep Termes that the *Ateneos* showed clear Catalanist sympathies, he is mistaken in arguing that they were representative working-class institutions and that their Catalanism can automatically be extended to other working-class bodies (Termes 1987: 9–11).

On the contrary, there was considerable antagonism in the leftist press, reflected in the commonplace identification of the Catalanist movement with 'the bourgeoisie'. It was the Spanish Socialists, whose opposition to regionalist or nationalist demands was well known, who most vociferously denounced such links. In 1899, for example, they celebrated the lack of working-class participation in the *Tancament*, arguing that 'by not adding their voice to that chorus of hatred, *Els Segadors*, they had 'clearly shown that they recognise their class interests and know that they have stronger ties with the workers of Castile' than with the industrialists in their own region.[4] This stance was supported by the Catalan Socialists, who had a virtually negligible impact on the Catalan political scene but who were active within the trade union movement.[5]

However, it was not only the Socialists who adopted an anti-Catalanist rhetoric. When *El Socialista* criticised the *Tancament* in 1899 it received letters of support from the Barcelona-based coachmen's and railway workers' unions. This last letter was written by the union's General Secretary, Luis Zurdo Olivares, a republican who had developed close contacts with the Barcelona anarchists. In anarchistic terms Zurdo Olivares urged workers not to be fooled by 'the conjuring tricks of the bourgeoisie, who bled us in Melilla, in Cuba and in the Philippines, and who take advantage of any event so that jesuitism – which in these commotions plays the first card – might show its hand', and

3. This section is based on a reading of: *Revista del Ateneo Obrero de Barcelona*, 1886–1908; *Boletin del Ateneo Obrero de Gracia*, 1904–1906; *Fomento Martinense (Ateneo Obrero)*, 1905; *Rayo de Luz, Boletin del Ateneo de San Andres de Palomar*, 1908–1911. The only important work on the *Ateneos* is Solà (1978).
4. *El Socialista*, 20 October 1899. *Els Segadors* was adopted by Catalanists as the Catalan national anthem from the turn of the century. See Marfany (1995: 317–20).
5. See, for example, the article by Amparo Martí in *Revista Fabril*, 20 April 1900. This was the mouthpiece of a new Catalan textile federation established in 1899 in which the Socialists had considerable influence.

instead to rally to the 'universal brotherhood' of the working class.[6]

In anarchist circles a similar approach was in general adopted. It is true that a number of anarchists grouped around the magazine *L'Avenir* were favourably inclined towards Catalanist demands. Their leading figure, Jaume Brossa, maintained that workers should support the Catalanists in their call for the reactionary Spanish State to be dismantled because they would then enjoy greater freedom to pursue their demands (Rosell 1940: 12–13; Olivé Serret 1977: 622–4; E.R.A.80 1977: 16–170). Yet they were not central figures within Barcelona anarchism. There were two major groupings of anarchists in Barcelona at this time. In the first place, a number of anarchists centred on the figure of Francisco Ferrer, an ex-republican who had been converted to anarchism while in exile in France in the 1890s, and who during the first decade of the century became the principal benefactor of Catalan anarchism. In 1901 he subsidised a new publication called *La Huelga General*, and was also behind the establishment of a series of 'rational' educational establishments in Catalonia known as Modern Schools. Ferrer, at the same time, established close contact with Anselmo Lorenzo, the 'grandfather' of Spanish anarchism. Secondly, there was a group of anarchists and anarchist sympathisers who were closely linked to the Barcelona trade union movement. As labour agitation grew from 1899 they quickly strengthened their position and to an important degree came to dominate the organised labour movement between 1902 and 1903 (Smith 1997).

Both sections of the movement showed no sympathy for Catalanism. Lorenzo was well known for his hostility. Ferrer, for his part, suffered from an 'anti-Catalanist phobia', and ensured education in all his schools would be in Castilian (Rosell 1940: 26). The anarchist union militants adopted a similar approach. Hence they stated that they were opposed to all 'particularisms', and proclaimed that the future anarchist society would be a 'great region, a single fatherland covering all the earth, which would not legislate on custom or dress and would proclaim the people's right to live outside (or perhaps beyond) the harsh rule of the exploiters, however they be disguised'.[7] This was to be the dominant current in Catalan anarchism up until the outbreak of the First World War.[8] These anarchists did not defend the use of Catalan but argued that all people should speak a single universal language. They believed this

6. *El Socialista*, 27 October 1899. The Jesuits were commonly seen in leftist circles as the richest, most powerful and reactionary religious order.

7. *El Productor*, 13 July 1901.

8. This assertion is based on a reading of the two major anarcho-syndicalist papers of this period, *El Productor* (1901–1905) and *Solidaridad Obrera* (1907–).

language could be Esperanto, and therefore encouraged working-class unions and cultural associations to teach it.[9] Nevertheless, as we have seen in the case of Lorenzo's classes, their practice was not entirely language-neutral, for by establishing a link between Catalanism and reaction they tended to favour the Castilian language for educational purposes and in the press. Again this can probably be related to the generic tendency within much of the Left to see 'progress' as coming from within the established nation-state.

Nor were these anarchists afraid to take their anti-Catalanist message to mass union meetings. Thus, for example, in a meeting held in 1901 to protest at the repression of a strike in La Coruña, 'Teresa Claramunt attacked Catalanism, and defended human brotherhood and the universal fatherland. She said that the Catalanists wanted a free Catalonia but the Catalans to be slaves'.[10] Later in the same year after the mouthpiece of the *Lliga, La Veu de Catalunya*, had on several occasions criticised the calling of strikes and the conclusions reached at union meetings, at another meeting held to protest at the events in La Coruña, Segalás, a representative of one of the unions present and an anarchist sympathiser: 'Began by stating that he was speaking in Catalan, but that he was ashamed of addressing them in the same language in which *La Veu de Catalunya* was written.'[11] A large crowd was present but as far as one can tell no protests were to be heard. In fact, so widespread was criticism of Catalanism within the trade unions that in a meeting held in 1900 the leading figures in the remnants of the Barcelona TCV, Ramon Fontanals and Joan Vidal, who were trying to dispel their class collaborationist image, joined in.[12] Indeed, it became common during strikes for anarchist or syndicalist publications to stress that though the industrialist stated he wanted freedom for Catalonia he was at the same time enslaving his workers.[13] And it was no doubt this atmosphere that led Claudi Ametlla, a Catalanist republican, to note in his excellent memoirs that at the turn of the century in Barcelona: 'The people, by which I mean the artisan and the worker, were either non-political, or they were Spanish republicans or lived seduced by the universalist-

9. *El Trabajo*, 12 November 1904, 13 October 1906; Bonamusa (1976: 53–6, 89). *El Trabajo* was the mouthpiece of the Sabadell labour federation.
10. *La Publicidad*, 21 July 1901, Night Edition. *La Publicidad* was the principal republican daily in Barcelona. Teresa Claramunt, the best known female anarchist agitator of these years, was at this time struggling to unionise the female cotton textile weavers.
11. *La Publicidad*, 11 August 1901, Night Edition.
12. *La Publicidad*, 8 May 1900, Night Edition.
13. See, for example, *Solidaridad Obrera*, 1 May 1913, p.3, 5 February 1914, p.4. *Solidaridad Obrera* was the weekly newspaper of a syndicalist labour federation of the same name founded in Barcelona in 1907 and which was the precursor of the CNT.

humanitarian myths which did so much harm in working-class circles' (Ametlla 1963: 120).

The changing social landscape which underlay this critique of Catalanism was schematically but, nevertheless, effectively brought out by the Catalan Socialist, José Comaposada, who observed that the protectionist campaigns launched by the cotton textile industrialists between 1884 and 1886 were supported by all sections of the population including the working class. As a result of this pressure, he continued, the manufacturers were able to get their protectionist schemes approved. Under the new conditions the industrialists were to earn great sums of money. However, the workers, he observed, did not benefit from the new conjuncture. On the contrary, any move they made to improve their working conditions was bitterly opposed by their employers. It was, he concluded, these same industrialists who were now the leading figures within Catalanism, and who again called for the workers' support. The workers, however, had learnt from experience to take no notice.[14] Indeed the TCV, which had supported the employers' protectionist campaigns, was, despite its moderation, all but destroyed in a joint employer-state offensive between 1889 and 1891. This was of key importance for the future development of the Catalan labour movement, for the TCV had been the focus of reformist labour politics and the new cotton textile unions founded from the turn of the century, chastened by their experience, were considerably more radical (Smith 1991: 346–71).

Catalanists, Lerrouxists and Anarchists: The Politics of Catalanism and *Españolismo*

The division between on the one hand conservative Catalanists and a supposedly internationalist or even *españolista* Left remained at the heart of Catalan politics through to 1914. The outrage which followed the 'Disaster' of 1898 led urban society to become rapidly politicised, and in Barcelona and its surrounds the monarchist *caciques*, who had manipulated elections since the inception of the Restoration in 1875, were at last driven out by new mass political parties. Along with the growth of unionism the years between 1901 and 1903 saw the Barcelona republicans rapidly organise. The key figure was Alejandro Lerroux, who was the leading representative on the Left of the Spanish nationalist republican tradition (Alvarez Junco 1990: 320). He had cut his teeth in Madrid republican politics, and between 1897 and 1899 had gained widespread working-class sympathy in Barcelona when as director of the republican weekly, *El Progreso*, he spearheaded a

14. *El Socialista*, 15 June 1900.

Sardana, Zarzuela *or Cake Walk?*

campaign for a judicial review of the Montjuïc trial.[15] Lerroux had realised that in order to prosper republicanism needed a working-class base, and that Barcelona offered the most attractive environment. Hence, he transferred to Barcelona in March 1901 and was quickly able to dominate local republican politics. Over the next two years, under his leadership, the structure and language of republicanism in the city was overhauled. At a political and ideological level, although he integrated more moderate republicans into his movement, he adopted a leftist discourse which combined support for the labour unions, a philo- or psuedo-anarchistic rhetoric and fierce anticlericalism (Romero Maura 1975; Culla i Clarà 1986; Alvarez Junco 1990).

Yet the republicans were from the first faced with a powerful foe. The *Lliga Regionalista* also grew rapidly in strength, and the duel between these two formations dominated Barcelona politics throughout the decade. It was a fight in which no holds were barred. This should be related to the mental universe in which the propagandists of each of the formations moved. The new nationalist movement was exclusivist in nature, distinguishing between good Catalans who were within the Catalanist orbit, and the others, who must be either dupes or interlopers. The *Lliga*, in consequence, accused the Lerrouxists of being the dregs of society, rootless troublemakers or immigrants (*forasterada*), who had been sent to Catalonia by the authorities in order to disrupt the harmony of Catalan society through their violent and anarchistic doctrines. The republicans were not slow to respond. The enemy was in leftist republican cosmography an amalgam of reactionary Vaticanists and plutocrats, and so Lerroux tore into the *Lliga* with vehemence, accusing it of being a nest of clerical vipers, whose 'separatist' ideas were a backward-looking anachronism (Ametlla 1963: 240–1; Culla i Clarà 1986: 50–3; Alvarez Junco 1990: 347–50). Lerroux, therefore, was not unwilling to play the anti-Catalanist card. It is important to stress that in this as in much else Lerroux built on the currents already visible in the Catalan republican Left in the 1890s (Duarte 1987: 121–40). And it is difficult to believe that this would have been possible without some approval amongst the working-class base. Indeed if there had been a strongly defined working-class Catalanist culture it is hard to see how Lerroux, whose image was, to quote Ametlla again 'between that of a captain of Flanders and a Madrid "*xulo*"'(Ametlla 1963: 167),[16] could have been accepted as the head of Barcelona republicanism. Further-

15. This trial, held in 1896 after the bombing of a religious procession, was of infamous memory in leftist and working-class circles for torture had been used to extract false confessions of guilt.
16. The Castilian word *chulo* (translated into Catalan by Ametlla) referred originally to the Madrid lower classes, who were reputedly cocky and impudent.

more, the republicans' concept of the ruling class did not differ markedly from that of other groups on the Catalan Left. In general the Spanish State was seen as dominated by a reactionary, clerical oligarchy and within this block the Catalan 'bourgeoisie' was from the turn of the century seen as a key component.[17]

The Trials and Tribulations of the Catalanist Left

For Catalanist reformists this identification of Catalan nationalism with bourgeois interests would prove difficult to break down. In 1904 the republican and more strongly nationalist elements of the *Lliga* broke away, and two years later formed their own party, the *Centre Nacionalista Republicà* (CNR). Yet the leadership of the party, epitomised by such figures as Jaume Carner, Ildefons Sunyol and Pere Coromines, hailed from the cultured, wealthy, Barcelona middle classes, and though they might want to throw a protective cloak around a hypothetical reformist labour movement, they had little taste for the politics of insurrection, general strikes and plebeian anticlericalism. There was a group of leftists in the party who in general came from the populist, federalist, tradition, who were influential in the party's daily, *El Poble Català*, and who controlled a highly popular educational establishment, also used for frequent conferences, the *Ateneu Enciclopèdic Popular* (Popular Enciclopedic Athenaeum). This group did interest some workers, including the future leader of Catalan anarcho-syndicalism, Salvador Seguí, in Catalanism, but within the party it remained in the minority (Salut 1938: 140–2; Ferrer 1974: 40–1).

This was shown during the events of Tragic Week in 1909 (see Chapter 6). First the party refused to participate in a campaign launched to protest the call-up of reservists, then its leaders stood aloof during the strike organised by the syndicalist labour federation, *Solidaridad Obrera*. After the strike and church-convent burning had ended, the CNR's leading figures, at least privately, seemed to condone the repression unleashed by the Conservative government of Antonio Maura, and the party only tentatively participated in the campaign, organised by *Solidaridad Obrera*, for the release of political prisoners (Hurtado 1969: 162–3; Coromines 1974: 105). This of course has to be seen in its social context. Middle-class Barcelona was genuinely shocked by the events of Tragic Week, and both the politicians of the *Lliga* and leading figures in the CNR reflected this anxiety and the gen-

---

17. This was very clearly expressed in the protest meetings before Tragic Week. See, for example, *El Trabajo*, 6 June 1908; *Solidaridad Obrera*, 12 July 1908; *El Progreso*, 19 July 1909. *El Progreso* was the Lerrouxist daily from 1908.

eral state of mind that something had to be done. Yet it meant that the party would be unable to forge a solid working-class base.

The only time during these years when it seemed Catalanism could become an alliance taking in large numbers of all social classes was during the *Solidaritat Catalana* (SC) campaign of 1906–7. The campaign grew up as a result of attacks by army officers on the newspaper offices of the *Lliga* in November 1905, and the Liberal Segismundo Moret Government's decision to make all criticisms of the army in future subject to military jurisdiction. In response a wide-ranging alliance was forged in Catalonia, which from the first took in the *Lliga*, Carlists and the CNR. Furthermore, these events led to a split in Catalan republicanism, for while Lerroux declared he would not collaborate with what he termed as reactionary Vaticanists, many more moderate republicans migrated to the SC fold. These events were important on a number of levels. From this date in Catalonia the right-wing *españolista* tradition of republicanism was dead, and hence cooperation between the more reformist elements of Catalan labour and the liberal Left would in the future be refracted through a Catalanist mirror. This was the basis on which the nationalist movement would in the 1930s gain a sympathetic ear from wider sections of labour. Second, within SC the *Lliga* accepted universal manhood suffrage, and the coalition's so-called Tívoli programme called for a democratisation of the Spanish State. As a result, Catalanism could for the first time present itself as a civic protest movement against the reactionary army and monarchy (Alvarez Junco 1990: 354–5). Relatedly, though organised labour showed little enthusiasm for the SC campaign, as it reached a crescendo in the general elections of April 1907 many workers were – as *Solidaridad Obrera* admitted – pulled in the direction of the *Solidaritat* candidature.[18] Hence SC gained 51,000 votes in comparison to the Lerrouxists' 23,000, and was victorious in many of the more working-class districts.

This does indicate that a protest movement aimed at the abuses of the central state and military could attract widespread support. It was during this campaign that some workers began to identify with the new symbols of Catalan nationalism (Salut 1938: 147–8). Yet Lerroux, it seems clear, was able to retain most of his working-class base (Culla i Clarà 1986: 153–7). Detailed sociological profiles of the SC voters are not, of course available, and the fact that there was a considerable interclass component in all the Barcelona districts makes any social analysis of electoral results necessarily rather speculative. Nevertheless, it may be suggested that SC's core lower-class vote tended to consist of white collar and shopworkers, and workers who laboured in small workshops

18. *Solidaridad Obrera*, 19 October 1907.

and in an interclass community environment, and that in order to attract additional support it would need to fashion a policy more clearly in tune with workers' needs and aspirations.

Events following the collapse of the SC coalition in 1908 tend to bear this out. In the two municipal elections of 1909 the CNR formed a coalition with other republican groups that had formed part of the SC, and shortly before the May 1910 general elections they formed a new party, the *Unió Federal Nacionalista Republicà* (UNFR). The party gained support from all the city's districts, but in working-class areas it was largely eclipsed by the Lerrouxists, and was most strongly supported in districts such as Gracia and Sant Andreu, where there was still a strong, populist, interclass tradition. Hence, the description of Catalanist republicans as dominated by 'liberal elements, small tradesmen and artisans' (Bueso 1976: 14). A similar conclusion can be reached if one looks at the working-class organisations which clearly supported Catalanist demands. The CNR strongly defended the *Ateneos Obreros* from right-wing charges that they were centres of dangerous, revolutionary doctrines, and indeed their reopening was the party's foremost preoccupation after Tragic Week. Within the labour movement they received greatest support from the shopworkers (Lladonosa and Ferrer 1977: 292–7). The lower-middle classes and the shopworkers were certainly to give Catalanism a popular edge, yet this did not necessarily mean that the Catalanism would further spread into the working class. There was, indeed, some considerable antagonism between blue and white collar workers, the latter being accused of wishing to imitate the middle classes and looking down upon their manual brethren.[19]

Labour and the Cultural Politics of Catalanism

These divisions cannot, of course, simply be seen in political or even social terms, but must be viewed within the community, cultural milieu and value system in which they operated. In this sense all political ideologies need to be seen as part cultural, a set of shared values which serve to give coherence, an emotional bond and a sense of purpose to the group. Barcelona had since the mid-nineteenth century become a city increasingly divided along class lines. Elites had moved out of the Old Quarter to the space and light of the newly built *Eixample* (Extension), while the established commercial classes plied their trade in the sixth district on the right of the main *Ramblas* thoroughfare, which divided the old city in two. Other districts, such as Gracia and Sant

19. See, for example, *Solidaridad Obrera*, 9 October, 9 November 1907; Sans Orenga (1975: 45–6).

Sardana, Zarzuela *or Cake Walk?*

Andreu, as has been noted, still retained an interclass environment, with small employers, merchants, artisans and workers intermingling. Yet other areas were becoming increasingly proletarianised. This included the port district of the Barceloneta, the fifth district on the left of the *Ramblas*, and outlying districts such as Clot, Sant Martí, Sants and Hostafrancs. The middle- and working-class worlds were becoming in many respects mutually exclusive. Workers could easily feel excluded from the wealth of middle-class districts while proletarian Barcelona was for many middle-class observers a threatening place. The contrast is illustrated by the chasm which separated the solid respectable sixth district from the working-class fifth district, with its ill-lit, dirty, unhygienic backstreets, its bawdy Avenida de Paralelo and the notorious streets around Conde del Asalto, where prostitution was rife.[20]

The new Catalan nationalist movement was centred on middle-class Barcelona. It was a movement in part in tune with the propertied classes and commerce, but which also had strong rural roots. This was reflected in the spiritual and cultural representation of the new nation. The *volksgeist* of the Catalan people presented by the Catalanists was that of the serious, thrifty, hard-working family (in contrast to the supposed laziness and profligacy of the Castilians); its cultural symbols a nationalist rendition of traditional rural folk songs and the popular rural dance of the Empordà, the *sardana*, which was adopted as the new national dance (Romero Maura 1975: 427–9; Marfany 1995: 293–353). Simultaneously, the mountain of Montserrat and the benedictine monastery near its summit became the nation's spiritual heartland.

Of course this carefully constructed ideal of national culture differed markedly from the heterogeneous cultural influences in operation throughout urban Catalonia. Nevertheless, it may be suggested that the mismatch was greatest in the working-class areas. This is not to say that the workers were not Catalans. In the more working-class areas non-Catalan migrant workers formed approximately 25 per cent of the population at the turn of the century (little more than the average throughout Barcelona) (Ayuntamiento de Barcelona 1903: 132–5), and Emili Salut, in his recollections of his youth in the fifth district, also maintains that it was the district which best conserved the traditional festivities (Salut 1938: 118–19). But entertainment differed wildly from the Catalanist ideal. For the youth the public dance represented without doubt the favourite Saturday night out (Valdour 1919: 250). Older workers preferred the theatre (and later cinema), either in the premises of leftist associations or the new theatres which were opening in the

20. A feel for the chasm which divided the fifth and sixth districts can be gained from comparing the recollections of Salut (1938) and Regàs i Ardèvol (1960).

Paralelo. Here Catalan (and Catalanist) playwrights, especially Angel Guimerà and Santiago Rusiñol, did have some impact, but they were overshadowed by French melodramas, which often acquired strong social overtones. This was reflected in reading habits with Victor Hugo's *Les misérables* a perennial favourite. Worse from a Catalanist perspective, as the Paralelo and adjacent streets expanded in the early years of the century flamenco (especially around the turn of the century) and then the zarzuela (*género chico*) and cuplé dominated the dancing and music scene. Bullfighting was at the same time extremely popular in working-class circles.[21] Later in the decade the American cake walk, Brazilian rumba and machicha and Argentinean tango began to be played regularly by the street pianists (Cabañas Guevara 1945). Catalan workers were not heavy drinkers, though the bars and taverns rapidly filled on Saturday evening. However, prostitution was totally generalised, with most young working men's first sexual experience being in a brothel (Rosell 1940: 65–6). And what must have appeared as moral laxity can only have been confirmed by the frequency of cohabitation in working-class quarters (Salut 1938: 113). The diversity of interests, leisure pursuits and lifestyles can be seen in the rather bizarre diversity of sales in the Sunday morning bookshops and book market which opened in the upper Paralelo, and which were characterised by, 'books by Ibsen, Tolstoy, Gorky, Mirbau, Blasco, a lot of melodramas, a lot of esperanto and quite a bit of pornography' (Cabañas Guevara 1945: 151).

In these circumstances it is not surprising that, as Emili Salut comments, 'the working class was never interested in a Catalanism too full of traditions; the *Jocs Florals*, the Virgin of Montserrat and a poetic folklore which so contrasted with the prosaic business of the rich industrialists' (Salut 1938: 145). Indeed, moral conduct and cultural pursuits became a political battleground between Catalanists and Lerrouxists, with the latter portraying young Catalanists as frustrated virgins, whose dances and folklore were, like their politics, out of touch with the modern world. Nor was abuse merely verbal, as testified by the scandal aroused when a group of Lerrouxists disrupted a recital of the *sardana* with an impromptu rendition of the cake walk (Romero Maura 1975: 454).

This is not to say that workers could not be attracted to the Catalanist fold. Amongst Catalan workers there was without doubt a sense of being Catalan. Indeed, skilled workers, it seems, often looked down

21. According to Pere Manat in *La Veu de Catalunya*, 'the principal elements ...which do most harm to our fatherland (are) bull fights, the *género chico* and the *cafés-concierto*'. Cited in Romero Maura (1975: 428).

upon the unskilled migrants from other parts of Spain (Valdour 1919: 78). And in less conflictive trades, particularly where promotion was a possibility, the sense of vertical national identity could no doubt predominate over class identities.[22] Moreover, as has been noted, from the formation of the SC Catalanism took on a more democratic air. While working in Badalona the French traveller, Jacques Valdour, describes the figure of Puig, who was employed in a sugar refinery, and who staunchly defended the Catalan language and read the satirical Catalanist weekly *Papitu* (though he switched to the Lerrouxist *El Progreso* when there was a strike) (Valdour 1919: 174, 208–9). Yet it seems that for most workers the concept of Catalonia as a nation had not penetrated. For example, in a campaign against a flare-up in the Moroccan conflict in 1911, Joaquín Bueso, a key figure in Barcelona trade unionism since 1907: 'States that those who for centuries and centuries fought for their independence have no right to usurp the independence of other peoples. If in the past the Spanish threw the Moors (*moros*) out of Spain, then the Moors have the same right to throw out of Africa whosoever should want to seize it.'[23] Yet, as the quote makes clear, this is not to say that there was a fiery sense of Spanish patriotism. Hence, while Lerroux could rail again the 'reactionary' Catalanists he needed to keep his own Spanish nationalist rhetoric in check. Opposition to Spanish imperialism was, of course, amply demonstrated by the events of Tragic Week (see Chapter 6). Indeed, rather than a sense of national belonging there seems little doubt that horizontal identities – attachment to the working class or the 'people' (*pueblo*) – were more important.

Nevertheless, despite this lukewarm attachment to the Spanish nation, for Catalanism to extend its influence in working-class circles two interrelated developments were needed. First, the hegemony of the *Lliga* over Catalanist politics would have to be broken, and a new, more wholeheartedly reformist, Catalan nationalist party be constructed. Second, broader sectors of labour would have to be convinced of the practicability and desirability of collaborating in an interclass project of reform. Only in the Second Republic would these factors begin seriously to operate. Yet, at the same time, in so-called 'outcast' Barcelona, in the fifth district and in the peripheral working-class quarters, large numbers of unskilled workers saw no benefits flowing from the Republic and became enmeshed in a rebellious, lawless subculture, hostile to Catalanism and dominated politically by hardline anarcho-syndicalists (Ealham 1995). The growth of this subculture was not,

22. However, these formed only a minority of workers engaged in the skilled trades at this time. See Smith (1996).
23. *Solidaridad Obrera*, 11 August 1911.

however, simply the consequence of the waves of Murcian and Andalusian immigrants that arrived in Barcelona from the First World War, but, as has been made clear, also drew heavily on the lifestyles and mentalities which were already being forged at the turn of the century.

References

Alvarez Junco, José (1976), *La ideología política del anarquismo español, 1870–1910*, Madrid
—— (1990), *El emperador del Paralelo. Lerroux y la demagogia populista*, Madrid
Ametlla, Claudi (1963), *Memòries polítiques, 1890–1917*, Barcelona
Ayuntamiento de Barcelona (1903), *Anuario estadístico de la ciudad de Barcelona 1902*, Barcelona
Bengoechea, Soledad (1994), *Organització patronal i conflictivitat social a Catalunya. Tradició i corporativisme entre finals de segle i la dictatura de Primo de Rivera*, Barcelona
Bonamusa, Francesc (ed.) (1976), *Congreso de constitución de la Confederación Nacional del Trabajo*, Barcelona
Bueso, Adolfo (1976), *Recuerdos de un cenetista*, vol.1, Barcelona
Cabañas Guevara, Luis (1945), *Biografía del Paralelo, 1894–1934*, Barcelona
Coromines, Pere (1974), *De la Solidaritat al catorze d'abril. Diaris i records de Pere Coromines*, vol.2, Barcelona
Cucurull, Félix (1978), 'De la restauració monàrquica al "tancament de caixes"', in *Història de Catalunya Salvat*, vol.5, Barcelona
Culla i Clarà, Joan B. (1986), *El republicanisme lerrouxista a Catalunya, 1901–1923*, Barcelona
Duarte, Angel (1987), *El republicanisme català a la fi del segle XIX*, Vic
—— (1993), 'Republicanos y nacionalismo. El impacto del catalanismo en la cultura política republicana', *Historia Contemporánea*, no.10, pp.157–76
Ealham, Christopher (1995), 'Anarchism and Illegality in Barcelona, 1931–1937', *Contemporary European History*, vol.4, pp.131–51
E.R.A. 80 (1977), *Els anarquistes, educadors del poble: "La Revista Blanca" (1898–1905)*, Barcelona
Ferrer, Joaquim (1974), *Francesc Leyret, 1880–1922*, Barcelona
Gabriel, Pere (1986), 'Anarquisme i catalanisme', in Termes, Josep et al., *Catalanisme: història, política i cultura*, Barcelona, pp.195–210
Hobsbawm, E.J. (1992), *Nations and Nationalism since 1780. Programme, Myth, Reality*, 2nd edn, Cambridge
Hurtado, Amadeu (1969), *Quaranta anys d'advocat. Història del meu temps, 1849–1930*, Barcelona

Sardana, Zarzuela *or Cake Walk?*

Izard, Miguel (1973), *Industrialización y obrerismo. Las Tres Clases de Vapor 1869–1913*, Barcelona
Lladonosa, Manuel and Ferrer, Joaquim (1977), 'Nacionalisme català i reformisme social en els treballadors mercantils a Barcelona. El CADCI', in Balcells, Albert (ed.), *Teoría y práctica del movimiento obrero en España, 1900–1936*, Valencia, pp.281–329
Lorenzo, Anselmo (1974), *El Proletariado Militante*, prólogo y notas de José Alvarez Junco, Madrid
Marfany, Joan-Lluis (1995), *La cultura del catalanisme*, Barcelona
Olivé Serret, Enric (1977), 'El moviment anarquista català i l'obrerisme, 1900–1909', unpublished PhD thesis, Universitat Autònoma de Barcelona
—— (1984), '"La Tramontana", periòdic vermell (1881–1893) i el naturalisme de Josep Llunas i Pujals', *Estudios de Historia Social*, nos 28–9, pp.319–26
—— (1987), 'L'Anarquisme i el catalanisme. Entre el mite i la confusió', *L'Avenç*, no.102, p.5
Regàs i Ardèvol, Miquel (1960), *Confessions, 1880–1936*, Barcelona
Reventòs, Manuel (1925), *Assaig sobre alguns episodis dels moviments socials en Barcelona en el segle XIX*, Barcelona
Riquer, Borja de (1977), *Lliga regionalista: la burgesia catalana i el nacionalisme, 1898–1904*, Barcelona
Romero Maura, Joaquín (1975), *La Rosa del Fuego. Republicanos y anarquistas: la política de los obreros catalanes entre el desastre colonial y la Semana Trágica*, Barcelona
Rosell, Alba (1940), *Recuerdos de educador*, vol.2, unpublished memoirs, Montevideo
Salut, Emili (1938), *Vivers de revolucionaris. Apunts històrics del districte cinqué*, Barcelona
Sans Orenga, M. (1975), *Els treballadors mercantils dins el moviment obrer català*, Barcelona
Smith, Angel (1991), 'Social Conflict and Trade Union Organisation in the Catalan Cotton Textile Industry, 1890–1914', *International Review of Social History*, vol.36, no.3, pp.331–76
—— (1996), 'Trabajadores "dignos" en profesiones "honradas": los oficios y la formación de la clase obrera barcelonesa, 1899–1914,' *Hispania*, no.193, pp.291–326
—— (1997), 'Anarchism, the General Strike and the Barcelona Labour Movement, 1899–1914', *European History Quarterly*, vol.27, no.1
Solà, Pere (1978), *Els ateneus obrers i la cultura popular a Catalunya, 1900–1939. El Ateneu Enciclopèdic Popular*, Barcelona
Solé Tura, Jordi (1974), *Catalanismo y revolución burguesa*, 2nd edn, Madrid

Termes, Josep (1972), 'El federalisme català en el període revolucionari de 1868 a 1873', *Recerques*, no.2, pp.33–69

—— (1974), 'El nacionalisme català: *problemes de interpretació'*, *Primer Col.loqui de historiadors*, Barcelona, pp.43–54

—— (1987), 'Els Ateneus Populars: un intent de cultura obrera', *L'Avenç*, no.104, pp. 9–11

Ucelay da Cal, Enric (1982), *La Catalunya populista. Imatge, cultura i política en l'étapa republicana, 1931–1939*, Barcelona

Valdour, Jacques (1919), *La vie ouvrière. L'ouvrier espagnol. Observacions vécues. Tomo 1. Catalogne*, Lille/Paris

–11–

The Role of Commemorations in (Ethno)Nation-Building. The Case of Catalonia
Josep R. Llobera

Love thou thy land, with love far-brought
From out the storied past, and used
Within the Present, but transfused
Thro' future time by power of thought.

Tennyson

Introduction

In 1977 a monograph entitled 'Rural Catalonia under Franco's Regime' was published. The author, Edward Hansen, was then an up-and-coming American anthropologist who had done the standard fieldwork stint in the Catalan provincial town of Vilafranca del Penedès (the commercial centre of the *cava*-producing area) in the late 1960s. Hansen's general conclusion was that modernisation had eradicated Catalan national identity (Llobera 1990: 17–8). Hansen was not, however, the only social scientist to have written off Catalan national identity in the 1960s and early 1970s.

With hindsight this might seem a rather ill-considered conclusion, but in fact it responds to an attitude that fails to understand the irreducible, *sui generis* character of national identity, and hence it cannot account for its amazing tenacity and resilience. What it tends to miss is what I would call the materiality of culture, the materiality of the ideational. It is as if some contemporary scholars have not learnt the lesson beautifully inscribed in a passage written by Mauss and Fauconnet in 1901, that reads as follows: 'Sociological explanation assigns a preponderant role to. . .collective beliefs and sentiments' (Mauss 1968: 29). But lest I should be misunderstood, what the Durkheimian School is suggesting is not an ideational explanation, but just a corrective to those (and they are still legion today) who give primacy to economic or social structures. 'There is nothing more vain than to enquire if ideas create societies or whether the latter, once formed, generate collective ideas. In fact, these are inseparable phenomena, and it is nonsense to try to establish any kind of primacy, either logical or chronological' (ibid.: 28).

Unfortunately for Hansen *et alia*, on 11 September 1977, one million Catalans demonstrated peacefully through the streets of Barcelona in favour of self-government, that is, the re-instatement of the 1932 Statute of Autonomy. Franco had been dead for only two years. In Spain the political transition from dictatorship to democracy was a peaceful process which took place in a relatively short period of time. By 1978 the new Spanish Constitution had been approved and in 1979 a new Statute of Autonomy of Catalonia was in place. The force of Catalan nationalism had to be reckoned with in the shaping of the new Spanish state; and without the Catalan and Basque pressures there would have been no decentralised Spanish state.

What Hansen and many other observers of the Catalan reality had missed was that under conditions of severe repression, nationalist sentiments are to be found at different registers from the usual ones appropriate for liberal-democratic countries. Where there is no free press and where political parties are banned, the culture of resistance will of necessity express itself in subtle ways. The ethnonationalisms that made their first public appearance in Eastern Europe in the late 1980s came as total surprise to the Western social scientific community. Communism, is was believed, had solved the national question. But, as Graham Smith has shown for the Baltic Countries, nationalism had never disappeared, it had just taken other cultural forms (1994).

The parallelism between the Catalan case and that of the Baltic Countries in the transition from dictatorship to democracy has been emphasised by Hank Johnston, among others. He mentions seven main points of convergence: the vitality of nationalism after many years of repression, the memory of previous political autonomy, the crucial national role of the Church, the liberalisation of the state, the conflict between hegemonic and subordinated nations within the state, the presence of an important immigrant population and the progressive delegitimisation of the ancient regime (Johnston 1991: 202–3).

It is interesting to note that Hansen had decided to ignore the evidence presented by a colleague, under the excuse that he was a petty-bourgeois Catalan nationalist. Oriol Pi-Sunyer, an American anthropologist of Catalan origin, had suggested, as early as 1971, that at least three levels of ethnonationalist affirmation could be observed in the Catalan case (1971: 130):

1. At the family level Catalan national identity was preserved in a variety of ways. Speaking the native language was an act of Catalan affirmation, particularly as it meant fighting against the tide of Castilianisation; reading books in Catalan was another. The latter was not easy in the early period of Francoism, but many middle-class families had preserved small Catalan libraries. At a more general level, the family was the only channel of socialisation into a sort of romantic and mythological history of Catalonia. Last but not least, Catalan lore (songs, proverbs, games, etc.) were also transmitted mainly through the family.

2. At a more formal level, a variety of groups (some social and recreational, others more intellectual and cultural) also contributed to the maintenance and transmission of Catalan identity. A good number of these organisations worked under the umbrella of the Catholic Church. These groups reflected a thriving civil society. Typical of such groups were excursionist clubs, choral societies, folk dance groups, cinema clubs, alumnae associations, literary organisations and gatherings, etc. Some sections of the Church itself played a decisive role in the first major movement of 'communitas' (Turner, in Pi-Sunyer 1971) which took place in Catalonia in the post-war period. The ceremony of enthronement of the Virgin of Monserrat in 1947 was the first occasion in which Catalans of all persuasions had the chance to express their national identity, albeit through a disguised religious veil. Around 70,000 people attended the rituals in which a variety of symbols of Catalan identity was present (including a huge illegal Catalan flag and the limited use of the Catalan language). This episode became, in the long years to come until Franco's death, a reservoir of national strength; many resistance organisations which prospered in the 1950s and 1960s stem from this first popular re-encounter with the idea of a Catalan community (Frigolé 1980).

3. At the level of the underground political parties. Although they were of different ideological signs, they were all committed to a national (if not nationalist) vision of Catalonia.

It is possible to conclude provisionally that the Catalan case shows that while history was written by the winners – that is, a crypto-fascist Spanish national-Catholicism bent on eradicating Catalan separatism – the losers managed to preserve their ethnonational identity in the ways just described. However, the resilience of Catalan national identity would have been unthinkable had there not existed a reasonable degree of (ethno)national consciousness by the 1930s. This, in turn, was the result of one hundred years of (ethno)nation-building which had started with a cultural renaissance (*Renaixença*) between 1833 and 1885 and had continued with a movement for political autonomy – a process which culminated in the 1932 Statute of Autonomy (see Chapter 1).

History and Memory in the Recent Literature

What happens when, as is the case of Catalonia after 1979, with the coming of political and cultural autonomy, there seems to arise a need to connect with a suppressed past which becomes the indispensable foundation of the *geistliche Gemeinschaft* (i.e. the spiritual community)? Does this mean a return to the era of romantic nationalism as some critics claim? In an ethnonationalism which is forward-looking, would not the idea of Habermas's 'constitutional patriotism' or that of Schnapper's 'community of citizens' suffice? Or is there always bound to be at least a residual dimension based on the ideas of common history, common language and common culture? What has been the discourse of the Catalan autonomous government and that of the wider Catalan civil society concerning the (re)making of Catalan identity?

What kinds of theoretical tools do we possess to look at the central issue of this paper, that is, the role of historical memory in ethnonation-building? The modern literature on the topic seems to emphasise the invented, the fabricated character of this history (Hobsbawm and Ranger 1983). Even if this were the case, why are some invented histories more successful than others? Furthermore, perhaps there are other types of history. Bernard Lewis definitely thinks so. In a thin, but significant book he identifies three types of history: remembered history, recovered history and invented history. Remembered history is the collective memory of a community; what the social group 'chooses to remember as significant, both as reality and symbol' (1975: 12). It is common to all types of societies and 'it embodies poetic and symbolic truth as understood by the people, even where it is inaccurate in detail. . . It is preserved in commemorative ceremonies and monuments,. . .official celebrations, popular entertainment and elementary education' (ibid.: 11–12).

Recovered history is the consequence of a retrieval of past events by academic scholarship. These are events which for one reason or another have been forgotten and after a shorter or longer period of time are recovered by scholars studying archives, conducting archaeological digs, deciphering obscure languages, etc. Hence, a forgotten past is being reconstructed. And this is an activity fraught with dangers. What separates recovered history from invented history is that while both imply a reconstruction of the past, the latter (when necessary) fabricates facts to suit a political purpose.

A look at the literature of the past few years shows a growing interest in the issues of history and memory (Lowental 1985; Namer 1987; Connerton 1989; Middleton and Edwards 1990; Fentress and Wickham 1992; Hutton 1993; Gillis 1994). All these developments are tributary to the work of a leading French Durkheimian, Maurice Halbwachs, who in three classic studies (*Les Cadres sociaux de la mémoire* (1925), *La topographie légendaire des evangiles en Terre Sainte* (1941) and *La mémoire collective* (1950)) did the essential groundwork for a sociology of memory.

A recent major contribution to the study of historical memory, inspired by Halbwachs's method, is a collection in seven volumes directed by Pierre Nora and entitled *Les lieux de la mémoire* (*The Sites of Memory*); it was published between 1986 and 1992. It deals with the representation of the French national memory. An array of specialists offer us an inventory of the different traditions that have shaped the French national memory. Nora and his contributors follow the diverse paths (republican, national and cultural traditions) which provide a key to French national identity. For Nora 'the memory of the past is central to the identity in the present' (Hutton 1993: 89). And this is even more the case after the demise of the communist utopia.

In an earlier work, Nora had distinguished between collective memory and historical memory. By collective memory he meant what 'is left from the past in the actual experience of groups (including nations) or that which these groups make of the past. . .. Collective memories evolve with the groups and constitute an inalienable asset which can be manipulated; they are both a tool for the struggle for power, as well as a symbolic and affective stake (*enjeu*)' (1978: 398). Historical memories are the 'result of a scholarly and scientific tradition; they are the collective memory of a specific group: the professional historians. Historical memories are analytic and critical, precise and distinctive. They have to do with reason – which instructs without convincing. . .. Historical memories filter, accumulate, capitalise and transmit' (ibid.: 399).

This distinction between collective memory and historical memory reminds us somewhat of Lewis's remembered history and recovered history. Some recent critics have strongly objected to Nora's idea that memory and history are different, and more importantly to the implication that the latter is superior to the former. Elizabeth Tonkin, for example, does not accept that history is 'just reconstruction of what no longer exists' and insists that 'however carefully and critically historians reconstruct, they have also been formed by memory. This means also that their choice of topic is unlikely to be independent of social identity, a historical construction rich in the imaginary, which claim us all' (1992: 119).

What is important in Nora, whether we agree or not with his distinction between historical memory and collective memory, is his creation of a history of France through memory. His crucial theoretical tool is that of '*lieu de mémoire*' (site or place of memory). The history of any modern country is made of an 'array of sites of memory that have been invested with enduring and emotive symbolic significance'. A *lieu de mémoire* is 'a meaningful entity of a real or imagined kind, which has become a symbolic element of a given community as a result of human will or the effect of time' (Wood 1994: 123–4). However, 'all that we refer to today as memory is not really memory but already history. . ... The need for memory is a need for history' (Nora 1986: I.XXV). As to the *lieux de mémoire*, they are 'memories worked over by history, – which is to say, worked over by professional historians who are concerned to respond to the felt emotional and psychological needs of their fellow citizens' (Englund 1992: 305).

A Catalan Case Study

We can now return to the issue of the role of historical memory in the (re)making of Catalan national identity after Franco's death. There is little doubt, as I have already implied, that historical memory is one of the central components of contemporary Catalan identity (language being perhaps the most important one). The point of departure of my enquiry are the sites where the Catalan nation 'places voluntarily its memories or rediscovers them as a necessary part of its personality' (Nora 1978: 401). In this chapter I shall concentrate on what Nora refers to as symbolic sites. I have chosen two key anniversaries for consideration: the commemoration of 11 September (National Day) and the celebration of 23 April (Book Day). In addition, I shall be examining the speeches of Jordi Pujol (the President of the Catalan Autonomous Government) delivered on the National Day commemorations. Finally, I propose to consider the centenary commemorations of the First Convention for Catalan Autonomy (*Bases de Manresa*).

A Commemoration (11 September)

The reason why commemorations are so important from the perspective of nation-building is because they strengthen what Halbwachs called the 'habits of mind', bringing about specific recollections of the past in the form of images. Commemorations tend to be selective, structuring time and space in a certain way. Only a few events and places can profitably be remembered (Hutton 1993: 79–80).

Commemorations are particularly useful when the sense of continuity of a nation has been lost through conquest or occupation (and later recovered) or has been changed through revolution. In these cases, a commemoration signifies a rupture with a certain undesirable past. Furthermore, commemorations are also useful when there exist divergent representations of time past and an unitary version of national identity is required. Finally, fragile nations and new nations are in special need of commemorations (Gillis 1994: 8–9). To conclude, human societies in general, and nations in particular, seem to have an irrational fear of historical emptiness; hence a connection with the past appears as extremely desirable (Llobera 1994: X). This 'possession in common of a rich heritage of memories' that Renan (cited in Bhabha 1990: 19) referred to seems to be a constant point of reference of national commemorations, but also of celebrations – which are perhaps more festive in character but nonetheless as important.

The 11 September is at present Catalonia's National Day (*Diada Nacional*). It commemorates the fall of Barcelona to the troops of Philip V (the Bourbon contender to the Spanish throne) in 1714. The defence of the city was led by Antoni Villaroel and Rafael Casanova, two names who are remembered with streets in Barcelona's *Eixample*; Casanova has also a monument in the city centre. The defeat, in addition to the ferocious repression that followed, meant the end of autonomy for Catalonia and the beginning of the political centralisation of the Kingdom of Spain (*Decreto de Nueva Planta*, 1716).

During the period of the *Renaixença* (1833–85), the 11 September began to acquire a certain meaning by making its appearance in some of the historical novels of the period. But in fact the tradition of commemorating that date began in 1901, when a group of young people decided to place a wreath in the monument to Casanova in Barcelona (*Arc de Triomf*) on 11 September; they were rudely interrupted by the police and sent to jail. There followed an act of protest organised by the *Unió Catalanista* (a political association created in 1891 with the goal of promoting Catalanism) against the detentions; and another wreath was placed in the monument to Casanova (Albareda 1991: 62–3).

It is from 1901 onwards, then, that we can say that a tradition of patriotic commemoration of the 11 September started. The state authorities tended to repress these patriotic demonstrations, particularly during the Dictatorship of Primo de Rivera (1923–30). During the short Republican period the commemorations were legal and encouraged by the Catalan autonomous government. With the coming of the Francoist dictatorship demonstrations were completely banned and the monument to Casanova was withdrawn (though the street name was preserved). Nonetheless, 11 September was always marked in a more or less public way by a small but active minority. From 1964 onwards the number of people demonstrating grew noticeably and 1971 was the first time that the Catalan national anthem (*Els Segadors*) was sung publicly (Albareda 1991: 63).

The tradition of commemorating 11 September was allowed once again in 1976. There followed a mass demonstration in Barcelona which proceeded to Sant Boi de Llobregat (Casanova's death place), on the periphery of the city. As I have already mentioned, on 11 September 1977 there was a mass demonstration of about one million people in favour of the Statute of Autonomy. In 1980 the Parliament of Catalonia passed unanimously a bill declaring 11 September the National Day of Catalonia (Albareda 1991: 757–8). It has been customary since 1980 for the President of the Generalitat (Jordi Pujol) to address the country on the occasion of the National Day. Before analysing the content of his speeches which are, I think, essential to understanding the whole process of nation-(re)building in the 1980s and 1990s, I would like to discuss briefly the other key anniversary of the Catalan calendar, that is, the 23 April, which celebrates St George's Day.

A Celebration (23 April)

What does St George's Day mean for the Catalans? It is essentially a day on which all those who are either Catalans by birth or who live and work in Catalonia and want to be Catalans feel a certain sense of pride in themselves. The 23 April is not only a celebration of the patron-saint of Catalonia; it was also chosen because it coincides with the anniversary of the death of two great writers: Shakespeare and Cervantes. It is interesting to note in passing that the initiative for Books Day originated with the Spanish state in 1926, at the instigation of publishers. However, its popularity started only in 1931 and its was circumscribed to Catalonia.

The image projected by the day's events is fundamentally a festive one. The towns of Catalonia, but particularly Barcelona, awaken to hectic cultural activity which will last until late in the day. To the superficial observer 23 April will appear as just another, perhaps glorified, book fair – which the innumerable street bookstalls confirm. In fact, 23 April is much more than a book fair because, alongside books, red roses and Catalan flags are present. It is customary to buy a book and a rose (decorated with a small red and yellow ribbon) for loved ones. St George's Day is an extremely popular festivity which brings together natives and immigrants. In Barcelona thousands of people participate in the ritual struggle through the crowded *Ramblas* to choose the right book (and the rose) for loved ones (including oneself).

The celebration contributes in no minor way to the creation of a sense of community, even if diffuse, which is focused not on past values but on perennial ones. wo essential values are enhanced here: cultural sensibility and amity. These are features which are typically based not on the principle of ethnic exclusion, but on the idea of int ration: they generate what has recently been labelled ivic nationalism. By focusing on universalist values (literary appreciation and love of others) it is possible to transcend the dangers of chau inism which are present in all nationalisms (Durkheim **dixit**).

The success of Book Day (*Diada del Llibre*) has recently prompted the Generalitat of Catalonia to undertake two initiatives at the international level: first, to send a book of a Catalan author in translation, as well as a rose, to a select list of world heads of state on 23 April; second, to suggest to UNESCO that 23 April should become International Book Day.

The contrasts between 23 April and 11 September could not be more striking, and can be expressed in the following list of opposites:

23 April	**11 September**
Popular	Official
Universalist	Particularist
Present-oriented	Past-oriented
Non-heroic	Heroic
Profane	Sacred
Civic	Ethnic
Culture of leisure and love	Culture of resistance and grievance

The 11 September Speeches of Jordi Pujol

I have mentioned above that, in the context of the commemoration of the National Day of Catalonia, I would refer to the speeches of Jordi Pujol (1993). In many respects Pujol is no ordinary politician. He has presided over the Generalitat (Catalan Autonomous Government) since 1980, having won four successive elections – which is no mean achievement. A medical doctor by training, he has always been a man of strong religious and nationalist convictions. He was active in the resistance movement against Franco from the 1950s, and he spent some three years in jail for his political activities. In the 1960s, without abandoning politics, he was involved in policies of nation-building (*fer pais*) at economic and cultural levels.

At present Pujol represents the political centre, having evolved from a social-democratic position to a more liberal one. He is the unchallenged leader of *CiU* (a centre-right coalition which has governed Catalonia since 1980). Concerning the Catalan national question, Pujol has pursued a policy of both firmness and compromise *vis-à-vis* the Spanish state. Although not a supporter of outright independence, he is still in favour of taking the Statute of Autonomy to its virtual limits. An astute politician, Pujol has a clear European vocation and sees in the European Union a Europe of the regions in which small stateless nations like Catalonia can flourish and be free (see Chapter 11). Although neither a prolific nor an intellectual writer, his books and his collections of speeches are politically cunning and historiographically sophisticated; they are also an indispensable tool for the understanding of contemporary developments in Catalonia.

What are, then, the leitmotivs of Pujol's 11 September speeches? At one immediate level, 11 September commemorates not a defeat, but the heroic deeds and sacrifices of the Catalans of nearly two hundred years ago. In the face of an overwhelmingly superior army of foreign invaders, the Catalans defended the will to survive as a people, as a nation. Hence, 11 September honours the brave ancestors of the Catalan people of today. From a more contemporary perspective, the commemoration implies the will to maintain a country with a millennial history, a common culture, a common language and common institutions. Of course, each historical period commemorated 11 September in different ways: from the 1940s to the 1960s was a time of resistance, the 1970s a time of popular mobilisations and the 1980s and 1990s a time to consolidate Catalan autonomy.

But the heroic register is not the only one mentioned by Pujol. In many of his speeches he asks rhetorically what happened on 12 September 1714. And the answer is that on that day the Catalans went back to work; that is, they channelled their energies in productive directions. This was not a betrayal of lofty ideals, but a reflection of Catalan pragmatism. In this way they reconstructed, through their own efforts, a country which had been ravaged by a cruel war. This can only be done by a people which is self-confident and willing to keep its language and culture in the face of adversity. This was a collective effort undertaken by a hard-working people with a civic spirit.

These two features of heroism and tenacity, which constitute the essence that can be distilled from this episode of Catalan history, is not all that Pujol wants to emphasise. He also looks at three current variables: economic progress, social integration and development of the autonomous community. In relation to economic progress, the speeches obviously reflect the vagaries of the growth and decline of the GNP, the level of unemployment, the degree of competitiveness of the country, etc. Perhaps the main message here is the attempt to infuse self-confidence in the historically demonstrated economic abilities of the Catalan people. As a convinced European, Pujol also believes that modernisation means Europeanisation: that the country has to prepare itself to compete advantageously in the EC. Social integration, that is the fate of the immigrant population in Catalonia, is another leitmotiv of the speeches. As I have mentioned before, this is an old concern of Pujol who, in 1965, had already stated that 'a Catalan is whoever lives and works in Catalonia and wishes to be Catalan'. The danger of the creation of two opposed communities is what has prompted Pujol's attempt to integrate the immigrant population in a democratic way.

Concerning development of the autonomous community, the speeches reflect the constant battle with the central government over the speedy implementation of the Statute of Autonomy. This is a theme that appears every year and that reflects the frustration of the stop-go policies of the state. However, Pujol does not despair; rather, he shows an amazing amount of tenacity in pursuit of higher levels of autonomy short of independence. According to Pujol, the events of 1989 in Eastern Europe gave a boost to the rights of peoples to self-government. In this sense, he asserted the right of the Catalan people to see in recent events a new justification and a reinforcement of its national claims. On the positive side, the Statute of Autonomy has allowed the Catalans a number of achievements; linguistic progress is an obvious one, following on the Law of Lingusitic Normalisation of 1983 (see Chapter 4).

A final point: Pujol is well aware of the importance of commemorations as a means to preserve identity and enhance patriotism. He often emphasises the importance of origins, using organic metaphors (trees, roots). History is essential for the making of the nation. In his speeches there are often references to other commemorations sponsored by the Generalitat: the millenary in 1988 of the birth of Catalonia out of the Carolingian matrix, the 350th anniversary of the War of the Reapers, the centenary of the *Bases de Manresa* in 1992, etc.

A Centenary Commemoration: The Bases de Manresa

The Centenary of the *Bases de Manresa* (First Convention for Catalan Autonomy) was celebrated in 1992. Although there was an official initiative for the commemoration which stemmed from the Generalitat, there were also active voices arising from the Catalan civil society. The Managing Committee of the Centenary consisted of a variety of literary, recreational, sporting, cultural and political organisations; more than seven hundred non-governmental groups adhered to the commemoration and signed a document putting forward a number of demands which essentially amounted to a manifesto for the self-determination of the Catalan nation. The fact that the Centenary of the *Bases de Manresa* coincided with the year of the Olympic Games meant that the celebrations of the former were largely eclipsed by the multitudinous repercussions of the sporting event. In any case, the Olympic Games could hardly be instrumentalised as a purely Catalan happening, while the *Bases de Manresa* could.

Independently of the way in which the *Bases de Manresa* have been historically interpreted, it is clear that there is a tendency to see them, as Rovira i Virgili amongst others has, as a conservative combination of federalism and traditionalism. Nonetheless, it is a document which represents the starting point of the Catalan claims for self-government that will eventually lead to the statutes of autonomy of 1932 and 1979. It is in that sense that they constitute a important milestone in the annals of Catalan historiography. In spite of its limitations, the document came to symbolise the nationalist demands of Catalonia.

It would be, of course, historically naive to expect that the *Bases de Manresa* were unanimously accepted, although they were the political platform of the *Unió Catalanista*. Indeed, a leading Catalanist like Valentí Almirall did not participate in the assizes or contribute doctrinally to the document. Nonetheless, the participants represented a wide range of middle-class opinion; in addition, the most influential Catalan intellectuals of the time were also present. The political moment was also appropriate: the 1890s was a period of expansion for the Catalan political press. An initiative like the *Bases de Manresa* was bound to have an echo through the media. Doctrinally, many of the statements on Catalan nationalism uttered in the 1890s and later are concrete reflections of the general principles exposed in the *Bases de Manresa*. It is worth also remembering that the famous *Compendi de doctrina catalanista* (a cathecism of Catalan nationalism), written by Prat de la Riba and Muntanyola in the form of questions and answers was published in 1894 and that 100,000 copies were printed.

On the other hand, the reactions of the Spanish politicians were predictably hostile, rejecting the moderate home rule programme of the document. For many years, the *Bases de Manresa* were envisaged from the Spanish centre as the first well-articulated manifestation of a dissenting particularism. However, from the point of view of the Spanish state, the project was more utopian than illegal. The animosity against the *Bases de Manresa* continued unabated during the first third of the twentieth century: when the Francoist troops conquered the city of Manresa in 1939, the Falangist press reminded its inhabitants of the negative role that their city had played in the 'deplorable political process' of Catalan separatism (Figueres 1992: 48).

Role of Commemoration

The commemoration of the *Bases de Manresa* consisted essentially in an itinerant exhibition, a series of lectures and a number of publications (Figueres 1992; Termes and Colomines 1992; Ferrer 1993). The media reflected these events which culminated in a formal ceremony, presided by Jordi Pujol, on the 25 March 1995. Perhaps the *pièce de resistance* of the commemorations of the centenary was the roving historical display which was visited by more than 100,000 people. The catalogue printed to accompany the exhibition was divided into four major sections: origins of Catalanism (1868–1914), Catalan society (same period), biographies of illustrious Catalans and symbols of Catalan identity. It is plain that the catalogue-book's objective is to enlighten, perhaps at a rather crude level, a population which is largely ignorant of Catalan history. Ethno-nation-building is the term that comes to mind when assessing the content of the exhibition. On the other hand, some critics (for example, Martinez-Fiol 1993: 48) have suggested that the whole thing should be seen as an exercise aimed at glorifying Pujol and his nationalist policies.

It may well be the case that the exhibition portrays the Catalan past in a selective way, but the purpose of commemorations is not strictly academic, but political. The question is whether what is conveyed is an invented history or a recovered history – to use Lewis's terms. In the present circumstances, nationalist mythology may be both unacceptable and counter-productive. On the other hand, to highlight certain episodes of history for political purposes may be permissible provided that it does not involve blatant distortions.

Conclusions

That historical memory seems to be one of the central components of (ethno)national identity seems to be amply demonstrated by the recent experience of stateless nations both in Western and in Eastern Europe. Indeed, the phenomenon is much wider as can be shown by the case-study of nation-states such as France (Nora 1986–92).

What is perhaps less clear is how effective the different sites of memory are in securing the intended national anchorage. Unfortunately, we do not possess adequate and precise instruments to measure, for instance, the results of the specific policies of (ethno)nation-building of the Catalan Generalitat or of the variety of voluntary associations of Catalan civil society. By 1995 twenty years have elapsed since Franco's death, and no doubt great strides have been made to rekindle the hidden Catalan national identity that had eluded some foreign researchers in the early 1970s. Whilst being cautious about what they are worth in ascertaining the degree of national identity, both regular elections and surveys confirm that nation-building has proceeded at a steady pace.

The specific sites of memory that I have presented for consideration are a very small part of the possible range of instances. For better or for worse, in contemporary societies the role of the mass media is paramount in shaping, but also in diluting, national identity. Both the press and radio/television echo in multitudinous ways nationalist initiatives that have arisen either at the official level or at that of the voluntary associations; this, of course, is within the context of their political and cultural agendas. Indeed, there is a constant reminder of Catalan commemorations, anniversaries, celebrations, etc. in all the media. On the other hand, the mass media are also the carriers of constant messages which refer to the Spanish nation. And all this is taking place in the context of the increasing media presence of an American-inspired global culture. By mirroring foreign models, it is alleged that national cultures are being emptied out of their original contents. The dangers of being swamped by the process of Americanisation of the world (both at the lingusitic and at the cultural level) are all too real to be brushed off. Even the French do not believe any longer that their precious cultural and linguistic castle is impregnable. In the Catalan case, however, the main danger is that of being acculturated by the powerful and ever-present Spanish culture.

What is the role of historical memory in such a situation? I have maintained elsewhere (Llobera 1994) that, for reasons which are not altogether clear, the idea of historical continuity appeals to nations. The search for origins, particularly if they show a separate political entity with clearly defined cultural and linguistic features anchored in a more or less distant past, is a generalised pursuit of (ethno)nations trying to make their presence felt. This exercise in historical memory may be fraught with romantic and essentialist traps (Martinez-Fiol 1993).

This is not to say that a sense of national identity may not only be a necessary corrective to a prior political situation which was experienced by the majority of the population as oppressive, but it may also provide the needed energy to dynamise a society. The crucial issue is whether the right kind of balance between civic and ethnic nationalism can be established. Equally important is the time-frame and the means used to implement the policies of national redress. It would be naive to expect that situations which require compromise from the different participating actors will not be conflictual. Language, culture and national consciousness are often highly valued assets, hence the entrenched positions. What matters, however, is how to minimise the conflict, that is, how to develop procedures to manage conflict in a properly democratic and tolerant way.

Only in rarified intellectual atmospheres can nationalist historians get away with their myths and fables. Unfortunately, this is what has happened in the ex-Yugoslavia, where extremely skewed national histories have been used to justify horrendous crimes. There is no panacea to human folly except a free, vigorous and vigilant civil society. Totalitarian regimes of whichever persuasion (fascist, communist or those derived from religious fundamentalisms) will tend to monopolise historical memory with the avowed aim of creating and imposing a certain type of uniform national identity; as a consequence, ethnonational identities will be at best ignored or repressed, at worst obliterated.

References

Albareda, J. (1991), 'L'Onze de Setembre: realitat i "mite"', *L'Avenç*, vol.15, pp.62–5

—— (1991), 'L'Onze de Setembre', *Diccionari d'Història de Catalunya*, Barcelona, pp.757–8

Bhabha, H. (ed.) (1990), *Nation and Narration*, London

Connerton, P. (1989), *How Societies Remember*, Cambridge

Englund, S. (1992), 'The Ghost of Nation Past', *Journal of Modern History*, vol.64, pp.299–320

Fentress, J. and Wickham, C. (1992), *Social Memory*, Oxford

Ferrer, J. (ed.) (1993), *Les Bases de Manresa 1892–1992. Cent anys de Catalanisme*, Barcelona

Figueres, J.M. (ed.) (1992), *Les Bases de Manresa i el futur de Catalunya*, Barcelona

Frigolé, J. (1980), 'Inversió simbòlica i identitat ètnica: una aproximació al cas de Catalunya', *Quaderns de l'ICA*, vol.1, pp.3–27

Gillis, J.R. (ed.) (1994), *Commemorations. The Politics of National Identity*, Princeton

Halbwachs, M. (1925/1975), *Les cadres sociaux de la mémoire*, Paris

—— (1941/1971), *La topographie légendaire des évangiles en Terre Sainte*, Paris

—— (1950/1968), *La mémoire collective*, Paris

—— (1992), *On Collective Memory*, Chicago

Hobsbawm, E. and Ranger, E. (eds) (1983), *The Invention of Tradition*, Cambridge

Hutton, P. (1993), *History as an Art of Memory*, Hanover

Johnston, H. (1991), *Tales of Nationalism: Catalonia 1939–1979*, New Brunswick

Lewis, B. (1975), *History. Remembered, Recovered, Invented*, New York

Llobera, J.R. (1990), 'Catalan National Identity. The Dialectics of Past and Present', *Critique of Anthropology*, vol.X, nos 2 and 3, pp.11–28

—— (1994), *The God of Modernity*, Oxford

Lowental, D. (1985), *The Past is Another Country*, Cambridge

Martinez-Fiol, L. (1993), 'Commemoracions, Catalanisme i Historiografia', *L'Avenç*, vol.175, pp.42–7

Mauss, M. (1901/1968), *Essais de sociologie*, Paris

Middleton, D. and Edwards, D. (eds) (1990), *Collective Remembering*, London

Namer, G. (1987), *Mémoire et société*, Paris

Nora, P. (1978), 'Mémoire collective', in Le Goff, J. et al. (eds), *La Nouvelle Histoire*, Paris

—— (1986–92), *Les lieux de la mémoire*, 7 vols, Paris

Pujol, J. (1993), *La Diada nacional de Catalunya*, Barcelona

Pi-Sunyer, O. (1971), 'The Maintenance of Ethnic Identity in Catalonia', in Pi-Sunyer, O. (ed.), *The Limits of Integration: Ethnicity and Nationalism in Modern Europe*, University of Massachusetts, Research Reports No.9

Smith, G. (ed.) (1994), *The Baltic States*, London

Termes, J. and Colomines, A. (1992), *Les Bases de Manresa de 1892 i els origens del catalanisme*, Barcelona

Tonkin, E. (1992), *Narrating Our Pasts*, Cambridge

Wood, N. (1994), 'Memory's Remains: Les lieux de mémoire', *History and Memory*, vol.6, pp.123–49

–12–

Bilingualism and Multinationalism in the Basque Country[1]
Jeremy MacClancy

It is an unfortunate fact, one insufficiently stated, that nationalists' efforts to create 'one nation, one people, one language' tend to produce the very opposite of what they originally intended. This idea of 'linguistic nationalism', largely a product of the German Romanticism of the late eighteenth and early nineteenth centuries (Edwards 1985: 23–34), has been so successfully propounded and taken up by nationalist ideologues and their followers, that the exclusive association of one language with one nation now appears almost natural to many people (see Chapter 4). According to this scheme of things, if a self-defined people are to form a nation, it is best if they have their own language. Yet despite their efforts (or rather, partly because of the nature and style of their efforts), nationalists usually fail to realise their dream. Instead they normally assist in the production of a complex cultural arena, one characterised not by unity and singularity, but by divisive conflict and plurality.

The aim of this chapter is to substantiate this point by reviewing the example of Basque nationalism. For today in that region of northern Spain, where nationalism has for so long dominated the political agenda, there is not a single language spoken by all but a variety; its inhabitants do not participate in a homogeneous culture but a postmodernist diversity, and the majority do not support a coherent nationalism but a spectrum of nationalisms.

Basque nationalism, which arose in the late nineteenth century, explicitly valued Basque distinctiveness and made it a crucial part of its *raison d'être*. According to the leaders of the nationalist forces, the

1. Much of this article is based on my intensive fieldwork in the Basque Country, in which, over the last decade, I have spent more than four years. I am grateful to the ESRC, the Nuffield Foundation, the Faculty of Anthropology and Geography of Oxford University and the Ministerio de Asuntos Exteriores of the Spanish Government for their financial support.

Basques were different to others and had to be recognised as such. A potential key component of this distinctiveness was Euskera, the Basque language, the only non-Indo-European language still spoken in Western Europe. The following grammatical examples may give an idea of just how very different it is from any language spoken by neighbouring peoples today: the definite article is not a separate word but a suffix; nouns used with numerals remain in the singular; auxiliary verbs vary according to the number of objects as well to the number of subjects; instead of prepositions, Euskera employs a host of suffixes and prefixes which vary depending on whether the word to which they are attached refers to something animate or inanimate.

The origin of Euskera is so obscure and yet so fascinating a question to many linguists that a number of them have produced some almost fantastical pseudo-answers. One of the more sober attempts has been the connexion made between Basque and the Caucasian languages Georgian and Circassian which, like Euskera, are non-Indo-European. Some linguists have taken the 7 per cent overlap in vocabulary between Euskera and the other pair of languages as evidence suggesting the former existence of a Basque-Caucasian proto-language. However, as the linguist Karl Schmidt has pointed out in a critical review of this work, any attempt at reconstructing this hypothetical language 'can only be made under the supposition that this proto-language possessed a common phonological system. But at present it would be quite impossible to reconstruct this system' (Schmidt 1987: 121). A similar proviso would apply to any attempt to link Euskera with Berber just because they share 10 per cent of their vocabularies.

The German linguist von Humboldt considered Euskera to have been the last vestige of Iberian, the ancient language of the Peninsula. But while there are some philological and phonological parallels between both languages, Iberian, so far as we can tell at present, lacks some of the most distinctive morphological aspects of Euskera, such as the nominal case system, pronouns and the tense system, as well as the analytic and periphrastic features of the verbs. Any rigorous comparison is also hampered by the fact that we do not know anything definite about the form of Euskera used twenty-five centuries ago, i.e. when Iberian was spoken in the Peninsula. All we can say is that speakers of Iberian and of Euskera appear to have been in sufficiently close contact in the western region of the Pyreneean mountains to have produced some linguistic blending between the two languages (Anderson 1988: 103–37; Untermann 1990: 151–2). Despite all this vagueness about the degree of connection of Euskera with other languages we can however state that its mere survival, as the only non-Indo-European tongue left in Europe, strongly suggests the continued existence of a group (or groups) of people who, at the very least, maintained the linguistic aspect of their cultural inheritance over several thousand years. If we cannot say that 'the Basques' have been living in the area for millennia (because we do not know how these prehistoric people(s) classified themselves), we can at least state that some form, however attenuated and vaguely defined, of 'proto-Basques' have inhabited the region for a prolonged period (MacClancy 1993).

The earliest successful organisers of Basque nationalism were members of the petty bourgeoisie who, in the 1870s, correctly perceived the rapid industrialisation of their country (especially the province of Vizcaya) as a real threat both to their position within local society and to the traditional way of rural life. The rise of the coal, iron-and-steel-making and shipbuilding industries, together with the movement of villagers into the towns and the mass immigration of non-Basque Spaniards looking for jobs, helped create an emerging society in which customary values did not hold as much sway as before. The first ideologues conceived of this social change as one affecting the very nature of Basque society and, in reaction to this unwanted flux, they propounded a nationalism which aimed to arrest the potentially destructive effects of *laissez-faire* capitalism within their own land.

Many early nationalists used the same racial terminology as, and adopted many of the attitudes held by, European anthropologists of the late nineteenth century. These racist academics hierarchised the different races of the world and gave their ordered system explicit moral overtones. According to their conception of human diversity, certain races were 'pure' and hence superior, while others were mere mongrel breeds, the unwanted products of misguided intermarriages. Pure breeds were extolled, half-casts were to be despised.[2]

To Sabino Arana, the founder and leader of the Basque Nationalist Party, the purity of a language was a good indicator of the purity of a race. According to this logic, the patent originality of Euskera and its lack of 'contamination' by other languages convincingly demonstrated the purity of the Basque race. But the Basque language (like the Basque Country) was not particularly important in itself, for Arana believed that nationhood was based neither on language nor on territory, but on race. As far as he was concerned, it was better to have a society of pure Basques who spoke Spanish and lived anywhere in the world than a population of Vizcaya-based half-breeds who babbled in Euskera:

---

2. This section on Basque racism is indebted to Larronde 1977: 119–31; Corcuera Atienza 1979: 383–90; Apalategi 1985: 86–9; Gurruchaga 1985: 110–12; .

Well, the extinction of our language is of no importance whatsoever; nor the loss of our history; nor the loss of our very own and holy institutions, nor the imposition of strange and liberal ones; nor the political enslavement of our patria; none, absolutely none, of this matters in itself, when compared with the rubbing together of our people with the Spanish, which, within our race, immediately and necessarily leads to ignorance and a drop in intelligence, to weakness and corruption of the heart, and to total estrangement; in a word, to the end of all human society. (Arana-Goiri 1897)

Other nationalists of Arana's time valued Euskera more highly. They were worried about the decline of its use. By the middle of the century Euskera was no longer spoken in the southern Basque province of Alava or the southern half of Navarre, and its daily use was mainly confined to the fishing communities and rural peasantry of the northern provinces of Vizcaya and Guipúzcoa and the Pyreneean valleys of Navarre – in total about half a million. Usage declined further with the establishment in the 1880s of primary schools, where Castilian was the medium of instruction. As this process accelerated, Euskera came to be stigmatised as an unrefined language for unrefined people, a primitive tongue for bumpkins.

In an effort to stem this trend, nationalist writers began to extol the virtues of Basque literature (the little that existed) while nationalist linguists tried to purge their languages of imports from Castilian and of the 'Castilian' letters *c*, *ch*, *f*, *g*, *h*, *v*, *w* and *ll* (Juaristi 1987; Heiberg 1989: 47). In the 1920s these efforts to revive the usage of Euskera and to stimulate its revaluation became much more systematic. The first *ikastolas* (schools using Euskera as the primary medium of instruction) opened; members of the recently founded Basque Studies Society 'sought to rationalise and professionalise language studies' (Urla 1989: 170). They collected statistics on its use and attempted to create a standardised version, drawing on its seven major dialects. All these efforts came to a sudden halt with the outbreak of civil war and the consequent imposition of a military dictatorship over the country. The Basque Government, which had been formed in 1936, went into exile, the PNV (Basque Nationalist Party) effectively went into hibernation, and the speaking of Euskera was brutally repressed.

In the late 1950s Basque youths reacted against the passivity of their parents by forming ETA (*Euskadi ta askatasuna*, 'The Basque Country and Freedom'). At first a broad cultural and humanist movement ETA gradually evolved – while passing through a period of great popularity – into a terrorist organisation with separatist, irredentist and revolutionary socialist ends. In the course of its evolution, ETA underwent a long series of schisms. In each case, those who kept their arms kept the name of ETA. Those who laid down their arms formed separate groups which, during the transition to democracy following the death of Franco in 1975, became political parties. During the dying years of the dictatorship, the PNV re-emerged as the major political force in the area but it too has experienced schism and the formation of a separate party, *Eusko Alkartasuna*, by the deserters from its ranks (Cueva 1988). (It already experienced schism in the 1930s when a group of radical nationalists broke away to form the *Asociación Nacional Vasca*.) The sum consequence of this political process is that the Basque nationalist political spectrum, which gains over 70 per cent of the vote in the Basque Country, now runs from PNV on the centre-right to EA a little more towards the centre to a variety of left-wing groups whose most extreme pole is defined by *Herri Batasuna*, the political wing of ETA. *Herri Batasuna* unswervingly calls for the independence of the Basque nation, to be organised as a radically socialist state. PNV used to make similar demands for independence but in recent years has lowered its political horizons to a high degree of autonomy within the frame of the Spanish State for the Basque Country, to be run on social meritocratic lines.

Members of ETA and their sympathisers do not think of themselves in racial terms, but in cultural ones (Clark 1984). Instead of worrying, as Arana had done, about the purity of their blood and the dangers of miscegenation, they are far more concerned about the survival of Euskera. To them, the Basque language is the central cultural prop, a besieged form of distinctiveness which was being attacked by the Francoist regime and which had to be maintained. As some of its earliest protagonists stated:

> There is no creation more strictly and permanently national, present and lived, popular and collective, than the national language. One is dealing, perhaps, with the only creation in which all the regions, all the social classes, and all the successive generations have collaborated. . . .
> In a strict sense only the Basque language maintains at an unquestionable level the objective unity of Euskadi, across the Basque-speaking zones of the Spanish and French states. . ..
> . . .Since the times of Machiavelli it is an extremely well-known political counsel, and one which works infallibly, that to kill a *pueblo* there is nothing more deadly than to kill its national language. A *pueblo* which stops speaking its language is a *pueblo* which has died. A *pueblo* which changes its language for that of its neighbour, is a *pueblo* which changes its soul for that of its neighbour. (ETA 1979, vol.1: 105–6)

To *etarras*, Euskera is 'the maximum expression of the national personality'. As the essential factor of national identity it must not be lost nor any effort spared to maintain, or revive, its use.

Etarras revalued Euskera so highly partly because of their readings of structuralist theorists (Saussure, Lévi-Strauss, Lacan) and of the work of Sapir and Whorf on the interrelation between language and thought. Nationalists' interpretations of these writings gave a scientific edge to their promotion of Euskera and they came to the view that if language and world-view were inextricably interlinked then the loss of their ancestral tongue would necessarily entail the disappearance of a distinctively Basque mode of thought. It thus became almost a duty for intellectual *etarras* both to assist in the recuperation of Euskera and to investigate its nature according to the latest methodologies, whether that be Chomskian or sociolinguistic (Urla 1988: 385).

In the 1960s nationalist activists took advantage of a mild increase in the tolerance of the regime to revive the *ikastolas* (see Chapter 13) and to set up AEK, a system of Euskera night-schools for adults, each run on a co-operative, communal basis. The pedagogical style of AEK relies on the communicative method of language teaching. On its intensive, boarding-school courses teachers insert their groups into the social milieux of the area where the course is being held, students being taken, for example, on visits to local organisations and businesses in order to practise their Euskera. By bringing together students and locals in this way, AEK hopes both to enhance pupils' ability to speak Euskera and to reinforce the speaking of it among those who use it, at least to a certain degree, within their workplace. For a tenet of AEK is that a language dies, not because people do not know it, but because those who do know it do not use it, or do not use it in a quotidian manner. As a self-styled 'popular' organisation, the management structure of AEK is as democratic as possible, the participation of both teachers and students in decision-making meetings being actively promoted (Valle 1988: 83–5).

Once the Basque Country had gained a certain degree of autonomy however, the Basque government began in 1981 to create an alternative, competitive network of language academies called HABE. Unlike the cheap, sixty to ninety-minute classes four nights a week offered by AEK, HABE classes cost somewhat more and 'tend to be intensive three to five-hour blocks of time and more fast-paced' (Urla 1993: 112). HABE is more appealing to those people who wish to gain a formal qualification in Euskera. Possession of this qualification increases a person's chances of getting a job in a school or the civil service of the Basque government.

AEK and HABE do not work in unison, but have an unhappy history of conflictive relations. Proponents of AEK argue that its long history of activity (compared to that of the more recent HABE) allow it to claim a leading role in the teaching of Euskera. Proponents of HABE contend that the democratically elected nature of the Basque government legitimates its claim to the same leading role. AEK prides itself on being a popular organisation open to all who wish to learn the language and thus some of its members criticise the HABE preliminary exam for prospective students as 'discriminatory'. In turn, members of HABE criticise AEK instructors as having, in the majority of cases, no qualifications in teaching or Euskera. The Basque government has been prepared on several occasions to help fund the running costs of AEK but negotiations have always collapsed because the representatives of AEK will not surrender a degree of their autonomy for the sake of a subsidy (Valle 1988: 102–14).

At the root of this continuing controversy are contrasting conceptions of the roles the two Euskera-teaching institutions play in the contemporary Basque Country. We might say that while HABE has the restricted, somewhat 'technical' aim of promoting the speaking of Euskera, AEK has broader aims: teaching people *Batua* (the standardised Basque finally agreed upon by Basque linguists) *and* raising their nationalist consciousness. In the words of a senior official of HABE:

> What we (HABE) have to do is set up some centres, an academy in the academic sense, in which there is a didactic act of teaching, full stop. That is to say, as a public entity we cannot get involved in other things. We have to increase the use of Euskera among the people to the maximum level. . . .What AEK does is very different, what is important to them is to stir people up: if they learn Euskera, good, but that is not so important as stimulating patriotic consciousness. (quoted in Pérez-Agote 1987: 26).

To opponents of AEK the organisation is in the hands of the radical nationalist Left and, rather than dedicating itself to the population in general, has tended to side with marginal groups within Basque society. Supporters of AEK, however, claim it is the sort of democratic grassroots organisation which 'the people' should support while HABE is the sort of formal hierarchic organisation set up by the powers-that-be which 'the people' should reject.

To members of *Herri Batasuna*, Basque patriots are *abertzales*, a status not defined by birth but by performance: an *abertzale* is one who actively participates in the political struggle for an independent Basque nation with its own distinctive culture. You are not born *abertzale*; you make yourself one. I have met people whose parents emigrated from southern Spain and who, though not born in the Basque Country, identify with the Basque movement, learn Basque and join demonstrations against the latest threat to the integrity of the Basque people. One told me: 'Not being born Basque doesn't matter. I *feel* Basque.' His gathered friends nodded in agreement.

Radical ideologues speak of *la gran familia abertzale*, a social unit where political attitudes are often inherited and one broad enough to accommodate both militant nationalism and revolutionary socialism. Members of *Herri Batasuna* have so successfully appropriated left-wing metaphors that in the Basque Country it is now difficult to be left-wing but not *abertzale*. Almost all left-wing issues are discussed within a Basque frame. To *abertzales*, *el Pueblo Trabajador Vasco* ('the Basque Working People') is a *pueblo* oppressed by the occupying forces of the Spanish State and exploited by centralist capitalists. Following their line of metaphors, the Basque people is already a 'nation' with its own 'popular army' (ETA) and whose gunmen are its 'best sons'. Basque politicians who do not advance the Basque cause are 'traitors' the attempt to build a nuclear power station on the Basque coast becomes 'genocide', the entry of Spain into NATO is damned as subversion of 'Basque sovereignty', and anti-nationalists' calls for the teaching of French or English in schools instead of Euskera becomes 'linguistic imperialism'. In this way radical Basque nationalists have created an explanatory world-view with great interpretive extension. In comparison, the PNV does not dare to define 'Basqueness' but appears to uphold implicitly a conventional ethnic definition in terms of genealogy, culture, language and residence, while its explanatory world-view 'Basquises' far fewer events than that of *Herri Batasuna*.

Abertzales wish to increase the number of Basque speakers, to increase the sorts of occasions on which it is spoken and thus, if necessary, to create social events in which Basque is the language of communication. In an attempt to 'Basquise' Castilian, *abertzales* impose Basque orthography on Castilian: *tx* is used in place of *ch* (e.g. *txorizo*, 'sausage, thief'), *b* instead of *v* (Nabarra). Where possible Basque, rather than Castilian, terms are used (e.g. *arrantzale*, 'fisherman'). Political slogans are preferably shouted in Basque, words for new Basque institutions came from the Basque, not the Castilian, lexicon (e.g. *irrintzi*, a cry, the radio) and parents give their children Basque names – a practice banned during Francoism. In Basque-speaking areas place signs are often bilingual and with the Castilian toponym usually painted out by some midnight *abertzale*. Bars run by radicalised youth are given Basque names and barpersons will reply in Basque if spoken to in the same tongue, though neither they nor their clients may be able to utter more than a few phrases. In one new bar I saw the sign, 'Castilian is also spoken'.

In fabricating their own social events, their own fiestas and, to some extent, their own language, *abertzales* create a novel, functioning subculture of their own, one broad enough to include urban activists, punks, young villagers and skinheads. (Some *abertzales* are particularly proud of the fact that Basque skinheads, unlike their bald counterparts elsewhere in Europe, are not automatically associated with the violent ends of the right wing.) Students of Basque collectively camp out for days, and sponsored thousands run in marathons pacing out the extent of the Basque Country, all for the sake of raising money to promote the teaching of Basque (Valle 1988). They also participate in fiestas celebrating marked aspects of 'Basque' culture, such as wood-choppers, stone-lifters, dancers, troubadours, Basque musicians and the *olentzero* (the Basque equivalent of Father Christmas). In fact there are so many of these modern fiestas that committed nationalists can spend many of their spring and summer weekends going from one event to another. Public gatherings held in homage to murdered *Batasuna* leaders, to dead gunmen (or their mothers), or to *abertzales* killed by police in demonstrations become the frequent occasion for further, congregated celebration of the radical version of how to be 'Basque' (Aretxaga 1988; MacClancy in press). The range of this constructed culture is shown by the articles in the *Batasuna* newspaper, which may laud the pre-capitalist way of life of Basque villagers in the last century, or describe the latest developments in 'the Basque novel', 'Basque painting', 'the Basque cinema', 'the Basque video', 'Basque sports', 'Basque cuisine', or (very popular) 'radical Basque rock'.[3]

At about the same time as the creation of '*el rock radical vasco*', *Herri Batasuna* began to use the slogan '*Martxa eta borroka*' (perhaps best translated as 'liveliness and struggle'.) This rallying-cry connoted both the need for young *abertzales* to enjoy themselves while still working for the cause, *and* their need to remember the cause whilst enjoying themselves in town and village fiestas. '*Martxa eta borroka*' is a way both to enliven the struggle for Basque independence and to politicise traditional fiestas in a radical mode. For, as so many examples show, these collective parties of sanctioned licentiousness, with excited and inebriated crowds filling the streets, can easily turn into major demonstrations. The bloody conflict between the festive participants and massed groups of the police in the Pamplona fiestas of 1978 was so sustained that the municipal council was forced to stop the festivities after only two days of the week-long event. In the same fiestas eight years later two hapless *nacionales* (members of *Policia Nacional*, a nationwide force of armed policemen) who had to change the wheel of their police-car in the main Plaza were surrounded for the duration of the operation by some sixty whistling youths. Since they were not being violent, the *nacionales* did not reply. They did not want to provoke a

---

3. On further, marked aspects of 'Basque' culture, and on their relations with Basque politics, see MacClancy 1996, forthcoming.

major riot. Outside of fiestas, the same scene would have been unthinkable; the police vans would have arrived in minutes to clear the area of the disrespectful whistlers.

Though *abertzale* culture is a mix of modern events and a selective taking-up of former ways, it gains prestige by association with the glorious past of Basque culture and history. But by claiming to be the rightful heirs to Basque tradition, nationalists can be criticised by others for acting inconsistently. When I watched a display of Basque dancing in a fiesta for world peace, one Pamplonan friend said to me that it was good dancing, but what was it doing here in Pamplona? The dances performed came from a fishing village miles north of Pamplona. Traditionally it would not have been staged in Pamplona, and certainly not by Pamplonans. Though the annual festival of Basque dance brings together performers from many different areas, it also decontextualises and reduces the distinctiveness of regionally based dance routines by making them all assimilable parts of a generalised 'Basque culture'. The confusion here is between culture as a static bounded entity, its content legitimated by traditional use, and culture as a dynamic, interpretative product, its content continually redefined by its present practitioners. *Abertzales* want the reflected prestige of the Basque past: they do not want to be confined by it. The culture they manufacture is a modern mix of the present and the past in the present, a continuing construction. Here, marked 'cultural' events are appropriated by a party programme which, in turn, is judged by political effectiveness.

Some Basques, like my critical friend, regard the social milieux created by *abertzales* as akin to a cultural monster, an unwanted hybrid threatening the existence of supposedly 'purer' growths. Yet, as defenders of this novel subculture argue, these invented contexts are absolutely necessary if Euskera is to survive, let alone thrive. Since the rural social structure which underpinned the traditional usage of Euskera is gradually disappearing, defenders of Basque need to create new arenas within which its usage may be considered customary. However, even this imaginative fabrication of novel contexts together with the expansion of the system of *ikastolas* is not enough to ensure the continued existence of Euskera as a viable language into the next millennium. In the Navarran village where I do fieldwork, some of the young men and women (the offspring of Basque nationalists but native Castilian speakers) were educated solely in *ikastolas*. Yet they do not normally speak Euskera because some of their friends do not understand it. For if a circle of acquaintances gather, even if only one of the group is not a speaker of Basque, the language used is Castilian. Similarly, professional teachers of Euskera, who have learnt the language as youths or as adults, do not usually employ it when talking casually to one another. As one put it to me, shame-faced, to them, emotional terms in Euskera do not carry the same personal psychological force as their Castilian equivalents. She confessed they 'ought' to speak Euskera amongst themselves but failed to do so because it did not provide a sufficient degree of personal satisfaction. Its words were not charged with the autobiographical associations that imbue the terms of one's mother tongue. In these sorts of circumstances, the danger is that, in social encounters, initially speaking some Euskera becomes a form of tokenism, a dutiful acknowledgement of its symbolic importance, before getting down to the business of the day, the latest gossip, or the deeply felt expression of opinions about recent events. Usually, when I was first introduced to committed nationalists, we would utter a few formal phrases of greeting in Euskera and then switch to Castilian. But that was normally enough for me to be accepted. The fact I had studied their language intensively for a few months was taken as sufficient evidence that I took their language (and implicitly their political aims) seriously.

A further obstacle to the perpetuation of Euskera is the very process of politicisation which galvanised its revival in the last decades of the dictatorship. For some Basques, uninterested in or disenchanted with the nationalist struggle, have reacted against the language movement as part of their rejection of politically motivated Basque patriotism. Some locals who, though the children of Basque-speaking, Basque surname-bearing parents, deliberately make no effort to speak the language and may even go so far as to claim they are not Basque. To them, the ethnic adjective has become so tainted by terrorist acts that they do not wish to be associated with it in any way.

The politicisation of Euskera has also affected, negatively, its usage among non-*abertzale* nationalists. For if, in the time of the dictatorship and the first years of the Transition, learning the language was an integral part of the general oppositional culture of nationalists, then the granting of autonomy and the establishment of a Basque government with steadily increasing powers has, for many, removed the justification for the continued existence of this culture. Hence a major reason for learning the language has effectively disappeared: speaking Euskera is no longer a way of manifesting opposition to Franco and his epigones but just a means of personally defending a nationalist notion of Basque culture.

In this contemporary context of democracy where many nationalist forces seek an advantageous accommodation with the central government, *Herri Batasuna* remains exceptional. Unlike other Basque parties which have diluted their demands or modified their position, the political wing of ETA persists in defining the radical edge of nationalist politics. On almost any issue that is under discussion, *Herri Batasuna* take an extremist stance, in order partly to show up their nationalist opponents' moderation and preparedness to compromise. The disadvantage of this ideological immobility is that what adherents might value as a morally upright steadfastness can appear to others as a refusal to accept the changing realities of the day. When the British Hispanist Michael Jacobs visited an *abertzale* in Bilbao, he comes to regard his host as out of touch: 'I spent that night on a sofa below a crowded bookcase, in a time-warp. I had regressed to a world of innocence and idealism. The books were those which might have been found in a student flat of long ago: Marx, Engels, Walter Benjamin, Rosa Luxemburg, Lenin, Che Guevara, Regis Debray, Marshall McLuhan, Mao Tse-tung, Simone de Beauvoir. . .' (Jacobs 1994: 311).

The advantage of this immobility is that *abertzales*, by not shifting their position, do not have to worry about the present nature of their identity. By not changing their political place, they have the satisfaction of continuing to know where they stand. The point is made by the Spanish writer José María Merino in his short story *Imposibilidad de la memoria*. The central thread of his tale is contemporary Spaniards' loss of identity through the persistent compromises necessitated by the establishment and maintenance of democracy:

'We would go mad if we were capable of understanding up to what point we can manage to change. We convert ourselves into other beings. That double ghoul of some horror story,' he thought, repeating a topic habitual in his reflections.

Javier had changed much, but perhaps it was true that the loss of identity was one of the signs of our times, and that there no longer remained in the world anything human which could conserve its substance. He himself had affirmed it in rotund phrases, on one of those occasions in which they had a conversation which rose above the strictly domestic.

'Identity now only exists in the day-dreams of ayatollahs, of abertzales, of people like that.' (Merino 1993: 114)

Unlike the protagonist Javier who disappears in a highly mysterious manner, *abertzales* do not lose their identity, do not have to question their own integrity. By continuing to uphold the slogan 'Those not with me are against me' they maintain a strong sense of political and linguistic conflict which serves to animate their efforts to see Euskera re-established as the common vernacular of their homeland.

References

Anderson, J.M. (1988), *Ancient Languages of the Hispanic Peninsula*, Lanham, Ma.

Apalategi, J. (1985), *Los Vascos: de la Autonomía a la Independencia*, San Sebastian

Arana-Goiri, Sabino (1897) 'Efectos de la invasión', *Bizkaitarra*, no.10 reprinted in *Obras completas*, Bayona, 1965

Aretxaga, Begoña (1988), *Los funerales en el nacionalismo radical vasco*, San Sebastian

Clark, Robert P. (1984), *The Basque Insurgents. ETA, 1952–1980*, Madison

Corcuera Atienza, Javier (1979), *Orígenes, ideología y organización del nacionalismo vasco 1876–1904*, Madrid

Cueva, Justo de la (1988), *La Escisión del PNV. EA, HB, ETA y la deslegitimación del Estado español en Euskadi Sur*, Bilbao

Edwards, J. (1985), *Language, Society and Identity*, Oxford

ETA (1979), *Documentos*, 18 vols, San Sebastian

Gurruchaga, A. (1985), *El código nacionalista durante el franquismo*, Barcelona

Heiberg, Marianne (1989), *The Making of the Basque Nation*, Cambridge

Jacobs, Michael (1994), *Between Hopes and Memories. A Spanish Journey*, London

Juaristi, Jon (1987), *El linaje de Aitor. La invención de la tradición vasca*, Madrid

Larronde, J-C. (1977), *El nacionalismo vasco. Su origen y su ideología en la obra de Sabino Arana-Goiri*, San Sebastian

MacClancy, Jeremy (1993), 'Biological Basques, Sociologically Speaking', in Chapman, M. (ed.), *Ethnicity. Biological and Social Aspects*, Oxford, pp.92–139

—— (1996), 'Nationalism at Play: The Basque Community and Football', in MacClancy, J. (ed.), *Sport, Identity and Ethnicity*, Oxford

—— (in press), 'To Die in the Basqueland. Martyrdom in northern Iberia', in Pettigrew, J. (ed.), *The Anthropology of Martyrdom*, Amsterdam

—— (forthcoming), 'Negotiating "Basque Art"', in MacClancy, J. (ed.), *Anthropology, Art and Contest*

Merino, José María (1993), 'Imposibilidad de la memoria', in Valls, F. (ed.), *Son Cuentos. Antología del relato breve español 1975–1993*, Madrid, pp.111–25

Pérez-Agote, Alfonso (1987), *El nacionalismo a la salida del franquismo*, Centro de Investigaciones Sociológicas, Madrid

Schmidt, K.H. (1987), 'The Two Ancient Iberias from the Linguistic Point of View', Proc IV Coll Lenguas Prehistóricas Hispánicas, *Veleia* vols2–3, pp.105–21

Untermann, J. (1990), *Monumenta Linguarum Hispanicarum* vol.3 (1), Wiesbaden

Urla, Jacqueline (1988), 'Ethnic Protest and Social Planning: A Look at Basque Language Revival', *Cultural Anthropology*, vol.3, pp.379–94

—— (1989), 'Reinventing Basque Society: Cultural Difference and the Quest for Modernity, 1918–1936', in Douglass, W.A. (ed.), *Essays in Basque Social Anthropology and History*, Reno, pp.149–76

—— (1993), 'Contesting Modernities. Language Standardisation and the Production of an Ancient/Modern Basque Culture', *Critique of Anthropology*, vol.13, pp.101–18

Valle, Teresa del (1988), *Korrika. Rituales de la lengua en el espacio*, Barcelona

Language and Basque Nationalism: Collective Identity, Social Conflict and Institutionalisation

Benjamín Tejerina Montaña

Introduction

The Basque language has undergone profound changes in the past three decades. In the 1960s, Basque nationalism redefined its discourse so that the language became the key element of collective identity and distinctiveness. In the context of the political repression of Franco's regime, the ethnolinguistic movement induced the recovery of the Basque language and culture with few resources and many difficulties. The most important features of this language shift were the appearance of schools teaching children in Basque (*ikastola*), schools for adult literacy in Basque (*euskaltegi* and *gaueskola*), and an increase in Basque literature and cultural production. In the 1970s, with a more favourable political structure, the ethnolinguistic movement spread throughout Basque society. The success of the movement extended to the knowledge and use of the Basque language, as well as to the symbolic value of the language for collective identity. At the same time, the linguistic sphere and the movement itself became the object of much political discussion. During the 1980s, the ethnolinguistic movement was divided by internal and external conflicts. Internally, the opposition between professionalisation and mass movement tendencies was the origin of the conflict. Externally, the linguistic policy of the Basque government resulted in a progressive institutionalisation of the goals and part of the resources of the movement. This chapter will discuss these conflicts as it traces the recuperation and vitality of the Basque language in recent years.

Basque Nationalism and Language during the Franco Period

The Reformulation of Basque Nationalism

During the late nineteenth century, the first attempts were made at defining the Basque national consciousness and nationalist formulations of its collective identity (see Chapter 1). In its definition of the Basque collective identity, language was always subservient to other elements on which the group differentiation was supported – basically the ethnic characterisation of the Basque people. It was not until well into the Franco period that a reformulation of Basque nationalism took place, with the language gradually emerging as the critical element of the identity/differentiation of Basqueness.

The Franco regime (1939–75) systematically repressed all non-Spanish symbols in the immediate post-war period. The Basque language was most strongly repressed in the schools and on the streets. It became impossible to use Basque in public social settings, which led to the withdrawal of Basque to the areas of private and family life. Since the family was the only place in which Basque was allowed, family life became the fundamental mechanism for conserving the language by passing it on from one generation to the next. In this way Basque was reinforced, though it never became fully autonomous. The passing on of the language from one generation to the next within the family was the only form immune from direct repression. This was interrupted, however, due to the interiorising of repression in the family sphere. In some cases parents' fear of repression against them personally or against their children led to the breakdown of the mechanism of language reproduction which operated in this setting. In this sense, not only personal attitudes but also the role of the small local community were important in the abandonment of language.

The repression of Basque in official settings and public places was joined by a large-scale internal immigration process in the 1950s and 1960s. These factors led to a reduction in the use of the language in both geographical areas and social spaces of usage. Paradoxically, the reduction in the use of Basque led to an awareness that the language was being lost. Consequently, the traumatic realisation of this loss reinforced the symbolic role of the language. Two things had to happen – two projects coinciding in time and in some cases with the same protagonists – before this situation, and the realisation of this situation, could take on a political dimension in the generic sense of doing something to change it: the recovery of the language led by the ethnolinguistic movement and the redefinition of nationalist discourse.

Basque literature in the early post-war years was non-existent. In the words of Joxé Azurmendi, 'the Basque writer is an unexpected artist writing in a language which does not exist, but which is however understood by those who have to understand him' (cited in Torrealday 1977: 51). In fact it was not until 1949 that the first book was published in Basque after the end of the Civil War (a religious poem by Salbatore Mitxelena). Just five years later a tenuous recovery of cultural activity began to take shape. During those years, in the privacy of seminaries and other ecclesiastical institutions, Basque and literature in Basque were cultivated. When the 'social shut-down' imposed on these manifestations of Basque culture was lifted, it gave rise to one of the most vitally creative periods of the Basque language and encouraged a cultural recovery movement of great social significance. The symbolic value of the Basque language – especially considering the context of repression in which this occurred – was to take on a more and more prominent nature as an element of definition of collective national identity and to become the fundamental element of the nationalist reformulation, which developed in and around ETA, *Euskadi ta Askatasuna* (Basqueland and Freedom).

This process of linguistic and cultural recovery coincided with a redefinition of national consciousness. The profound socio-economic changes which had taken place and which were becoming more marked at that time posed a serious problem for the Basque Nacionalist Party's nationalism. Its traditional nationalism had trouble fitting in with the new reality that was emerging. The first twenty years of the Franco period had seen the spread of a feeling that Basque nationalism was dying, and the most visible feature of this was the decline of the language. In the context of the changes in social structure as a result of industrialisation, urbanisation and the massive influx of immigrants, two immediate tasks had to be faced: on the one hand, something had to be done about the lethargy of older people, who were still frustrated that the Civil War had been lost and Basque nationalism thus defeated; and on the other hand, Basque nationalism had to be redefined and adapted to the new reality of Basque society.

The refusal to accept the religious element or racial character which had played a fundamental role in historical nationalism as objective support of national identity led to a situation of orphanhood when it came to defining the objective element or elements on which a particular idea of the Basque nation was to be founded (Jauregui 1981: 270). The idea that the language constituted the support of the Basque nation was not completely clear from the outset, but was arrived at as other 'objective' elements used for this purpose were ruled out. It was gradually realised that nationality, the differentiation of the Basque people, could not rest on biological elements (race). The influence of Federico

Krutwig and his work *Vasconia, Estudio dialéctico de una nacionalidad* (*Basconia, A dialect study of nationality*) (1963) would provide the necessary elements for ETA to work out the ideological formulation on which their redefinition of Basque nationalism was based.

The feeling that the language was dying, and the need to respond to the widespread inability to react among the older generation, gave rise to a regenerationist attitude among ETA militants. The immediate aim was to recover the Basque language, since '*Euskera* (Basque language) is the quintessence of Euskadi (the Basque Country): while *Euskera* lives, Euskadi will live', so that 'when *Euskera* ceases to be a spoken language, the Basque people will have died; and in a few years the successors of today's Basques will be no more than Spaniards or Frenchmen' (Sarrailh de Ihartza 1963: 160).

In ETA's ideology, the Basque language came to prevail over all other elements as a fundamental component of the Basque collective identity. The language became the empirical correlate of the different identity of the Basque people. However, the feeling of belonging to a community was critical. It was a patriotic feeling that acted as the vehicle for national identity. Importantly, as the language was recovered, the Basque collective national identity spread, and activities favouring the recovery of the language would, it was realised, help spread that identity. These are in fact two complementary dimensions of the same problem. There was therefore no sense in taking up the task of recovering the language unless it was accompanied by a collective national identity. For ETA, the problem of *Euskera* and the national identity of the Basque people were part of a wider context. In that context, it was the political oppression of the Basque people which prevented it from developing and expressing itself: the lack of a political framework for expression was the restrictive element generating the present situation. It would only be possible to attain these objectives in a political structure which guaranteed the persistence of the language and national identity, i.e. by the achievement of a politically independent Euskadi. In this situation, the recovery of the language and with it national identity were dependent on the political goal of self-government for the Basque people.

This reformulation of Basque nationalism and the role played by the Basque language had a permanent reference point in the work of Sabino Arana (see Arana Goiri 1965; Chapter 1 of this volume). It is logical to think of a continuity between the two formulations, but if we bear in mind that the one was made up to contrast with the other in a constant dialogue, the differentiating elements show up immediately:

Criteria will coincide only on one single point: the need to recover the language. The reasons why this is necessary, the role to be played by the language in recovering national identity, its function in the Basque society of the future, its process of adaptation to new needs (modernisation of the language, unification of its dialects) are aspects in which great contrast will be found between the two concepts of nationalism. (Sarrailh de Ihartza 1963: 162–3)

The Reappearance of the Ethnolinguistic Movement

There has been a long tradition of empowerment and defence of the Basque language. It is possible to find many examples of this linguistic awareness and of projects aimed to encourage its development and growth even before the beginning of the eighteenth century. Nevertheless, it was from the nineteenth century on that linguistic awareness gained a new dimension as a consequence of the influence of nationalist thought spreading through Europe at the time. During the latter part of the nineteenth century and the early part of the twentieth century many activities aimed at cultural and linguistic recovery took place. These attempts would serve as sources of inspiration for the most recent social movements for the defence of the Basque language.

The reformulation of nationalist discourse during the 1960s had a twofold influence on the situation of the language. On the one hand, the language became the most socially significant element for the construction of the differentiality of Basque collective identity, as an empirical correlate of the existence of a differentiated community; this affection for the language reinforced its value as a symbol of belonging to the community. On the other hand, the same feeling for the language as a symbol of belonging to a social group with a differentiated collective identity led individuals who had never spoken it to learn Basque, thus increasing the extent of its knowledge and use. Why did the members of a certain collectivity feel the need to recover their language at a time of accelerated retrocession?

In the Basque Country the Basque language had been losing importance as a means of communication for several decades, falling back territorially before the advance of other languages. This meant a reduction in the percentage of Basque speakers and the disappearance or loss of the language in certain social settings. During the Franco regime Basque was repressed and political pressure accentuated this drop. This political pressure led people to become aware that the language was being lost. These features of the social situation of the language enable us to propose the following hypothesis: if a language is lost traumatically, there is an increase in conscious awareness of the loss of its use.

The growth of that awareness leads to an increase in the affective adherence to the language as a symbol of belonging to the group. This reinforces the symbolic role of the language as an important element of the group's collective identity. In addition, the decrease in the use of the language lessens as a result of the influence of its symbolic importance. The latter acts in two ways: the awareness that the language is being lost moves those who speak it to use it more, and also there is greater motivation to learn it among those who do not speak it. It is also possible that those who do not experience the loss as a problem may slowly abandon its use. This may be due to the fact that they are not aware of the process or that, even if they are aware, they do not experience any conflict in its abandonment because of personal motivations or social conditions which encourage them to use another language and renounce their own (Michelena 1977: 22; Pérez-Agote 1986: 425).

There were three main manifestations of the awareness that the use of Basque was being lost and that there existed the need to recover it: the creation of *ikastolas*, the literacy movement including the teaching of Basque to adults and the increase in the number of publications in Basque.

The most important of these manifestations, having the greatest force as a symbol of linguistic recovery, is the appearance of the *ikastola*, a school charged with educating and socialising new generations in Basque (see Table 13.1). Its very existence was to take on a threefold

Table 13.1. Number of *ikastolas* between 1960 and 1975.

	Alava	Guipuzcoa	Vizcaya	Navarra	French B.C.	Total	T. Acum.
1960	–	3	–	–	–	3	3
1961	–	–	–	–	–	–	3
1962	–	2	–	–	–	2	5
1963	1	3	2	–	–	6	11
1964	–	4	4	–	–	8	19
1965	–	5	4	1	–	10	29
1966	–	11	1	–	–	12	41
1967	–	9	5	1	–	15	56
1968	–	6	5	–	–	11	67
1969	–	10	6	2	1	19	86
1970	–	8	4	3	2	17	103
1971	1	7	2	2	4	16	119
1972	–	2	4	4	5	15	134
1973	2	1	8	1	1	13	147
1974	–	–	–	5	2	7	154
1975	2	–	–	3	1	6	160
Total	**6**	**71**	**45**	**22**	**16**	**160**	**160**

Source: Siadeco.

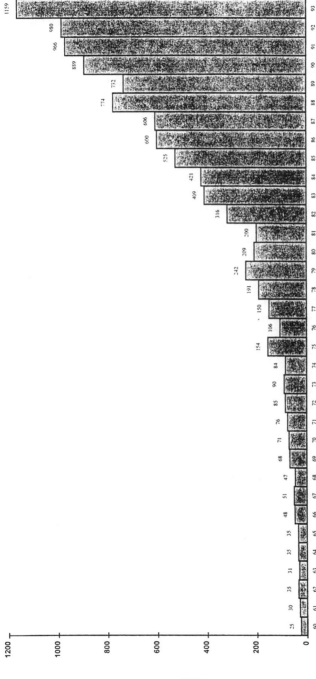

Sources: 1960–1975, Euskal Idazleak Gaur; 1976–1986, Euskal Hitz; 1987–1993, Dept. of Culture of the Basque Goverment

Figure 13.1. Books published in Basque (1960–1993)

social significance: a symbol for a culture undergoing an identity crisis, a cultural codification of the collective identity and a mythical stronghold of Basque identity in the context of repression.

During Franco's regime the repression of Basque in schools, the questioning of Basque-speaking culture posed by the pragmatism of the middle classes, the structural changes wrought by industrialisation, urbanisation and the arrival of immigrants and the greater cultural, administrative and political pressure exerted by the central state all had their most immediate consequence in the loss of any Basque-speaking cultural referent, and, 'furthermore, a rural culture more and more dominated and considered as retrograde or an ancestral relic suffers the corresponding identity crisis' (Arpal et al. 1982: 43). The collective identity crisis was the result of the processes of transformation in the structure of Basque society during the 1950s and 1960s. It was the crisis of society itself, but above all a crisis for the social definition of Basque-speaking cultural identity, which referred back to the social structure of traditional, rural society where the equivalence of cultural identity and Basque-speaking culture could still be found. This identification of Basque-speaking society, population and territory was to break down under the impact of immigration.

Paradoxically, it was in this context of a Basque identity crisis, once its presence was felt, that the need for cultural and linguistic recovery was considered. The *ikastola*, as an institution whose intention was to regenerate Basque language and culture, was to become the practical and symbolic referent for the realisation of Basque culture. The number of students enrolled in *ikastolas* rose from 596 in the academic year 1964–5, to 26,936 ten years later. The number of centres also rose from three in 1960 to a total of 160 in 1975, scattered over the Basque Country. There were fewer centres in Alava and Navarre, where the position of Basque was not as strong as it was in Guipuzcoa and Vizcaya (see Table 13.2).

Table 13.2. Number of students in *ikastolas* in the Basque Country between 1964 and 1975.

	1964–65	1969–70	1970–71	1971–72	1972–73	1973–74	1974–75
Alava	22	171	334	376	486	677	1,026
Guipuzcoa	520	5,770	8,181	10,673	13,245	15,272	17,971
Vizcaya	54	1,958	2,591	3,157	3,755	4,938	5,822
Navarra	–	348	765	950	1,377	1,631	1,892
French B.C.	–	8	14	47	101	175	225
Total	**596**	**8,255**	**11,885**	**15,203**	**18,964**	**22,693**	**26,936**

Source: Siadeco.

The political pressure exerted upon the language and its manifestations helped ensure that the phenomenon was not restricted to the educational and linguistic spheres, but rather to acquiring a political and ideological dimension transcending the limits of education systems in normal situations. In the late 1960s, the *ikastolas* had become highly significant in the cultural codification of the collective identity, connecting the new definition of Basque nationalism with wide sectors of traditional nationalism and the Basque Nationalist Party, thus becoming the 'mythical stronghold of Basque identity' (Arpal et al. 1982: 51).

Apart from setting up *ikastolas* in order to educate young people in Basque, it was also necessary to teach reading and writing skills to people who could speak the language but had no formal education in Basque because it had been kept out of the education system. Moreover it was also necessary to teach the language to the rest of the population, who did not have any contact with Basque. This attempt started in 1966, under the promotion of the Real Academia de la Lengua Vasca-Euskaltzaindia (Royal Academy of Basque Language). Although at first this attempt had had mainly a cultural and linguistic content, very quickly it gained a strong political significance, which increased against the backdrop of social and political convulsions that characterised that period.

The Ethnolinguistic Movement in the Process of Political Institutionalisation of Nationalism in the post-Franco Period

During the process of political transition to democracy, and under the pressure of a growing demand for the democratisation of social structures as well as policies which already existed, two basic problems arose. On the one hand was the question of how to establish a democratic political system similar to that of Western countries, where the Left and Right would be reconciled on the basis of political pluralism. On the other hand was the need to respond to the demands for self-government made to the State by various areas of its territory, where national identity and singular consciousness had been maintained. This meant establishing a political and administrative structure different from the centralist state imposed during the Franco regime: the model proposed was the 'State of the Autonomies' (*Estado de las Autonomias*), aimed at reconciling the centre with the periphery. This political rationalisation persists through the recognition of a plurinational reality, a nationalisation of the State and adaptation to the new socio-political and institutional context.

Since 1975 there has been a different perspective for the ethnolinguistic movement, resulting from opportunities from the new political structure. The central feature that defined Basque identity had been its strong politicisation. The burst of public expressions exposed differences in aims and in the strategic ways to reach those aims. With the crisis of Franco's regime, the city streets turned into arenas where nationalist claims were unleashed through demonstrations and social mobilisations. Those social and political expressions of nationalist claims gradually gained social and political importance.

The Basque language was one of the symbols that the nationalist movement wanted to use in order to restore their long-denied collective identity. The language is the centre of most of the attempts directed at the restoration of identity signs. This was reinforced by the existence of a generalised, anguished feeling of loss of the language during the Franco regime. Consequently, all practical attempts aimed at the restoration of linguistic normalisation of Basque lead different people from different social sectors to try to learn the language.

This second step in the development of the ethnolinguistic movement showed that there was a lack of means with which the language teaching could be carried out. The precariousness of material and human resources was compensated for by a great willingness. The situation was clearly characterised by improvisation and a lack of didactic planning. This was clear when all the means available proved to be insufficient to satisfy the huge and unexpected demand for Basque. This situation motivated the development of new methods of teaching Basque. Moreover, it was also necessary to improve the coordination between institutions. Against this backdrop, in 1977, AEK (*Alfabetatze Euskalduntze Koordinakundea*) – a coordinating body for literacy and Basque education – appeared, during the Basque Fair of Books and Records in Durango, trying to provide an answer to those teaching needs. Concomitantly, a group called UZEI and later one called ELHUYAR led to the process of standardisation of Basque.

As the process of linguistic recovery increased (Table 13.3), the material and human resources and the coordination of institutions

Table 13.3. Number of students in *ikastolas* between 1975/76 and 1981/82.

	1975–76	1976–77	1977–78	1978–79	1977–80	1980–81	1981–82
Alava	1,429	1,812	2,654	3,293	4,277	5,086	5,509
Guipuzcoa	21,325	25,314	29,652	31,423	34,733	37,145	39,128
Vizcaya	8,634	10,977	13,422	14,875	16,136	17,157	19,107
Navarra	2,158	2,621	3,094	3,744	4,909	5,369	5,727
French B.C.	305	341	382	390	474	516	564
Total	**33,851**	**41,065**	**49,204**	**53,725**	**60,529**	**65,273**	**70,035**

Source: Federation of *Ikastolas*.

improved. Between 1975 and 1980 a network of language schools was set up in the territory of the Basque Country.

In this context, the debate for the professionalisation of teachers arose. For some people it was necessary to achieve at least some stability. The most importa. t issue in the AEK internal debate was centred on how to resolve the increasing social demand for Basque. Consequently it would be necessary to establish a structure abl .o unify the schools' administration in order to devel. p a more professional attitude to the work. This would enable teachers to live exclusively on their teachers' salary. Conversely, the debate also focused on whether it would be better to dedicate greater efforts to increasing public awareness and to working as a mass movement.

The Process of Institutionalisation of Linguistic Recovery

The process of political rationalisation had two consequences. At the structural level it led to the establishment of a highly rationalised bureaucratic organisation controlling the institutional sphere, which was to become the focus for discussion of matters affecting that area. This implied a de-politicising of social life and social relations. This lack of participation – except when electing representatives – made it necessary to establish times of collective participation: participation is thus ritualised into one-off situations which, paradoxically, legitimise the absence of participation. At the conscious level, the institutionalisation of the political sphere – and with it the matters on which it decides – does not presuppose its total disappearance from everyday life: it is still relevant, but it loses its public character and becomes a private matter. Politics is privatised, which means that it becomes a question of personal preference or choice. In this sense, the question we must ask is whether these processes of political institutionalisation of nationalism, which became a hegemonic political force after Franco's death, and of privatisation of life which has taken place in the Basque Country, have affected the process of linguistic recovery.

I assert that these processes have extended and reinforced the close relationship which traditionally existed between nationalism and language, while at the same time making the language sphere more complex in respect to the following items: (1) the loss of monopoly and the appearance of diversity of organisations, which has led to a situation of plurality in the language sphere; (2) the political confrontation between AEK and the government, represented by HABE (the institute for adult literacy and Basque reeducation); (3) the increasing professionalisation of this world as a consequence of the pluralism of organisations that appeared alongside AEK, and the politicisation of other organisations either rejecting or getting closer to the ideological line that framed the confrontation between AEK-HABE (see Chapter 12); and lastly (4) the shift of protagonism to public institutions (Departments of Linguistic Policy, Education and Culture of the Basque government) and the increasing economic dependence of the ethnolinguistic movement on institutions' programmes.

Table 13.4. Evolution of Basque speakers between 1981 and 1991.

Provinces	Basque sp. 1981		Basque sp. 1986		Basque sp. 1991	
	Total	%	Total	%	Total	%
Valles Alaveses	39	0.93	45	1.10	89	2.30
Llanada Alavesa	6,559	3.38	12,235	5.98	16,080	7.50
Montaña alavesa	20	0.56	77	2.21	172	5.40
Rioja Alavesa	80	0.86	307	3.20	662	7.19
Estrib. Del Gorbea	1,552	27.94	1,758	32.48	1,734	32.94
Cantábrica Alavesa	1,443	4.37	3,002	8.86	4,258	12.66
Alava	**9,693**	**3.88**	**17,424**	**6.67**	**22,995**	**8.59**
Bajo Bidasoa	15,992	25.47	18,754	28.64	20,429	31.14
Bajo Deba	30,818	47.51	32,893	53.01	32,563	55.19
Alto Deba	34,834	53.44	36,799	56.79	38,808	60.57
Donostialdea	80,643	26.05	93,964	30.37	98,625	32.34
Goierri	31,952	46.71	35,171	52.00	36,342	55.54
Tolosaldea	28,649	63.04	30,192	67.07	30,142	68.16
Urola-Costa	43,891	73.62	46,918	77.73	48,494	78.43
Guipuzcoa	**266,779**	**39.50**	**294,691**	**43.67**	**305,403**	**45.92**
Arratia-Nervion	10,422	47.91	10,918	50.96	11,123	53.09
Gran Bilbao	58,959	6.47	82,603	9.10	92,746	10.40
Duranguesado	32,227	36.58	34,898	38.96	36,515	40.98
Encartaciones	309	1.01	511	1.70	1,233	4.22
Busturialdea	32,196	71.55	33,100	73.33	33,676	75.59
Lea-Artibai	22,364	81.73	23,415	84.31	22,806	84.87
Uribe-Butron	15,207	46.80	16,264	49.95	17,120	49.25
Vizcaya	**171,684**	**14.90**	**201,709**	**17.48**	**215,219**	**18.94**
Total number in Basque Country	**448,156**	**21.50**	**513,824**	**24.58**	**543,617**	**26.27**

Source: figures taken from 1981, 1986 and 1991 Census.

Let us consider some reference data: between 1981 and 1991 the number of Basque speakers rose by 95,461 – i.e. from 21.5 per cent to 26.27 per cent of the population of the Basque Country (see Table 13.4). The majority of this growth was focused among the under-25 age group (see Table 13.5). The rise in the number of *ikastola* students coincides with the rise noted in the number of young Basque-speakers (see Table 13.6).

Table 13.5. Basque speakers in de Basque Country over the age of 2.

	Fluent Basque speakers		Fairly competent B.s.		Non-Basque speakers		Total
Age	Total	%	Total	%	Total	%	
2–4	16,513	22.40	12,077	16.38	45,142	61.22	73,732
5–9	47,091	28.97	49,017	30.16	66,427	40.87	162,535
10–14	48,210	26.24	71,324	38.81	64,222	34.95	183,756
15–19	42,283	23.25	60,733	33.40	78,840	43.35	181,856
20–24	42,949	23.40	37,435	20.40	103,163	56.20	183,547
Total (2–24)	**197,046**	**25.09**	**230,586**	**29.36**	**357,794**	**45.55**	**785,426**
25–29	39,005	22.86	28,923	16.96	102,655	60.18	170,583
30–34	31,567	20.89	22,073	14.61	97,457	64.50	151,097
35–39	31,740	21.10	19,183	12.75	99,507	66.15	150,430
40–44	27,703	20.64	14,552	10.84	91,938	68.52	134,193
45–49	24,875	21.05	10,292	8.71	83,010	70.24	118,177
50–54	31,352	22.87	10,518	7.67	95,195	69.46	137,065
55–59	31,557	25.43	8,660	6.98	83,885	67.59	124,102
Total (25–59)	**217,799**	**22.10**	**114,201**	**11.59**	**653,647**	**66.31**	**985,647**
60–64	28,121	27.92	6,826	6.78	65,767	65.30	100,714
65–69	22,430	31.23	4,607	6.41	44,782	62.36	71,819
70–74	19,564	32.76	3,485	5.84	36,660	61.40	59,709
75+	28,864	33.30	4,411	5.09	53,405	61.61	86,680
Total (60–75+)	**98,979**	**31.04**	**19,329**	**6.06**	**200,614**	**62.92**	**318,922**
Total number in B.C.	**513,824**	**24.58**	**364,116**	**17.42**	**1,212,055**	**58.00**	**2,089,995**

Source: figures taken from 1986 Census.

After years of growing demand for Basque classes, interest declined until the early 1980s. Then, interest increased considerably, coinciding with the inauguration of HABE (Table 13.7). Not long before, AEK had held the first *Korrika* (fun run held over several days in various locations in the Basque Country, in support of Basque) and had developed the coordination of a network of *Gaueskolas* (night schools) and *euskaltegis* (Basque-literacy schools).

Inside AEK there was no unanimity, and the differences of opinion were very strong depending on the size of the school, its location, etc. The ideological debate that provided the backdrop for the confrontation

Table 13.6. Number of students receiving education in Basque between 1982/83 and 1987/88.

	1982–83	1983–84	1984–85	1985–86	1986–87	1987–88
Alava	4,578	6,023	6,406	4,627	4,881	5,180
Guipuzcoa	51,567	51,563	54,121	56,596	59,507	60,026
Vizcaya	25,781	29,092	31,187	32,812	35,793	37,704
Total number B.c.	81,926	86,678	91,714	94,035	100,181	102,910

Source: figures taken from Eustat, 'Teaching Statistics 82–83/87–88'.

Table 13.7. Number of students (81–82 to 86–87) and number of enrolments by quarters (87–88 to 89–90) with economic support of HABE.

	81–82	83–84	84–85	85–86	86–87	87–88	88–89	89–90
Alava	2,730	6,356	6,138	5,529	8,261	3,345	3,169	2,552
Guipuzcoa	6,212	17,255	17,461	18,955	19,462	10,760	10,136	10,007
Vizcaya	13,212	32,901	41,298	46,354	49,765	18,772	17,828	15,790
Total number B.c.	22,154	56,512	64,897	70,838	77,488	32,877	31,133	28,349

Source: HABE.

between AEK and HABE (see Chapter 12) was not the central issue in the internal discussions, but little by little its importance increased. This process had at least three fundamental aspects: the problem related to the ownership of the centres, the question about how to deal with HABE (integration-relationship), and the ideological discussion about the degree of acceptance of the social and political reality.

Although the external image of AEK was clearly attached to an image of opposition against the government, inside AEK three elements overlapped: the professionalisation of the system of teaching, the ownership of the centres, and what could be called either the political dimension or the political opinions that accompany the multiple ways of understanding the process of linguistic recovery.

The central feature of linguistic recovery is diversity. Gradually, from a situation of indefinition – in which linguistic, political and ideological questions were mixed and lacked a clear profile, – there evolved a situation in which each of these aspects gained enough autonomy to work in quite differentiated spheres. The language sphere became increasingly more complex and diversified as a sign of the growing tendency to specialisation.

As for the linguistic recovery among adults, new institutions were founded, dedicated to the teaching of Basque, some of which stemmed from the direct action of the Basque government through HABE, and others either due to the fragmentation of AEK's *euskaltegis* or because of their unification with the so called '*euskaltegis libres*' (free *euskaltegis*), namely BERTAN and IKA. This plurality of organisation implied a radical change in the landscape of the linguistic recovery among adults. At first, there was a discussion about who should be the protagonist of that process. Gradually this discussion led to a conflict between AEK and HABE, between the legitimation of the history of the movement and the legitimation of the representative democracy. The increasing intervention of different institutions of the Basque government or the presence of new protagonists led to a situation in which AEK lost its monopoly to teach Basque to adults. This monopoly had existed until 1981, the year HABE was established.

From that moment on, the situation began to change. There were repercussions with respect to the awareness and degree of commitment to language. On the one hand, individual responsibility and personal awareness decreased and a new way of looking at the language emerged. On the other hand, although part of the individual responsibility had remained in the personal sphere or was lost (absence of commitment), a great part was assumed by public institutions: while some people reinforced their commitment to the language by engaging in the struggle for its transmission or use, other people gave up as a consequence of the high costs implicit in the contact with this world.

The process of political rationalisation through the *Estado de las Autonomias*, and the transfer of the powers of the *Estatuto de Gernika* (Statute of Guernica), entitled the Basque government to find solutions to social demands. The success of the ethnolinguistic movement and the necessity to improve the process of language recovery hastened the intervention of the government. The presence of a resourceful government shifted the centre of gravity of the linguistic recovery from the sphere of social movements to the sphere of institutions. The control of different resources along with the power to plan and carry out linguistic policies created a subsidiary relationship – one might even say a one-way dependence to some extent – between the government and the initiatives that arose in the civil society.

Conclusions

Basque nationalism was the driving force behind the need to recover the Basque language, as opposed to other social movements which did not give such importance to this objective. The recovering process speeded up over the 1960s and 1970s as Basque became, for nationalist discourse, the central symbolic element of collective Basque identity. This symbolic importance of the language pushed it into a more prominent position in schools, homes and social spheres.

On the death of Franco and the subsequent disappearance of direct repression, nationalist discourse and its symbols dominated Basque society. One of the objectives was to extend the usage of the language, then only spoken by 20 per cent of the population. A great majority of the Basque people supported this drive, although this support was strongest in sectors nearest the heart of Basque nationalism. The symbolic character of the language and the predominance of nationalist discourse explain the intensification of the recuperation process over the two decades.

The setting up of the *Estado de las Autonomias* led to conflict between the new Public Administration (the Basque government) and the ethnolinguistic movement studying the role and direction the linguistic recuperation was taking. Ideological fragmentation, internal conflicts in the movement and the progressive strengthening of resources mobilised by the Basque government led to an increase in the knowledge and usage of the Basque language, but a progressive institutionalisation of linguistic policies and planning.

References

Arana Goiri, Sabino (1965), *Obras Completas*, Buenos Aires

Arpal, J., Asua, B. and Dávila, P. (1982), *Educación y sociedad en el País Vasco*, San Sebastián

Jauregui, Gurutz (1981), *Ideología y estrategia política de ETA. Análisis de su evolución entre 1959 y 1968*, Madrid

Michelena, Luis (1977), 'El largo y difícil camino del euskera', in *EUSKALTZAINDIA, El libro blanco del euskera*, Bilbao

Pérez-Agote, Alfonso (1986), 'The Role of Religion in the Definition of a Symbolic Conflict. Religion and the Basque Problem', *Social Compass*, XXXIII/4

Sarrailh de Ihartza, F. (1963), *Vasconia. Estudio dialéctico de una nacionalidad*, Buenos Aires

Torrealday, J.M. (1977), *Euskal idazleak gaur. Historia social de la lengua y literatura vascas*, Oñate-Arantzazu

–14–

Language and Identity in Galicia: The Current Orthographic Debate

Tracy Henderson

In this chapter I will discuss the role that language plays in Galicia as an identity marker and in creating a sense of belonging or 'groupness'. I will link language and identity to what happens in practice in Galician schools, and then raise some of the sociolinguistic issues which I believe lie behind the current orthographic debate between the *Reintegracionista* and *Independentista* (or *Isolacionista*) tendencies. As we will see, I believe that the *Reintegracionista-Independentista* orthographic debate has repercussions for community- or nation-building in Galicia. It is, therefore, necessary to look at the historical process of identifying Galicia as a nation and the role that language played in this. First it is necessary to take a brief look at language and identity and the role which language, and in particular print language, plays in the process of nation-building.

Language and Identity

It is the social, rather than the personal, aspect of identity which concerns us here. Social identity is derived from membership of various groups. If the social aspect of identity obtains from group membership, then a feature of identity must be the distinction between groups, that is to say recognition of discrete group boundaries. Identity, therefore, is also about defining and maintaining the boundaries between 'us' and 'them'. There are both objective and subjective aspects to ethnic identity. Objective aspects include linguistic, racial, geographical, religious and ancestral characteristics, which are in some way 'given' and 'involuntary'. Subjective aspects are seen as a matter of belief in which common descent is perceived to be more important than common heritage; there is presumed identity, but it is not arbitrary, there must be some link between past and present.[1]

1. For more detail about identity see Edwards (1985), Grillo (1980) and Liebkind (1989).

Language is one of the most important features of identity, and therefore an important marker of social identity. Of course, it is not the only one, but it is perhaps the most salient, and immediately differentiates 'us' from 'them'. In addition, language, and particularly print language, has an important role to play in the creation of a sense of belonging to a community. In what follows I hope to illustrate this by discussing the rise of the nation, with close reference to the ideas of Benedict Anderson in *Imagined Communities* (1983).

Anderson puts forward the following definition of the nation: 'it is an imagined political community – and imagined as both inherently limited and sovereign' (1983: 15). The nation is imagined because 'its members will never know most of their fellow-members, meet them, or even hear of them, yet in the minds of each lives the image of their communion' (1983: 15). It is imagined as limited because 'even the largest of them. . .has finite, although possibly elastic, boundaries beyond which lie other nations' (1983: 16), and it is imagined as sovereign because it has its origins in 'an age in which the Enlightenment and Revolution were destroying the legitimacy of the divinely-ordained, hierarchical dynastic realm' (1983: 16).

For Anderson, capitalism, and particularly print-capitalism, was central to the popularity of the nation. According to him, the print languages laid the bases for national consciousness in three ways: first, they created a means of communication below Latin and above the spoken vernacular, such that speakers of a vast variety of vernaculars could understand one another via print and paper and thus became aware of others in their language-field; second, print-capitalism gave a new fixity to language, and therefore the rate of change in language slowed in the sixteenth century; and, third, print-capitalism created languages-of-power (see Chapter 4). Thus, the new communities were imaginable due to the interaction between a system of production and productive relations (capitalism), print and the fatality of human linguistic diversity (although the immense variety of languages were assembled into fewer print languages, these could not be assembled into a universal language) (Anderson 1983: 47–8). If written language allows speakers of different varieties of a language to understand each other via print, we could say that in the Galician case different types of national consciousness would be created according to the different orthographies. In the case of the *Reintegracionista* orthography, speakers of the Galician variety of Portuguese would become aware of other speakers of Portuguese, creating a national consciousness which included other Portuguese-speaking nations. In the case of the *Independentista* orthography, speakers of one variety of Galician would become aware of speakers of other varieties of Galician, creating a Galician national consciousness.

Language also contributed to the rise of the nation through the increasing administration which it demanded. Anderson applies the '"journey" between times, statuses and places, as a meaning-creating experience' of the anthropologist Victor Turner to the process of state-building (1983: 55). The journey is the pilgrimage, in both religious and secular terms. The secular pilgrimage or journey was created by the rise of absolutising monarchies and by the Europe-centred world-imperial states. The absolutising monarchies created a unified apparatus of power, which was controlled by and loyal to the ruler. Unification meant that both people and documents had to be interchangeable. Human interchangeability was fostered by functionaries who undertook administrative 'journeys' on which they met fellow 'pilgrims', a process which lead to a consciousness of connectedness. The interchangeability of documents was fostered by the development of standardised languages-of-state. We can apply this 'journey' or 'pilgrimage' to the Galician situation where people and documents are interchangeable through the functionary administrative system and the use of Galician in administration. In other words, this is another way in which the creation of a sense of Galician consciousness is aided by written language. (Prior to the Autonomy Statute, however, these administrative 'journeys' would have been carried out by Spanish officials.)

For Anderson, then, language is important for creating feelings of loyalty, and thus for building the 'imagined community' of the nation.

Galicia as a Nation

From AD 216 there was a province within the Roman Empire, in the Iberian Peninsula, called Gallaecia, which extended into what today is northern Portugal, as far south as the River Douro. Latin-speakers colonised the area administratively, and Latin forms the basis of the Galician language. Latin continued to be the language used in administration and the Church, but by the eighth century it differed so much from the spoken language that we can say two languages existed: Latin and Galaico-Portuguese, or Galician-Portuguese. The first texts written in Galaico-Portuguese appeared in the twelfth century, and between the twelfth and fifteenth centuries this was the language used by the intellectual class.[2]

2. See Siguan (1992) for more detail about the development of Galician and the other languages in Spain.

Portugal became an independent monarchy in the twelfth century. Land between the Miño and Douro rivers became part of Portugal, and with linguistic influences from the south, the language south of the River Miño developed into Portuguese. Literary production in Galician stopped in the fourteenth century. In the fifteenth century the Galician nobility was replaced by Castilian nobility, and under Castilian influence, the language of Galicia became a popular language, with no administrative or cultural uses. Galicians who wished to gain access to the ruling group adopted Castilian.

From about the middle of the last century, there was a growing awareness of Galicia's own culture and identity. The cultural-political movement which developed from this was *Galeguismo*, which has been categorised as three phases: provincialism, regionalism and nationalism. Beramendi (1985 and 1991), Máiz (1984, 1986 and 1991) and Portas (1993) provide accounts of these three phases.

Provincialism

Portas (1993: 73) describes the nineteenth century as one of deep social, political and economic transformations in Galicia. Political attention concentrated on whether the model of state should be one of absolute monarchy or one based on the liberal ideology to have come out of the French Revolution. It was in this context that the assumption that Galicians had the right to be masters of their own destiny was taken up by some Galician intellectuals.

Provincialism lasted during the 1840s, and both the economic backwardness of Galicia and the centralising policy of the monarchy were criticised. Its proponents rejected the provincial divisions of 1833, believing instead that Galicia should be recognised as one single province, as was the old Kingdom of Galicia. The provincialists argued that Galicia was distinct in terms of its history, countryside, economy, ethnicity and traditions. Language, however, was not at first considered to be a differentiating factor. The young intellectuals of the 1850s began to turn their attentions to cultural as well as political activities, and it was then that Galician began to appear in poetry. The language aspect of *Galeguismo* really took hold after the 1860s, and particularly in the last quarter of the nineteenth century, with an increase in the literary use of Galician and the appearance of Galician grammars and dictionaries. The first work written entirely in Galician was *Os Cantares Gallegos* by Rosalía de Castro, published in 1863, and this marks the beginning of the literary *Rexurdimento*, or Renaissance.

Regionalism

The regionalist phase lasted from the time of the restoration of the Bourbon monarchy until 1916. The regionalist movement organised its own political party, *Asociación Regionalista Gallega* (1891), which drew its theoretical basis from *El regionalismo* by Alfredo Brañas (1889) and *El regionalismo gallego* by Manuel Murguía (1889). In Murguía's writing there is a concept of Galicia as a nation, although the word 'region' is also used. Whilst his work is influenced by Mancini's concept of 'nation', in which national consciousness is a central element, it is not monopolised by it. Murguía's concept of nation is a hybrid of the organic and historicist concept of nation which was born in Germany at the beginning of the nineteenth century, in which nation is defined by race, language, customs, history and territory, and Italian nationalism of a liberal nature, centred on national consciousness and political will. However, race, history and language are central to Murguía's concept of nation, whilst in liberal Italian nationalism these elements are peripheral (see Máiz 1984). In his *Galeguista* ideology there is a desire for socio-political modernisation of Galicia and for industrialisation and a bourgeoisie, mixed with a desire to return to Galicia's ethnic origins.

In contrast to Murguía's liberal regionalism, there was also a traditionalist ideology which was theorised and politically headed by Alfredo Brañas. According to Beramendi (1985: 177), this ideology used the liberal concept of nation elaborated by Murguía, but added elements of a Catholic-traditionalist type, such that the aim of Brañas's regionalism was completely different to Murguía's. The only thing they had in common was the concept of Galicia and the necessity of political autonomy. These differences, according to Beramendi, account for the stalemate between the two types of regionalism and the political failure of the *Asociación Regionalista Gallega*.

The use of Galician was encouraged in publications (for example in the bilingual *A Nosa Terra*[3]) and public acts. The *Real Academia Galega* was founded in 1906 in La Coruña with Murguía as its first president. According to García Pereiro (1978), Murguía supported the idea that Galician and Portuguese were the same language.

---

3. Publication of *Solidaridad Gallega* and mouthpiece of the agrarian movement.

Nationalism

In May 1916 the first *Irmandade da Fala*[4] was founded in La Coruña by a group of *Galeguistas*. Others were set up all over Galicia, and there were even *Irmandades* in Madrid, Buenos Aires and Havana. They encouraged the use of Galician in literature, education, science, and any public use, both oral and written. They set up publishing houses in which they published newspapers, magazines, short stories, plays, and so on, in Galician. The most important of these publishing houses was *Nós*, founded in 1927 in La Coruña by Anxel Casal, and later transferred to Santiago, remaining active until 1936. It published the most important works of the *Nós* Generation[5] and the magazine of the same name, as well as the paper *A Nosa Terra*, by then written entirely in Galician. Máiz (1986: 215) points out that the *Irmandades da Fala* were not associations of a purely cultural nature primarily interested in the promotion and defence of the Galician language, as their name would seem to suggest. In fact their programme included social, political and ideological elements which were developed through *A Nosa Terra*.

The birth of modern Galician nationalism is generally considered to be in 1918 when the *Irmandades da Fala* had their first assembly in Lugo from which their *Manifesto* emerged. In this document, the *Galeguistas* affirm that 'Since Galicia has all the essential characteristics of a nation, from today we will call ourselves Galician nationalists, because the word "regionalism" does not encompass all the aspirations or include the intensity of our problems' (author's translation, quoted in Portas 1993: 103). Some of the proposals put forward in the *Manifesto* were: coofficiality of Galician and Castilian, and as such its use in domains such as education and the judicial system; and a series of measures aimed at achieving national sovereignty for Galicia. It defended an Iberian federation, which included Portugal, and the establishment of a Galician government and parliament which would exercise power in Galicia.

There were ideological divisions within the *Irmandades*, which gave rise to a split in 1922. On one side was traditionalist or conservative nationalism (Beramendi 1985: 180), heir to traditionalist regionalism, and on the other was liberal (Beramendi 1985: 178) or democratic

4. Originally called *Hirmandade de Amigos da Fala Gallega*, the objective of these 'brotherhoods' was to dignify the Galician language and encourage its public use. Using the name of what had been the publication of *Solidaridad Gallega*, the mouthpiece of the Irmandades was *A Nosa Terra*, which they published in Galician from 1916 to 1936.

5. The *Nós* Generation included Vicente Risco, Ramón Otero Pedrayo, Florentino López Cuevillas, Alfonso Rodríguez Castelao, Ramón Cabanillas Enriquez and Antón Lousada Diéguez.

(Beramendi 1991: 150) nationalism, heir to liberal regionalism.

For the traditionalists,[6] ethnicity and history were factors which formed the nation, and land and race were particularly important.[7] The traditionalists rejected capitalist modernity and this was complemented by a nostalgia for the past. They also rejected industrialisation as a solution to Galicia's backwardness, believing that Galicia should continue to be rural since the peasantry held the most pure national characteristics. The persistence of the rural nature of Galicia was seen as a defence against the modern economy and capitalism, and the rural nobility would conserve or recuperate their hegemony by their reconversion into a ruling elite.

Like the traditionalists, the liberal nationalists saw the nation as being determined by history and nature. However, spiritual elements predominated over physical ones in establishing ethnicity, that is, 'Volksgeist', language and folklore predominated over race and land (Beramendi 1991: 152). With the aim of a more equal distribution of resources amongst individuals, they supported the generalisation of small businesses in cities and small cooperatives in the country. They supported the creation of an urban ruling class.

All groups criticised the backwardness of Galicia and emphasised its problems, such as the lack of communications and education, linguistic and cultural oppression, emigration and the poor living conditions of, in particular, peasants and fishermen. In contrast to the provincialist and regionalist phases in which Spain was seen as the nation, containing regions or other nations, the nationalists denied the existence of a Spanish nation. They saw the centralist state and Castilian domination of other nations through the state as being responsible for Galicia's problems. They proposed a federation or confederation of Iberian nations, which would include Portugal if possible (unity with Portugal, *reintegración*, should be recuperated through an Iberian confederation). In Galicia, Galician and Castilian would be co-official, education would be 'Galicianised' at all levels and Galician culture would be encouraged (Beramendi 1991: 161).

The Nós *Generation*

The *Nós* Generation used Galician not only in literary work, but also in scientific, ethnographic, historic and geographic work. Perhaps the most

6. During the 1920s and 1930s the nucleus of traditionalist nationalism was Vicente Risco (the principal ideologue), Ramón Otero Pedrayo, Arturo Noguerol and Florentino López Cuevillas.
7. Risco's concept of a nation was that it was 'a natural fact, a biological fact, independent of the will of the people' (author's translation, see Beramendi 1991: 143).

important and famous of their collective work is the magazine *Nós*, which was published from 1920 to 1936, and which was the cultural expression of the *Galeguismo* of the *Irmandades*. The *Nós* Generation identified the Galician spoken in rural areas as the authentic Galician, and saw the language as the fundamental element in the recuperation of the cultural identity of Galicia (Noia 1988). They saw a need to elaborate a standard variety, different from the colloquial variety, and saw Portuguese as a great help in this respect. For Viqueira, Portuguese was the son of Galician, with less differences between them than there were between Andalusian and Castilian, and he proposed that Galician should be written like Portuguese (see Fernández 1979). One of the most influential figures of the *Nós* Generation and of *Galeguismo* was Castelao. In *Sempre en Galiza*, Castelao states that 'Galician is a widely-spoken and useful language, because – with little variation – it is spoken in Brazil, Portugal and the Portuguese colonies' (author's translation, Castelao 1977: 43), and '. . .fortunately our language is alive and flourishing in Portugal. . .' (author's translation, Castelao 1977: 232).

According to Máiz (1986: 217), the *Nós* Generation, in particular Risco, disagreed with the way to achieve the economic, political and cultural objectives of the *Irmandades*. For the *Irmandades*, achieving the nationalist objectives (recuperation and dignification of Galician language and literature, economic progress and modernisation), went hand in hand with the political battle in elections, parliamentary discussion and gaining social support for *Galeguismo* and seats in the Spanish Parliament. For the *Nós* Generation, the main objective of nationalism was to turn what was merely a sense of difference into a national consciousness of Galicia, which was to be achieved through *Galeguista* propaganda and culture, thus undermining the basis of Spanish political and cultural domination.

The political wing of the *Nós* Generation was the *Partido Galeguista*, which was founded in 1931 at the seventh and final assembly of the *Irmandades*. In its *Declaración de Princípios*, the *Partido Galeguista* considered the Galician language to be one of the most important features of Galician identity and expressed its intention to defend the language and contribute to expansion of its use and its social dignification. The party defended the right to use Galician and proposed a type of bilingualism which favoured Galician, thus helping to increase its use in different functions. The legal recognition of Galician was sought by its parliamentary representatives in the Cortes of the Second Republic. However, there were divisions within the *Partido Galeguista*, principally between the conservatives and the Left, although there were radical Left and separatist groups (Máiz 1986: 222–3). In 1935 the conservatives broke away and formed *Direita Galeguista* in Orense and in Pontevedra, whilst the pro-republican Left remained in the *Partido Galeguista*, which in 1936 became incorporated into the *Frente Popular*. The *Partido Galeguista* was instrumental in securing the Autonomy Statute under the Republican Constitution. The Statute was approved in 1936 by a regional referendum during the month before the outbreak of the Civil War, and submitted to the Spanish Parliament at the session which was held in Montserrat in Catalonia in February 1938, by which time Galicia was already under the control of Franco's Nationalists. The party was reconstituted in 1943, but by 1950 was defunct. The *Frente Cultural Galaxia* emerged in its place.

The Franco Dictatorship

Galicia was under the control of Franco's Nationalists very soon after the military uprising of July 1936. The Franco Regime saw Spain as being culturally and linguistically uniform. Galician disappeared from public life, and any domains which had been gained through *Galeguismo* were lost. *Galeguismo* in Galicia was silenced by the Franco Regime, but the work of linguistic recuperation was carried on by those in exile in Argentina, Brazil, Venezuela, Mexico and Cuba.

The cornerstone in the recuperation of the written use of Galician in Galicia was the founding in Vigo in July 1950 of *Editorial Galaxia*, which published periodicals and supported literature written in Galician. It was set up by an important sector of *Galeguistas* in the *Culturalismo* movement, headed by Ramón Piñeiro, who concentrated their efforts on cultural activity which they saw as the only viable action given the political conditions at that time.

During the 1960s with a certain opening up of the regime cultural associations were able to form. These associations supported the use of Galician in the transmission of Galician culture and questioned the social situation of the language through their courses and conferences. At about the same time, clandestine political parties, principally on the Left, began to emerge.

The creation in 1965 of the *Cátedra de Lingua e Literatura Galegas* at the University of Santiago de Compostela was of enormous symbolic importance. Three years later the research centre *Instituto da Lingua Galega* was set up. *Galeguista* demands increased through the 1970s.

In the post-Franco period, under the Spanish Constitution and the Galician Statute of Autonomy, Galician is recognised as co-official with Castilian within Galicia and as such it is used in public administration, education and the media (see Chapter 4).

The next section is an attempt to link the importance which language, and particularly written language, has for the 'imagined community' to the *Reintegracionista-Independentista* debate in Galicia.

The Movement for *Reintegración*

The *Real Academia Galega* and the *Instituto da Lingua Galega* approved an orthographic and morphological *norma* for Galician in July 1982, which was sanctioned by the *Xunta*, the Galician local government. In spite of this, there are still groups who contend that Galician should be written to a greater or lesser extent like Portuguese, rather than like these *normas*. In order to understand the two main positions on Galician orthography it is necessary to take a very brief look at the history of the Galician language.

The division of the old Galicia, the creation of Portugal and the development of Portuguese form the basis of the two broad linguistic tendencies in Galicia today, that is the *Reintegracionista* and the *Independentista* tendencies. The *Independentistas* believe that the political division between Galicia and Portugal was accompanied by a linguistic division, such that Galaico-Portuguese gave rise to two separate languages, Galician and Portuguese. The *Reintegracionistas*, on the other hand, believe that Galaico-Portuguese in Galician territory stagnated under political and linguistic influence from Castile, whilst Galaico-Portuguese in Portuguese territory was able to evolve: they see Portuguese as the projection of what Galician would have been had it not been for Castilian influence. Thus, the *Independentistas* see Galician as an independent language, whilst the *Reintegracionistas* believe that Galician is a variant of Portuguese, which also has varieties in Portugal, Brazil and the Portuguese-speaking countries of Africa.

Broadly speaking, the aim of the *Reintegración* Movement is to 'clean' the Galician language from Castilianisms, to recuperate traditional forms, and to 'reintegrate' Galician into its original environment, that is, into the Portuguese-speaking world. *Reintegracionistas* believe, therefore, that Galician should be written to a greater or lesser extent like Portuguese. (See Arribe Dopico et al. 1994.)

According to the orthographies they use, the *Reintegracionista* groups can be divided into what are sometimes referred to as the *mínimos* and *máximos*. Although the *mínimos* consider Galician to be a variety of Portuguese, the orthography they use does not differ a great deal from the orthography used by the non-*Reintegracionistas*, or *Independentistas*. There are two positions adopted by the *máximos*: AGAL (*Associaçom Galega da Língua*) uses an orthography which is substantially Portuguese, but which maintains the minimal differences peculiar to Galicia; *Irmandades da Fala* and ASPGP (*Associação Sociopedagogica Galaicoportuguesa*) adopt the orthography used in the Portuguese *Acordo Ortográfico* (signed in 1990 by representatives of the governments of Portugal, Brazil, Angola, Mozambique, Guinea-Bissau, Cape Verde, and São Tomé and Príncipe, and observers from Galicia), which proposes a simplified, standard orthography for the Portuguese-speaking countries. At an organisational level, these groups have no links with political parties.

Given that in the history of mankind speech developed long before writing, that individuals learn to speak before they learn to write and that writing is absent from some societies, we could take the view that spoken language is much more important than written language. If this is the case, we could say that it should not matter how a language is written. In the case of Galician, more than a decade after the *normas* were sanctioned by the *Xunta*, there is still debate about how the language should be written: groups supporting *Reintegración* still exist and they are still active. If spoken language is more important than written language, why do these different positions exist?

The process of prescribing *normas* is part of corpus planning. In *Language Planning and Social Change* Cooper (1989) points out that language planning is generally not carried out solely to improve communication, but rather in order to achieve non-linguistic ends, such as national integration, political control, economic development, and so on. In other words, one should distinguish between overt and covert goals in language planning.

Different Orthographies, Different Communities

We have seen that an important part of *Galeguismo* has been the use and promotion of Galician, both written and oral, and that by the Regionalist stage it was one of the main differentiating factors of Galician culture and identity. The belief that the Galician language is a key element of Galician identity is still widely prevalent.[8] Whilst there are many features of Galicia that can be found elsewhere, such as bagpipes, the mountains and the *rías*, the language is a differentiating feature, seen by some as the basis of Galician identity, and by others as the external manifestation of something interior and as the most external feature of identity.

---

8. Between January and March 1994 I carried out research in Galicia and Portugal, interviewing a number of academics, writers and politicians, of *Reintegracionista* and *Independentista* tendencies. All of those asked about language and identity expressed this view.

As far as the relationship between Galicia and Portugal is concerned, there have been closer ties and more commercial and economic contact in recent years between Galicia and northern Portugal. Galicians recognise that in terms of language and culture, they are closer to the Portuguese than to the Castilians, and many would like to see more contact between Galician and Portugal. The Portuguese, however, generally do not know about the Galician *Reintegracionista* Movement. One Portuguese supporter of *Reintegración* believed that rather than a lack of support this was a lack of knowledge due to a lack of communication (Da Rocha Valente, personal communication). On the whole, the Portuguese view Spain as united and do not want to 'interfere'.

Many commentators doubt that there is any real will to normalise Galician on the part of the *Xunta*. A recurrent remark in connection with the *Xunta* and their use and promotion of Galician is *fachada*, that is, facade. García Negro has referred to official policy as 'homeopathic tactics' ('táctica homeopática', 1993: 90) because 'bad' or 'prejudicial' elements are injected to neutralise growth and to combat from within.

Since 1983 (under the Language Normalisation Law) Galician has been recognised as official in all levels of education. Galician is a compulsory subject at all non-university levels. It is obligatory for students to receive three or four hours per week of Galician language or literature (depending on the level) and some other subjects are to be taught through Galician. At primary level at least history and geography should be taught through Galician, and at secondary level at least two of a selection of subjects are to be taught through Galician. Whilst at secondary level the legal requirements for the teaching of Galician language and literature are carried out, this is not always the case for the teaching of other subjects through Galician, the decision becoming in practice a personal decision of the teacher concerned. There appears to be no 'policing' of this aspect of the law by the authorities, once again raising questions about the will of the authorities to normalise the language.[9]

---

9. In November 1994 I carried out interviews in Pontevedra with Galician teachers, principally from secondary schools, but also from nursery and primary schools, a teachers' training college and the University of Santiago de Compostela. I concentrate here on the findings of interviews with secondary school teachers, since any teaching of non-official orthographies tends to take place at secondary rather than primary level, and at university level Galician is not compulsory. It should be stated that Pontevedra is a very 'Castilianised' city, so the vast majority of students are Castilian speakers, and in general the language most often heard in schools is Castilian – students probably all have the ability to speak Galician with varying degrees of accuracy and fluency, but the language they most often choose to use is Castilian. In more rural areas the use of Galician is likely to be much higher.

The orthographic and morphological rules approved by the *Xunta* in July 1982 are the ones which are obligatory in all schools in Galicia, and are the most widely used in schools. However, in some schools other orthographies are taught. It should be pointed out that many teachers who use the official orthography criticise it for being basically Castilian orthography which, therefore, makes Galician appear to be a dialect of Castilian, and also for the fact that every year there are changes, causing confusion amongst students. On the whole, when *Reintegracionista* orthography is taught it tends to be the *mínimos'* orthography, rather than the *máximos'* one. Teachers may come into conflict with the authorities when using *máximos'*, but not when *mínimos'* is used, because this is harder to detect. Some teachers believe that, as far as the *Xunta* is concerned, any conflict between teachers and students over orthography is 'beneficial'. Some commentators believe that the Galician government is against Galician and wants to impose Castilian, and since any conflict over orthography is damaging for Galician, the *Xunta* does not interfere.

Obviously, Galician could make much more progress if the two main sectors could find a way to work together for the promotion of the language. The *Reintegracionistas*, too, would be in a stronger position if they could reach an agreement amongst themselves. However, as we have seen, not only is there a broad split between *Reintegracionistas* and non-*Reintegracionistas*, but there are also divisions within the *Reintegración* Movement. An agreement on orthography between the *Reintegracionistas* and the *Independentistas* would appear, at the very least, to be difficult: if the *Reintegracionistas* cannot agree between themselves on an orthography for Galician, there would appear to be little hope of an agreement between them and the *Independentistas*. It seems to me that the only agreement that could possibly be reached, and that seems unlikely, would be between the *mínimos* and the *Independentistas*, and only because their respective orthographies are closer than those between either the *mínimos* and *máximos*, or the latter and the *Independentistas*. It is, however, difficult to see how an agreement could be reached given that there is a fundamental difference that neither side would be willing to compromise on and which underpins the two main positions: whether Galician is an independent language or whether it is a variant of Portuguese.

Language and identity, as we have seen, are intimately related. Calling the language spoken in Galicia Portuguese could, therefore, raise questions about Galician identity. If Galicians wrote Portuguese, would they consider themselves, or be considered by others, to be Galician, or Portuguese, or Spanish? Galician might be seen by some people as a foreign language in Spain, and others, although a minority, might think about political unions with Portugal. Galician orthography, then, could have political repercussions for the Spanish State.

Conclusions

We have seen that the Galician language is an important part of Galician identity, that is, it is part of the group boundary for 'us', the Galicians. However, according to whether *Independentista* or *Reintegracionista* orthography is used, the language within the group boundary 'us', and therefore within the group boundary 'them', will either be Galician or Portuguese. Thus the orthographic debate raises questions about the content of the group boundaries 'us' and 'them'.

We could argue that the *Independentista* orthography helps to construct a group of 'us' which includes only Galicians, and that the 'them' group would therefore include both Spain and Portugal. On the other hand, we could say that the *Reintegracionista* orthography would help to construct a Galician group of 'us' which included Portugal and possibly the other Portuguese-speaking countries. 'them' would therefore include Spain, but not Portugal. Given that the *Reintegracionistas* believe that the official orthography is too similar to Castilian and will eventually lead to the assimilation of Galician by Spanish, some would say that the *Independentista* view of 'us' includes Spain.

It is the *Independentista* orthography which is most widespread in education, and where *Reintegracionista* orthography is used it is usually the *mínimos'* rather than the *máximos'* orthography. Given the importance of written language and education as a means of identity and community-building, we could argue that education is helping to create an independent Galician 'imagined community' rather than one which includes Portugal. Where *mínimos'* orthography is used, the authorities do not usually take any action, in spite of the fact that it is against the law. The use of Galician in the teaching of other subjects seems to be a matter of choice for the teacher concerned. This leads one to question whether the *Xunta* really has the will to try to create a Galician 'imagined community' of any description, either independent or one which includes Portugal.

References

Anderson, B. (1983), *Imagined Communities: Reflections on the Origin and Spread of Nationalism*, London

Arribe Dopico, M.D., Gil Hernández, A. and Rábade Castinheira, J.C. (1984), 'Tese reintegracionista', in Barca Lozano, A. et al., *I Encontros labaca. Ponencias*, Sada (Corunna), pp.43–175

Language and Identity in Galicia

Beramendi, J. (1985), 'Achegamento ás ideoloxías do galeguismo (1846–1936)', in De Juana, J. and Castro, X. (eds), *Ias Xornadas de Historia de Galicia*, Orense, pp.167–84

—— (1991), 'El Partido Galleguista y poco más. Organización e ideologias del nacionalismo gallego en la II República', in Beramendi, J.G. and Máiz, R. (eds), *Los nacionalismos en la España de la II República*, Madrid, pp.127–70

Castelao, A. (1977), *Sempre en Galiza*, Madrid

Cooper, R. (1989), *Language Planning and Social Change*, Cambridge

Edwards, J. (1985), *Language, Society and Identity*, Oxford

Fernández, C. (1979), 'Teoria da língua en Xan Vicente Viqueira', *Grial*, no.66, pp.489–94

García Negro, M.P. (1993), *Sempre en Galego*, Santiago de Compostela

García Pereiro, M. (1978), 'Teoría da língua galega en Murguía', *Grial*, no.61, pp.363–6

Grillo, R. (1980), 'Introduction', in Grillo, R. (ed.), *'Nation' and 'State' in Europe: Anthropological Perspectives*, London, pp.1–30

Liebkind, K. (1989), 'The Identity of a Minority', *Journal of Multilingual and Multicultural Development*, vol.10, no.1, pp.47–57

Máiz, R. (1984), 'Raza y mito céltico en los orígenes del nacionalismo gallego: Manuel M Murguía', *Revista Española de Investigaciones Sociológicas*, vol.25, pp.137–80

—— (1986), 'El nacionalismo gallego: Apuntes para la historia de una hegemonía imposible', in Hernández, F. and Mercadé, F. (eds), *Estructuras sociales y cuestión nacional en España*, Barcelona, pp. 186–243

—— (1991), 'Federalismo y nación en el discurso del nacionalismo gallego de la II República', in Beramendi, J.G. and Máiz, R. (eds), *Los nacionalismos en la España de la II República*, Madrid, pp. 377–404

Noia, C. (1988), 'Usos e actitudes lingüísticas na "Epoca Nós"', *Grial*, no.100, pp.174–82

Portas, M. (1993), *Língua e sociedade na Galiza*, Corunna

Siguan, M. (1992), *España plurilingüe*, Madrid

Part III

Supra-National Structures and the European Union

Spain, European Regions and City States
Alan Whitehead

Spain gives the appearance of having a system of regional government that works. What is more, regional boundaries, unlike those of France and Germany, have been allowed to follow historical patterns, so that administrative devolution and sub-national or national identities within the country seem to have been neatly combined. To some, this feat of political balance should not theoretically be possible to achieve. David Coombes, for example, states that 'Regionalism as political doctrine verges on the absurd, failing to distinguish between the contrary values of national separatism or irredentism, on the one hand, and the general decentralisation of state authority, on the other' (1991: 148).

He is suggesting, essentially, that state structures can meaningfully be of two types. A federal state, with minimal powers reserved for the centre, may provide for some degree of cohesion by allowing the 'national' question to float within the system. Unitiary states, on the other hand, might introduce a degree of devolved administrative responsibilities, such as the English county system, in the absence of significant centrifugal force within the state structure which might destabilise such devolution. The two types of system, Coombes infers, cannot be mixed. Certainly, according to this doctrine, Spain's model of regionalism should be a political impossibility. Indeed, the break-up of the country under pressure from regional 'nationalism' was envisaged immediately after the death of Franco (Medhurst 1977).

In the eyes of some commentators (Keating 1988; Canel 1994), however, Spain has succeeded in squaring the circle. By a combination of ambiguous wording in its national constitution, and a judicious mélange of a basic regional structure incorporating the opportunity for differential rates of devolution of authority, the country has managed to maintain national cohesion, whilst at the same time developing a highly decentralised system of government. This success is underlined by being achieved within the span of a decade or so after the demise of Western Europe's most centralised state machine. María José Canel, an adherent of this view, describes Spain's transition thus:

It is difficult to say whether a high degree of decentralisation is due to a pragmatic phase in Spanish politics. It is obvious that an autonomic system was the only way in which Spain could have handled regional differences and nationalist problems in 1978. The question that remains is whether the model is nothing more than a transitional step towards federalism. The fact is that the different Spanish regions are greatly diverse, but, at the same time, Spain also has a strong tradition of centralism, which makes it difficult to think of federalism as an option. The autonomic system, with all the corrections needed. . .could be a model for a third way between federalism and unitarianism for Spain and for those countries with marked regional identities within them. (1994: 59)

The purpose of this chapter is to examine Canel's viewpoint not so much in the light of Spain's internal constitutional arrangements – although it will be necessary to touch on them – but more in the light of Spain's embrace of the European Union, and the active participation of its regions and cities in the networks that are springing up across Europe. That, combined with the developments of the Maastricht Treaty and beyond, which the Spanish government has endorsed, will undoubtedly influence and possibly fundamentally alter the best efforts of the Spanish body politic to maintain the 'compromise' of autonomy.

The ability to steer a middle course between the scylla of federalism and the charibdys of centralism derives from the magnificently paradoxical wording of the 1978 Constitution. Article 2, for example, reads as follows: 'The constitution is based on the indissoluble unity of the Spanish nation, common and indivisible fatherland for all the Spanish people, and recognises and guarantees the right of autonomy for nationalities and regions which make up the Spanish state.'

On the one hand, therefore, the unitary state is promoted, but on the other, its constituent parts are formally, directly and centrally acknowledged. This is, to some extent just a pragmatic recognition of history: the languages and national identity of Catalonia, the Basque Country and Galicia are a fact, and there was clearly no mileage in releasing the country from the centralism of Franco only to continue with his policy of suppression of sub-national culture. Indeed, had any state not willing to adopt fascist methods of state control attempted to do so, Spain would have blown apart very quickly.

There are however, other considerations, such as the differing legal systems arising from the historical experience of various parts of Spain. Thus the first 'disposition' of the constitution gives protection to the '*territorios forales*' – those territories with so-called 'foral rights' that some regions have gained through history and remain to the present day as distinct laws implying rights of self-government. The financial systems operational in the Basque Country and Navarre which allow them to impose and collect the majority of taxes and then give an agreed sum to the central government for centrally provided services are examples of these rights (Keating 1988).

Consequently, the constitution allows for a series of arrangements between regions and the centre which can neither be called federal nor merely consultative. Indeed, Article 145 of the constitution states: '. . .to no extent will federation of autonomous Communities be allowed.' This curious phrase implies a clear brake on the process of autonomy: whilst the constitution recognises a high degree of political and administrative devolution among Spain's regions, that authority is derived as an instrument of the central state. There is no further right, as is logically the case in Canada, for example, for states to declare that they wish to secede from the federation, or to ally with other states to produce an alternative federation. Autonomous communities, however, can elect their own representatives to the senate, can ensure representation on the constitutional court through the senate, and can present bills to the central parliament, with three members of the autonomous parliament to speak up for them.

Perhaps the key element in the development of Spain's 'third way' has, though, been the concept of a 'two-track' road to autonomy. This has undoubted salience in the current UK debate on regionalism, since a version of the system has been adopted by the UK Labour Party as a possible way out of the Party's difficulties with regional government. In effect, those communities which had long been regarded as indisputable regions because of linguistic and historic reasons were given leave to achieve full, immediate autonomy under the terms of Article 151 of the Constitution. Subject only to a majority vote of the deputies and senators to the Cortes from each region, Catalonia, Galicia and Euskadi were in business, as it were, straight away (Cuchillo 1993).

Other regions were offered two routes to autonomy. They could either aim for accelerated autonomy through a series of rather more rigorous procedures deriving from Article 151, or they could opt for a more gentle and gradual procedure under article 143 which involved the consent of two-thirds of the municipal councils of each region, followed by the agreement of the central Parliament. Only one region, Andalusia, opted for the exacting but accelerated path offered by Article 151, and, after a referendum, obtained full autonomy in 1981. All other regions followed the second path with ultimate success.

On constitutional matters, one ought to add two further observations. Firstly, the constitution not only allows for regional devolution in the way described, but also assumes considerable power of competence to local authorities. Whilst Article 148 states that each autonomous community will be empowered to decide on '. . .the boundaries of municipalities within its territory, and in general, every power belonging to the State Administration over the local corporations', local government itself is given wide discretionary power. The 1985 Local Government Act (the *Ley Orgánica de la Armonización del Proceso Autonómico*, known as the LOAPA) states that 'the municipality, in the furtherance of its interests and within the scope of its powers can promote all types of activity and provide those public services which contribute to satisfying the needs and aspirations of the local community' (Article 24 clause 1). This provides, as we shall see, for municipalities to exercise a high degree of freedom to act within the system.

Secondly, the state retains two cards to play in restraining the autonomous communities: the retention of Franco's administrative provinces, which remain outside the jurisdiction of the autonomous communities, despite attempts through the constitutional court by Catalonia to bring them under regional control (Brassloff 1995: 9–10), and a high degree of central control of finance (Brassloff 1995). Some 80 per cent of regional budgets derive from central government grant, except in the two Foral communities (Canel 1994: 55–6). This figure approximately equates to the level of central grant in the UK local government system, widely regarded as among the most centralised currently in the Western industrialised world.

Having set out the basis upon which the concept of Spain's 'third road' to regionalism is based, it is now necessary to ask the central question: will it be able to negotiate the twists and turns of the wider road, that of pan-European regionalism, down which Spain will inevitably have to take its organisational structure? This road poses problems for the Spanish system for several reasons. Broadly speaking, they can be categorised as follows:

1. Increasingly, European policy-making is emphasising the role of the 'Europe of the Regions'. This enhanced role for regions is accompanied by institutional structures in which Spanish regions will be invited to play a leading role. Spanish regions may, by that activity, gain additional 'leverage' on the Spanish State which might, in the wrong (or right) hands (depending on your point of view) cause the fragile compromise of 'autonomy' to blow apart.

2. The desire for administrative uniformity in European structures as they develop may cause Spain to revise its structures of authority between regions and the centre, thereby damaging the 'compromise'. This could indeed happen through a more standardised interpretation of the concept of 'subsidiarity' in the EU.

3. The existence of agencies within the EU such as DGXV1, which is

responsible for the development of regional policy, will have an inevitable effect of encouraging regions to undertake 'networking' both
in order to enhance their joint clout within the Union and to gain
funds for common purposes from the centre. In so doing, the regions
will increasingly bypass the central Spanish State and may thereby
unbalance the compromise.

4. The existence of parallel City networks alongside those of regions
    may cause some major cities in Spain to pursue links either to
    the detriment of their own regional arrangements, or, where Cities
    are effectively at the centre of a 'City-state' region, may provide an
    alternative avenue for a destabilised relationship with the central
    Spanish State.

All of these concerns suggest that, in time, the compromise may not
hold and might be replaced by a more explicitly federal structure for
Spain, or even the break-up of the nation-state as it is presently conceived. In order to assess the salience of these issues, each will be
examined in turn.

Policy-Making in the 'Europe of the Regions'

The view from Britain rather obscures the real developments that have
taken place in regionalism across Europe over the past few years. This
is, of course, because the UK has no politically elected regions, and to
a large extent, therefore, the daily small change of regional discussion,
decision-making and linkage passes us by. It ought to be noted,
however, that since early 1994, the UK has developed a system of Government Offices for the Regions (GORs) which have been allocated a
substantial amount of control over a series of regionally based funds,
including those relating to enterprise grants, transport funding, training
finance and the Housing Investment Programme (Mawson and Spencer
1996). According to Foster (1995) these 'have been likened to the district commissioners who ran the British empire, to Roman Pro-consuls,
French prefects, even to viceroys. They include several high-flyers
destined to become Permanent Secretaries, but their prerogatives and
comparative anonymity have led to all-party concern about the concentration of power in an unaccountable bureaucracy.' The description
is very reminiscent of the status of Spanish provincial governors under
Franco (Medhurst 1973).

Those in the UK who raise concerns about this state of affairs often
point to the model of European regionalism as an example of how
matters ought to be. However, one needs to be a little prudent when
discussing the issue of a 'Europe of the Regions' since in truth regional

government differs greatly across Europe and is by no means universal. The arrangements (set out in Appendix 1) range from a fully-fledged federal state in Germany, consisting of Länder with important legislative rights and the right to elect the members of the *Bundesrat*, or second chamber in the Federal Republic, through the regional structures of France and Italy to the unelected Nomoi of Greece. It is true to say, however, that the major players in the EU do have elected regional structures, and it is their interests that have been advanced through a number of structures increasingly characterising a swathe of European policy-making.

This is most noticeable in the establishment of the 'Committee of the Regions' (COR) in March 1994, the first serious attempt to provide regions and municipalities with a consultative role of permanent standing within the EU structure itself. Although provided for in clause 198a of the Maastricht Treaty itself, COR only started meeting in March of 1994. Its early meetings have been well supported by the Commission and by leading regional politicians within the community (Whitehead 1995). Significantly, Spanish interests have been well represented, with the emergence of leaders such as Jordi Pujol of Catalonia and Pascal Maragall of Barcelona as leading actors on the committee.

However, the dominance of these two figures over the proceedings of the new committee (Pujol chairs the influential sub-committee preparing for the Intergovernmental Conference of 1996 and Maragall will be the likely Committee Chair in 1996) throws some of the problems both of the committee and of Spain into relief. Spain has twenty-one members on the committee, seventeen of whom have been nominated from each of the regions. The remaining four have gone to the mayors of large cities, including Maragall. Pujol has explicitly stated that, as far as he is concerned, the committee should be for regions only, and that, indeed, his work in the years leading up to the 1996 IGC would not be that of COR itself but in campaigning for a different kind of body which would give strong voice to regional interests within Europe. Among other things, Pujol has suggested that COR might become a second chamber of the European Parliament, effectively mirroring at European level the arrangement between the *Länder* and the *Bundestag* in the Federal Republic of Germany (Gallagher 1995). Janice Morphet agrees substantially with this analysis of the possible future for COR and argues that despite its slow start, the Committee will provide an important conduit for regional matters into the EU's structure. She suggests that

> There is no doubt that local politicians will provide a conduit of influence and information that has been lacking before. The Committee will therefore lead to an enhancement of the role of 'shared responsibility'. In the longer

term, the committee could find itself reviewed and transformed into a more powerful body. There have already been proposals for a second chamber of the European Parliament to be based on directly elected regional representatives. (Morphet 1994: 59)

The significance of the possible development and of the fact that its leading champion is Jordi Pujol should not be overlooked in the context of the issues discussed here. It is clear that Pujol, at least, has in mind a substantially independent role in European policy-making for Catalonia, and, through European constitutional change, one that creates strong leverage for a federal structure within Spain. The 'opinion' on the future status of COR drafted by Pujol and adopted in April 1995 illustrates this ambition well. The opinion suggests that the 1996 Intergovernmental Conference introduces COR as an additional institution of the EU in article 4 of the EC Treaty, and that Clause 3b be reworded to mention 'regional and local authorities' specifically in the context of subsidiarity. On subsidiarity itself, the Pujol opinion has this to say:

> . . .the principle of subsidiarity needs to be looked at both in terms of its formulation in the Treaty and in terms of its applications, viz: the prior examination of new legislation; the examination of existing legislation; the analysis of the case for undertaking new policies or activities; subsequent monitoring by the Court of Justice. We believe in particular that the Committee of the Regions must be more deeply involved in monitoring application of the principle of subsidiarity and must be brought into the heart of the work done by the Commission in this area.' (Pujol 1995: 33)

Europe, Spain and 'Subsidiarity'

Spain, it could be argued, is already substantially more devolved than many European countries. The twin provisions of regional autonomy and general competence for local government would suggest that Spain has taken the doctrine to heart before it became enshrined in the proceedings of Maastricht. In the UK, also, the significance of 'subsidiarity' is of course, overlooked. From the point of view of the UK government, it has been presented as a doctrine which allows states to undertake actions deemed not to be appropriate for the European Union to undertake as a central organisation. It was therefore presented as, in effect, a triumph for intergovernmentalism over neo-federalism. This was the line taken by the British Member of Parliament Francis Maude in giving the UK government's view to a House of Commons Select committee. He defined subsidiarity straightforwardly as ensuring '. . .that things should not be done at community level unless they can be done at national level' (Norton 1992: 18).

In truth, it is not seen in this way by virtually anyone else in Europe. Clause 3b of the Treaty reads as follows:

> In areas which do not fall within its exclusive competence, the Community shall take action, in accordance with the principle of subsidiarity, only if and insofar as the objectives of the proposed action cannot be sufficiently achieved by the member states and can therefore, by reason of scale or effects of the proposed action, be better achieved by the community.

At first sight, this appears to be 'game, set and match' for the notion that the nation-state will decide, and that subsidiarity therefore preserves an intergovernmental interpretation of union rather than a federalist view. However, the clause in effect interprets competencies in accordance with 'subsidiarity' which itself must be separately defined. Interestingly , as several commentators point out (Norton 1992: 6–16; Green 1994: 291–2; Scott et al. 1994: 61–6), the concept of subsidiarity, whilst unfamiliar to English ears, is familiar to liberal/religious debates in Europe centred around Christian Democrat principles. Indeed, a succinct definition is contained in an 1936 encyclical of Pope Pius 1X who declared that 'it is an injustice, a grave evil and a disturbance of right order for a larger and higher association to arrogate to itself functions which can be performed efficiently by smaller and lower societies' (Green 1994: 290). This enshrines the idea that functions should be exercised, save on efficiency grounds, at the level closest to that which they concern – a principle supportive of regional structures if ever there was one. That this is so is reinforced by the actions of those who ensured the incorporation of 'subsidiarity' as a guiding principle at Maastricht, following the incorporation of a proto-subsidiarity clause into the Single European Act (Norton 1992: 18). The prime movers in securing the support of the German government were, as Green and others chronicle, the German Lander, fearful that their real degree of autonomy would be threatened by a possible centralisation of power post-Maastricht. The Commission itself also supported the insertion of the principle, conscious of its image within the national and regional policy-making environment (Wincott 1994). Consequently, 'subsidiarity' has been viewed very differently, and used for different purposes by various actors on the European stage, and, overwhelmingly, it has been used empirically, to justify devolution to regions, rather than to nation-states within Europe.

What might this mean for Spain? It would suggest, for a start, that the retention of the provinces as a 'counterweight' to regions might come under attack if there is any attempt to apply the notion of subsidiarity evenly across the Union. It would also suggest that the fiscal hold of the Spanish State over the regions could well be loosened. The European Charter of Self-government, for example, declares that sub-national authorities should have the right to '. . .regulate and manage a substantial share of public affairs under their own responsibility in the interests of the local population' (O'Neill 1992: 20).

It is difficult to interpret this statement as meaning other than that local government (and regional government can be included in this def-inition for this purpose), if established, should be able to manage its own affairs financially and not merely through delegated authority to expend grant funding. This interpretation, if combined with the prin-ciple of subsidiarity, could produce a potent challenge to the levers of ultimate authority over the autonomous system that the central gov-ernment presently exercises. It is not difficult, on this analysis, to appreciate the 'federalist' thrust of Pujol's hoped-for positioning of COR in the post-1996 EU.

The Impact of Regional Networking

Regions throughout the EU are in the process of developing networks, both through the 'Intereg' and RECITE programmes set up by the then Regional Commissioner, Bruce Millan, in 1990 (Benington and Harvey 1994). The two programmes have been defined as performing the fol-lowing functions:

RECITE

Open to any local or regional authority with responsibility for a population of more than 50,000. The rationale underlying RECITE is that each network promotes the economic interests of its partners enabling the programme as a whole to strengthen economic and social cohesion within the EU.

INTERREG

The objective of INTERREG. . . is to help border regions prepare for the single market through greater cooperation straddling national borders – both the EU's internal borders and its external borders with non-EU countries. . ..
(Hall 1993)

Spanish regions and municipalities have been active in both pro-grammes, and in RECITE in particular. A number of more formalised linkages marrying up regions and cities with similar interests have been established. Figure 15.1 depicts Spanish participation in the RECITE programme. It can be seen that, in purely numerical terms, Spain enjoys the second largest degree of participation of any member state. One such grouping is the Atlantic Arc, which links a number of regions on the periphery of Europe and includes the Spanish regions along the north coast.

THE DISTRIBUTION OF RECITE NETWORK
PARTICIPANTS BY MEMBER STATE

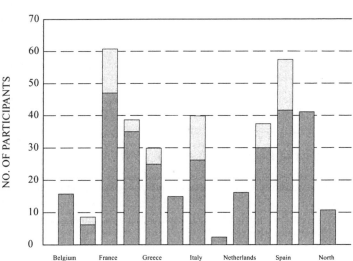

Source: Holland, S., Ward, M. and Emmerich, M. (1993), 'The Imperative of Inter-regional and International Networking', CLES, p.64.[1]

Figure 15.1

The most significant regional grouping for Spain is that which includes Catalonia. Dubbed 'the four motors', the grouping includes Baden-Württemberg, Lombardy and Rhône Alpes. If one looks at the map of the regions of Europe, Catalonia (and the other 'motors') already represent regions substantially overdeveloped in comparison to their national regional neighbours. According to Harvie this represented

1. We would like to thank the Centre for Local Economic Strategies for their kind permission to reproduce Figure 15.1.

a non-geographical nexus of factors which became critically important within the European community as it evolved towards a situation of 'mature' industrialisation. These were dominated by the functional requirements of multinational, or more correctly, 'post-national' high technology companies which, along with the internationalisation of capital markets, rendered 'national economic policies increasingly ineffective'. (1994: 60–1)

The 'four motors' is explicitly about mutual assistance and technology transfer to enhance this post-national economic advantage of particular areas of the EU on a basis that transcends national boundaries. Indeed, the former Minister-President of Baden Wurttemburg, Lother Spath, is reported to have defined the arrangement as 'a clear alternative to the existing Europe of sovereign states' (ibid.).

The Significance for Spain of Intercity Networking

Whilst regions have been busy networking in the new Europe, so have cities (Morris 1993). It is significant, for example, that whilst Catalonia has been establishing the 'four motors' Barcelona has been forging a different set of alliances with major cities across Europe and is a member of a grouping which includes, among others, Birmingham.

It is here that one can perhaps become a little speculative about the future structure of Europe: will it really be a 'Europe of the Regions' or will it perhaps consist of something more familiar to many on mainland Europe, a Europe of City States? It is worth remembering that a number of Spanish regions are, in effect, City Regions – that is to say, the city dominates the region that it is placed within. The populations of regions and that of selected Spanish cities expressed as a percentage of the region within which they sit is set out in Appendices 2 and 3. This demonstrates that for some Spanish regions, at least, they might more appropriately be called a city region rather than the more accepted view of a regional subdivision of a state. The substantial variation in regional size in Spain is, of course, another factor tending towards this mode of region.

This is relevant because it is possible to plot, on mainland Europe, and at brief periods of its history in Spain itself, a parallel history of city state development unfamiliar to someone weaned on the standard British history book fare of nations, kings and battles. This parallel history involves the complete separation at various historical times of a number of major cities from any connection with a larger territorial state; at other historical times many more cities only loosely and nominally responsible to a rudimentary state structure; and perhaps most significantly, a persistent history of networking on a non-territorial basis for both mutual defence and economic advantage.

For example, we might look at the political divisions in south and central Germany in the fifteenth century. The boundaries seem almost arbitrary and chaotic and represent a mélange of petty principalities, dukedoms and church lands. However, scattered among them are the 'imperial cities' or 'Reichstadte'. Peter Burke describes them thus:

> [there were] about 65 of them, subject only to the Emperor [i.e. the Holy Roman Emperor]. They were not quite as autonomous as Swiss cities, but the Emperor's weakness was their freedom. Some of them, notably Nuremburg and Ulm, came to dominate the countryside around them. Nuremburg, a City of about 20,000 people in 1500 had a 'territorium' of about 25 square miles. (1986: 146)

Further north, Burke notes, were a number of other cities, also more or less autonomous on the German model. He cites Bergen, Gdansk, Riga, Reval and Novogrod as examples, and says of Gdansk: 'Gdansk, which owned more than seventy villages, was one of the most fully autonomous cities in Central Europe in the sixteenth century, with its own currency as well as courts and taxes' (ibid.: 147).

These are perhaps among the lesser known autonomous cities of Europe. The Italian City States of the twelfth century and the independent Cantons of the Swiss confederation are much better known and documented. Italy in the twelfth century, for example, contained some two to three hundred cities in the north and centre of the peninsula which could be described as 'autonomous'. Far from the model of the nation-state, therefore, for long periods of the Middle Ages, and in the case of the Hanseatic Cities, up to 1806, the autonomous, or semi-autonomous city was, if not universal, a familiar political feature of the time, and an aspirational model for many cities less able to assert their own independence against territorial masters.

But what was perhaps more remarkable was that these cities tended, persistently, and on a widespread basis, to federate rather than attempt to accumulate adjacent territory. Some cities, such a Genoa, Pisa and Venice accreted small parcels of territory along their principal trading routes. These were more by way of commercial facilities than anything else: and it is remarkable that for all its power, at virtually no time in its history did Venice territorially occupy a significant area of mainland Italian soil.

The most famous of these federations was, of course, the Hanseatic League. The Hansa was a durable and effective trading group of up to seventy cities in the North Sea and the Baltic, capable jointly of enforcing advantageous trading deals on kingdoms, and independently or jointly, of resisting military adventures against them. Fernand Braudel characterises the success of the Hansa thus:

The products of the North and East – wood, wax, fur, rye and wheat – were only of value. . .when re-exported to the West. And in the other direction came the inevitable counterpart – salt cloth and wine. The system was a simple and well-founded one, but it had its problems. And it was the over-coming of such problems which welded together the urban league of the Hansa into a unit at once fragile and solid. Its fragility resulted from the instability of a group composed of so many towns – between 70 and 170 – all at some distance from each other, and whose delegates never all united in a single general assembly. Behind the Hansa there was no state, not even a firmly constituted organisation. It consisted simply of many towns, proud and jealous of their prerogatives. (1985: 102)

However, the Hansa was, if the most enduring, only one among many leagues and federations of cities in all parts of Europe and across differing ages. Kropotkin records that, in Italy,

when Frederick Barbarossa invaded Italy and supported by the nobles and some retardatory cities, marched against Milan, popular enthusiasm was roused in many towns by popular preachers. Crema, Piacenza, Brescia, Tortona went to the rescue: the banners of the guilds of Verona, Padua, Vicenza and Trevisio floated side by side in the cities camp against the banners of the emperor and the nobles. Next year the Lombardian League came into existence, and sixty years later we see it reinforced by many other cities and forming a lasting organisation. (1986 edn: 167)

Indeed, Kropotkin draws attention to the widespread organisation of villages into federations in many parts of Europe. Being essentially indefensible, they became relatively easy prey for territorial princes. Evidence of French village leagues is strong, and perhaps evidence of others has been lost because of their relatively transient nature. but where geography and politics combined to produce more fertile soil, those village leagues survived and grew to become the independent units of, for example, the Swiss confederation.

Neither autonomous cities nor federations were therefore exceptional in the medieval political system in Europe. Instead as Murray Bookchin remarks:

The emergence of the celebrated Swiss confederation. . .must be seen as an extension of the Rhenish and Swabian leagues, not an anomaly that stands at odds with the supposedly parochial traits imputed to European cities and their leagues. Switzerland was formed out of a milieu and modelled after examples that existed in Central Europe as a whole. (1992: 158)

In Spain itself we have the example of the 'Comuneros' where for a year from 1520–1, a series of cities in Castile threw out their Royalist local representatives (in the case of Segovia seizing the representative of the Cortes and hanging him) and developed a loose confederation including cities such as Toledo, establishing in Bookchin's words '. . .a parallel or "dual" power in opposition to the prevailing royal administration' (ibid: 167).

It is, perhaps, rather far-fetched to link easily the history of city states and leagues with the present development of intercity networks in Europe. Yet if we look at the modern map of business flights between cities, we will observe that, increasingly, flights are between centres that people want to get to from their starting point. Even ten years ago, it would have been relatively easy to pinpoint the capital city of each nation in Europe simply by looking at the air routes. Now it is by no means so clear-cut – and of course if one looks at the business air links between Barcelona or Seville and its partners, Madrid plays only a peripheral role. Perhaps of most resonance is what Burke has to say about the circumstances under which city leagues flourished in Europe. He advances the 'vacuum' theory of the city state and suggests that '. . .they and other small autonomous units. . .grow up when central authority is weak. . .and flourish in the interstices between major powers, as the small Italian states did in the no-man's land between empire and papacy' (Burke 1986: 152).

We might test this notion in the light of the evidence here presented of the potential destabilisation of the nation-state (especially one attempting to tread the fine line between centralism and federalism) by applying the 'Mabbott test' to national sovereignty. J. D. Mabbott in his book *The State and the Citizen* (first published in 1948) defined a 'state' thus:

> I am taking a State to be an association distinguished by
> (a) territorial limits
> (b) inclusiveness within these limits
> (c) the power in its officers to exercise force and the fear of force as instruments of policy
> (d) the possession of its officers of ultimate legal authority (1970 edn: 97)

Since the passing of the Single European Act, and certainly after the ratification of the Maastricht Treaty, it is no longer possible to regard Spain as a 'State' if we strictly apply these criteria. It has no longer any final right to control independently who crosses its borders. It is clear, therefore that it fails the test of section (a). It is no longer able to control the movement of foreign nationals within its boundaries to any great extent since Maastricht, and presumably fails on (b). I grant that it can still carry out (c), but it clearly fails on (d) as EU Law routinely takes precedence over Spanish legislation and is required, when enacted, to be incorporated by the *Cortes* into the next convenient piece of subsidiary legislation.

So if we can conclude that, already, Spain is a less than sovereign state. to whom has sovereignty been given? If we run the Mabbott test past the EU itself, it no more constitutes a 'state' than does the UK. It passes the test on (a) and (d) but arguably fails on (b) and certainly does not even merit consideration on (c). That perhaps brings us back to Peter Burke's definition of when city states (for which we might read regions) can flourish, and perhaps gives us a complete explanation of why Jordi Pujol is intent on making the Committee of the Regions the animal he has so clearly in mind for the end of this century.

References

Benington, J. and Harvey, J. (1994), 'Spheres or Tiers? The Significance of Transnational Local Authority Networks', *Local Government Policy Making*, vol.20(5), pp.20–30

Brassloff, A. (1995), 'Spain's Centre and Periphery: Is the Tail Wagging the Dog?', unpublished paper to Political Studies Association Conference, York

Bookchin, M. (1992), *Urbanisation without Cities*, Montreal

Braudel, F. (1985), *Civilization and Capitalism 15th – 18th Century*, vol.3, London

Burke, P. (1986), 'City States in History', in Hall, P. (ed.), *States in History*, Oxford, pp.142–65

Canel, M.J. (1994), 'Local Government in the Spanish Autonomous State', *Local Government Studies*, vol.20(1), pp.44–59

Coombes, D. (1991), 'Europe and the Regions', in Crick, B. (ed.), *National Identities: The Constitution of the United Kingdom*, Oxford, pp.134–51

Cuchillo, M. (1993), 'The Autonomous Communities as the Spanish Meso', in Sharpe, L.J. (ed.), *The Rise of Meso Government in Europe*, London, pp.210–46

Foster, J. (1995), 'MPs Attack Powers of Regional 'Viceroys', *Independent on Sunday*, 5 February

Gallagher, J. (1995), 'The Committee of the Regions: An Opportunity for Influence?' (monograph), Local Government International Bureau, London

Green, P. (1994), 'Subsidiarity and European Union: Beyond the Ideological Impasse', *Policy and Politics*, vol.22(4), pp.287–300

Hall, P. (1993), *Economic Development and European Networks*, Local Work no. 44, Centre for Local Economic Strategies, Manchester

Harvie, C. (1994), *The Rise of Regional Europe*, London

Keating, M. (1988), 'Does Regional Government Work? The Experience of Italy, France and Spain', *Governance*, vol.1(2), pp.184–204

Kropotkin, P. (1986 edn), *Mutual Aid*, London

Mabbott, J.D. (1970 edn), *The State and the Citizen*, London

Mawson, J. and Spencer, K. (1996), 'Pillars of Strength? The Government Offices for the English Regions', unpublished paper to Political Studies Association Conference 'English Regions: will they happen?', Southampton

Medhurst, K. (1973), *Government in Spain – the Executive at Work*, Oxford

—— (1977), 'The Basques and the Catalans', *Minority Rights Group*, report no.9

Morphet, J. (1994), 'The Committee of the Regions', *Local Government Policy Making*, vol.20(5), pp.56–60

Morris, K. (1993), *Ever Closer Unions*, Local Work no.48, Centre for Local Economic Strategies, Manchester

Norton, A. (1992), 'The Principle of Subsidiarity and its Implications for Local Government' (monograph), Local Government Management Board, Luton

O'Neill, N. (1992), 'European Regions after Maastricht', *Local Government Policy Making*, vol.19(3), pp.20–8

Pujol, J. (1995), *Opinion of the Committee of the Regions on the Revision of the Treaty on European Union*, Brussels

Scott, A., Peterson, J. and Millar, D. (1994), 'Subsidiarity: A 'Europe of the Regions" v. the British Constitution?', *Journal of Common Market Studies*, vol.32(1), pp.47–67

Whitehead, A. (1995), *Regional Government in England: What would it Look Like?*, Local Work no.57, Centre for Local Economic Strategies, Manchester

Wincott, D. (1994), 'Is the Treaty of Maastricht an adequate 'Constitution" for the European Union?', *Public Administration*, vol.72(4), pp.573–90

Appendix 1: Regional Structure of EU Member States as at end of 1994

EU Country	Regional Structure	Local Government Structure
Belgium	Federal: elected regional governments	Two tier: 9 provinces, 600 communes
Denmark	None	Two tier: 14 counties, 275 districts
Germany	Federal: 16 elected *Länder* – members of Bundesrat composed of members of *Länder*	Varies according to *Länder*: generally two tier – Kreis (county), and Gemeinde or Städte (district or city). Some Städtes, are unitary authorities, 'Kreisfreie' Approx. 120 Kreisfreie and 400 Kreise
Spain	17 'Autonomous Communities'	41 provinces and 10 island councils. Provinces overseen by centrally appointed Governor with delegates from municipalities. 8,000 municipalities
Greece	51 Nomoi. Government appointed units running devolved government functions	Single tier 500+ councils
France	22 elected regions	Two tier: 96 elected Departements, 36,000 Communes
Ireland	None	Two tier: 35 county councils, 84 municipal authorities
Italy	20 elected regions	Two tier: 95 elected provinces, 8,000+ communes
Luxembourg	None	Single tier: 118 communes
The Netherlands	12 elected provinces	636 municipalities
Portugal	Regional structure provided for but not implemented. Currently 18 provinces (non elected) as temporary measure	275 municipalities
United Kingdom	None: unelected Integrated Regional Offices in England perform some regional functions. Scottish, Welsh and N. Ireland Offices likewise in respective areas.	Two tier outside metropolitan areas, single tier in metropolitan areas. Currently undergoing review: unitary local authorities established in Wales and Scotland, variety of arrangements in England

Source: Gallagher, J., 'Committee of the Regions: An opportunity for Influence', LGIB, 1995.

Appendix 2: Comparison of Spanish Regions with UK Counties

Spanish Regions	Pop. (million)	English Counties	Pop. (million)
Andalusia	7.0	Hampshire	1.6
Catalonia	6.1	Essex	1.5
Madrid	5.0	Kent	1.5
Valencia	3.9	Lancashire	1.4
Galicia	2.7	Staffordshire	1.1
Castile-León	2.6	Devon	1.0
Euskadi	2.1	Surrey	1.0
Castile-La Mancha	1.7	Hertfordshire	1.0
Canarias	1.6	Avon	1.0
Aragon	1.2	Cheshire	1.0
Asturias	1.1	Derbyshire	0.9
Murcia	1.1	Leicestershire	0.9
Extremadura	1.1	Humberside	0.8
Balearics	0.7	Norfolk	0.7
Navarre	0.5	Berkshire	0.7
Cantabria	0.5	W. Sussex	0.7
La Rioja	0.3	E. Sussex	0.7

Sources: España: Anuario Estadístico 1992, OPCS Census 1991.

Appendix 3: Selected Spanish Cities: Population expressed as a Percentage of Regional Population

Spanish City	Pop. (million)	% of Region
Barcelona	4.69	76.6
Zaragoza	0.86	71.7
Madrid (Municipality)	3.01	61.2
Bilbao	1.16	54.8
Valencia	2.04	54.6
Las Palmas	0.85	51.9
Logroño (Municipality)	0.12	44.9

Source: España: Anuario Estadístico 1992.

N.B. There are two measures of the population of Spanish cities represented in the *Anuario Estadístico*. One represents the population of the city-province, and the other of the city municipality. The former measure is preferred here as better representing the 'territorium' of the city than the latter. The municipality is used where there is no provincial sub-division within the region.

Index

Index

Index

people lacking 143–4; disagreements about linguistic recovery 231–5; Euskera language 212–13, 226, 228–9, 230–1, 230–5; HABE 212–13, 231–5; literacy and standardisation of the vernacular 70; Spanish reforms 100

El Cid 152

Els Segadors (Catalan anthem) 197

Episodios nacionales (Pérez Galdós) 93, 96

España defendida (Quevedo) 91

España Invertebrada (Ortega y Gasset) 121

Esquerra Republicana de Catalunya (ERC) 16, 17

ETA *see* Euskadi ta askatasuna

European Union: Committee of the Regions 260–1, 269; intercity networking 265–8; networks between regions 263–5; Portugal joins 26; protection of linguistic and cultural identity 85; regional rights 23, 256, 258–61; Spain no longer a 'state' 268–9; subsidiarity 261–3; table of regional structure 271

Euskadi *see* Basque Country

Euskadi ta askatasuna (ETA): cultural recovery 223; formation 210–11; founded 22; political wing *Herri Batasuna* 211; as popular army 214; terror strategy 24

Euskera language: attempts to purge Castilian 214; and Basque nationalism 209–13; Batua 213; Franco's repression 211, 221, 228; language classes 226, 228–9; limitations and threatened existence 216–17; literature 222–3; origins in Basque country 208–9; programme of linguistic recovery 226–9; Royal Academy of Basque Language 229; some view as unsophisticated 209–10; standards of teaching 230–1; traumatic loss of language creates awareness of loss 225–6; tries to purge Castilian influence 210

Eusko Alkartasuna (EA) 211

exhibitions: commemorative politics 44

Falange: 26 points 151, 157

Farga Pellicer, Rafael 173

Ferdinand I of Spain 9

Ferdinand III of Spain 101

Ferdinand VII of Spain 92

Ferrer, Francisco 178

flamenco 186

Fontanals, Ramon 179

Foster, J. 259

France: arbitration of Africa dispute 62; creation of history 195, 196; effect of Revolution on nationalism 71; EU table of regional structure 271; influence on Portuguese culture 58; language 204; Napoleonic wars 91–3; regionalism 264; Spanish support split in WWI 124–5; Spanish xenophobia 90

Franco, General Francisco: anti-regionalism 81, 191–2, 221, 222; effect of Spanish-American War 155; repression and violence 21; resistance movement 199; social purification by repression and violence 157–62; strategy of autarky 149–57

Freedom of Expression Law (1966) 81–2

Freeland, Alan 5, 10, 11–12

Fuentes Irurózqui, Manuel 160

Galicia: autonomy within Spain 26; both Portuguese and Castilian influences 246–50; closeness to Portuguese language 2, 238–9, 241, 244; *Galeguismo* 14, 240, 244–5, 245; *Irmandades da Fala* 242–3, 244; language and identity 75–6, 80–1, 84, 237–9, 241; Left and Right split and Franco 244–5; liberals support nationalism 17; literature 17, 240, 242; longs for closer ties to Portugal 248; nationalist support divided 24–5; the *Nós* Generation 243–5; as province, region and nation 239–43; regional autonomy 256, 257; UPG founded 22

Gallagher, Tom 12

da Gama, Vasco 56

Ganivet, Angel 153, 154

García Negro, M.P. 248

Garrett, Almeida: *Camoes* 56–7; themes of loyalty and betrayal 59

Garrido, Fernando 93

Gdansk 266

Gebhardt, Victor: *Historia General de España* 100

Geller, Ernst 71

Le génie des Religions (Quinet) 64

Genio de España (Giménez) 155–6

Germany: EU table of regional structure 271; Hanseatic Cities 266–7;

Index

Index

Disaster 113–16; autarky 151; banal 34; complexity of ethnolinguistic movement 231–5; counter-culture 22; Galician language and identity 237–9; jingoistic rhetoric 99–100; and language 69–73; Mabbott test of sovereignty 268; myth and folklore 6–8; not necessarily linked to languages 207–8; renaissance of non-Castilian languages 74–5; repressive regimes versus liberal democracy 191–3; and republicanism 15–16; role of historical memory 203–5; rural folk culture 16, 185; shift towards conservativism 100–5

Navarre: language 83

navy: losses at Trafalgar 98

Negrín, Juan 142

The Netherlands 271

Nora, Pierre 195–6

North Atlantic Treaty Organization (NATO): Basque feelings against 214

Nós (magazine) 243–5

O Positivismo (Braga) 54

oligarchy: Spain's two ruling elites 119–20

de Olivares, Count-Duke 73–4, 97

de Oliveira Salazar, António 20–1

Olympic Games 202

oral tradition: symbolic and festive communication to illiterate 40–1

Orientales (Hugo) 94

de Ornella, Aires 49

Ortega y Gasset, José: *España Invertebrada* 121

Ortigao, Ramalho 58

Os Cantares Gallegos (Castro) 240

Os Lusiadas (Camoes) 42, 45; as national epic 56; science and industry 64–5; spirit in colonial policy 63–4

Os Maias (de Queiros) 60

Ottoman Empire: Portuguese divine mission 63

Ourique, miracle of 63

Paraíso, Basilio 114

Partido Socialista Andaluz (PSA) 22

Partit Socialista d'Alliberament Nacional dels Països Catalans (PSAN) 22

de Pascoaes, Teixeira 48, 49

Peninsular War *see* Spain: War of Independence

Pérez Galdós, Benito: *Episodios*

nacionales 93, 96

Pessoa, Fernando 48, 49

Philip II of Spain 97, 152; occupation of Portugal 55

Philip III of Spain 97

Philip IV of Spain 97; centralisation of Spain 73–4

Philip V of Spain: commemoration on National Day 197

Philippines: Spanish-American War 107

Pi-Sunyer, Oriol 192–3

Pi y Margall, Francesc 5, 109

Piñero, Ramón 245

Pius IX: rights of smaller societies 262

PNV *see* Basque Nationalist Party

poetry: Catalan 76

de Pombal, Sebastiao de Carvalho Marquis: commemoration of death 43; reforms 39

Popular Front: construction 134, 137–40; strategies and weaknesses 140–5

Portas, M. 240

Portugal: and Britain 12; commemorations for physiognomy 35–8; discoveries theme 11, 46–9, 63; divine mission 63; education 46; EU table of regional structure 271; fails the "threshold principle" 60; First Republic 40–1; growth and decay and messianic expectation 54–6; independence 1, 240; influence of other cultures 58; institutes liberal constitution 38; integrity as state 3; limited decentralisation 23–4; marginalisation 34; model of a nation 33–4, 99–12; new democracy 26–7; at odds with Britian over colonial policy 61–2; Philippine occupation 55, 57; 'Portuguese Integralism' 20, 48–9; recent adoption of Camoes as national symbol 53–4; Regeneration 40; reluctant to 'interfere' with Galicia 248; 'Renaissance' 48; republicanism 18–19; resentment of Spanish occupation 59; saves Europe from Muslim domination 45; support for Iberian unity 5

Portuguese language: and Galician 2, 80, 238–9, 241, 244, 246–50

Portuguese Republican Party (later Democratic Party) 46

Prat de la Riba, Enric 77, 202

Primo de Rivera, José Antonio 153, 197

Primo de Rivera, Miguel 4, 130

Index